THE BOOK ON RENTAL PROPERTY INVESTING

The Book on

RENTAL PROPERTY INVESTING

*How to Create Wealth with Intelligent
Buy & Hold Real Estate Investing*

BRANDON TURNER

BiggerPockets® PUBLISHING
Denver, Colorado

Praise for
Brandon Turner's Books

"An insider's perspective, full of encouragement and resources for new-comers... Interested readers will find the book substantially useful as a starting point."

—Kirkus Review on *How to Invest in Real Estate*

"I only wish this book had been written in 2005 when I was starting my real estate investing journey!"

**—Ken Corsini, Real estate investor
and star of HGTV's *Flip or Flop Atlanta***

"I think this should be required reading for anyone considering real estate investing... Countless hours, months, and—frankly—years this book would have saved me!"

**—Ben Leybovich, Real estate investor,
syndicator, and founder of JustAskBenWhy.com**

"There are very few books that provide a detailed, step-by-step framework for accomplishing real estate success. Brandon Turner's *The Book on Rental Property Investing* does that, and does it in a way that puts financial free-dom through real estate within reach of anyone who wants it."

**—J Scott, Bestselling author of
*The Book on Flipping Houses***

"I have not read a more comprehensive discussion in my 20 years of investing. This is a great reference for beginners and experienced rental owners!"

—Al Williamson, LeadingLandlord.com

"This book is an A-to-Z guide for the real estate investor—not just buying and selling, but also strategic planning, which is all too often forgotten. The real-world examples really drive it home."

—Brian Burke, CEO of Praxis Capital and bestselling author of *The Hands-Off Investor*

"*The Book on Rental Property Investing* fuses passion with a system-driven, business-mindedness that provides a very big resource to help establish and achieve your personal investment goals."

—Bill Syrios, Owner of Stewardship Properties

"I wish I had *The Book on Managing Rental Properties* before I made all of my expensive property management mistakes! Brandon and Heather Turner have covered the biggest challenges for landlords and solved each one with step-by-step systems. I literally gave the information in Chapter 6 on tenant pre-screening to my own team and said, 'Use this!' It's that good."

—Chad Carson, Bestselling author of *Retire Early with Real Estate*

"It's practical, real, and comes across very open and unbiased... This is great for beginners as well as anyone who is in another field of real estate investing looking to cross over."

—Lisa Phillips, AffordableRealEstateInvestments.com

The Book on Rental Property Investing
Brandon Turner
Published by BiggerPockets Publishing LLC, Denver, CO
Copyright © 2015, 2020 by Brandon Turner.
All Rights Reserved.

Library of Congress Cataloging-in-Publication Data
Turner, Brandon, 1985—
The Book on Rental Property Investing: How to create wealth and passive income through smart buy & hold real estate investing.
    p cm
Identifiers: LCCN: 2020937566
ISBN: 978-0-9907117-9-7 (pbk.) | 978-0-9907117-0-4 (ebook)
1. Real Estate Investment 2.Business- Real Estate I. Turner, Brandon II. Title

Published in the United States of America and printed on recycled paper.
10 9 8 7 6 5 4 3

Dedication

This book is dedicated to my many mentors who have brought me from where I was to where I am today. No words could do justice the appreciation I have for you.

TABLE OF CONTENTS

Prologue 14

About This Book 19

Chapter One
WHY I LOVE RENTAL PROPERTIES .21
Why Do I Love Rental Properties So Much? 22
The Four Wealth Generators .26
How Much Money Does One Need to
Invest in Rental Properties? .30
Top Five Difficulties of Rental Property Investing 34
Why Do So Many Rental Property Owners Fail? 38
Quitting (or Not Quitting) Your Job Through Rental Properties 41

Chapter Two
THE FIVE KEYS TO RENTAL PROPERTY SUCCESS 48
1. Think the Right Thoughts .49
2. Study the Right Source 52
3. Pick the Right Plan 58
4. Acquire the Right Asset 63
5. Manage the Right Metrics 63

Chapter Three
FOUR SAMPLE PLANS 66
Plan 1: How to Make $1,000,000 Through Rental Properties 67
Plan 2: Building Wealth Through Single-Family Homes 73
Plan 3: House Hacking 78
Plan 4: How to Make $100,000 Per Year
Using the BRRRR Strategy 81

Chapter Four
THE TEN MEMBERS OF YOUR REAL ESTATE TEAM......87
1. Spouse..88
2. Mentor/Accountability Partner..................91
3. Real Estate Agent.............................93
4. Lender(s)..99
5. Contractors and Handymen.....................100
6. Bookkeeper....................................105
7. CPA..105
8. Lawyer...106
9. Insurance Agent...............................107
10. Property Manager.............................107

Chapter Five
ANALYZING A RENTAL PROPERTY....................110
How to Analyze a Rental Property................111
What Is Cash Flow?..............................111
123 Main Street Analysis........................125

Chapter Six
INVESTING WHILE LIVING IN AN EXPENSIVE AREA...137
Are You Looking for Homes on Sale?..............138
Is the Price Relative?..........................139
What Is Working in Your Area?...................140
Have You Checked the Outskirts?.................140

Chapter Seven
TYPES OF RENTAL PROPERTIES.....................148
Single-Family Homes.............................149
Multifamily Real Estate.........................152
Condos..156
Townhomes.......................................157
REOs/Foreclosures...............................157
Fixer-Uppers....................................158
Commercial Real Estate..........................163

Chapter Eight
LOCATION, LOCATION, LOCATION! .165
Neighborhood Classes 166
Jobs versus Unemployment 170
Population Growth 171
Housing Starts and Building Permits 171
Proximity to Local Businesses 172
Price-to-Rent Ratio 172
Vacancy Rates 174
Property Tax and Insurance Rates 175

Chapter Nine
HOW TO FIND RENTAL PROPERTIES 178
1. The MLS 179
2. Direct Mail Marketing for Deals 183
3. Driving for Dollars 185
4. Eviction Records 186
5. BiggerPockets Marketplace 186
6. Craigslist 187
7. Wholesalers 188
8. Passion 188

Chapter Ten
WHICH PROPERTIES MAKE THE BEST RENTALS? 190
Eight Problems I Look for When Shopping
for Rental Properties 194
Three Problems I Avoid When Shopping
for a Rental Property 200

Chapter Eleven
SUBMITTING YOUR OFFER 203
How to Make an Offer 204
The Earnest Money Deposit 207
What Should the Offer Include? 210
How Much Should You Offer? 211
Sixteen Tips for Getting Your Offer Accepted 213

Chapter Twelve
REAL ESTATE NEGOTIATION 218
The Negotiation Process 219
When to Negotiate 222
Thirteen Tips for Successful Negotiation 223

Chapter Thirteen
FINANCING YOUR RENTAL PROPERTY 228
All Cash 229
Conventional Loans 234
Portfolio Lenders 239
Other Creative Methods 247

Chapter Fourteen
HOW TO GET A LOAN APPROVED, GUARANTEED 254
Understanding How a Loan Works 255
The Twelve-Digit Code You Need to Get Your Loan Approved ...257
Make Your Lender's Job Easier to Get Your Loan Approved 262

Chapter Fifteen
THE DUE DILIGENCE PROCESS 264
What Is Due Diligence? 265

Chapter Sixteen
GETTING READY TO CLOSE 277
Order Insurance 278
Do I Need an LLC? 283
Final Walk-Through of the Property 288
Sign the Docs 288

Chapter Seventeen
MANAGING YOUR RENTALS (PART I) 290
Self-Management versus Property Management 291
Business or Hobby: Getting in the Right Mindset 295
Getting a Property Ready to Rent 298
Five Ways to Find Great Tenants 299

Accepting Phone Calls. 301
Showing the Property to Tenants. 302
The Application Process. 303

Chapter Eighteen
MANAGING YOUR RENTALS (PART II) 314
Maintenance and Repairs 315
Landlord versus Tenant Responsibilities 318
Annual Preventative Maintenance. 319
Dealing with Difficult Tenants 320
If You Are Unhappy, Your System Is Broken 328

Chapter Nineteen
EXIT STRATEGIES AND 1031 EXCHANGES. 330
Hold Forever 331
Seller Financing 332
Cash Out. 332
The 1031 Exchange 333

Chapter Twenty
FINAL THOUGHTS 345
The Five Success Principles of Rental Ownership 346
Will You Take Action? 349

Acknowledgments. 351

PROLOGUE

What if I told you that you could make millions of dollars in real estate, doing nothing but sitting on a beach?

Piña coladas, little white umbrellas, endless sand—sounds pretty great, right?

Well, that is not going to happen, at least not anytime soon. If you were looking for an easy path to riches, rental properties are probably not the right avenue for you. I know I've probably just lost half of those who picked up this book, and that's okay. I know that millions more are willing to do what is necessary to find success, even if that path is more difficult than the late-night television infomercials would have you believe.

Obviously, people flock to real estate for a reason. In my opinion, real estate can provide the best, safest, fastest path to financial freedom compared with any other method used to build wealth. I've seen it in my own life, which I'll explain in a moment. But first, let's talk about what this book will *not* teach you.

If you were looking for a book written by the latest guru, you are going to be disappointed. You are not going to learn some secret strategy that I discovered and that no one else knows. After all, I'm not anything special. In fact, I'm just like you. I may be further along on my real estate journey than you are, or I may be years behind you—in which case, I hope to learn from you as well. The truth is that we're on the same journey together, playing the greatest game ever invented. In writing this book, I hope to share with you the lessons I've learned so far, both the successes *and* the mistakes. I believe these lessons will help you achieve a greater life than you have ever imagined.

Moreover, you should never learn from just one person, I believe, and anyone who says otherwise is probably trying to sell you something. The best education comes from experience, and by learning from the collective experiences of others, you can supercharge your real estate ambitions to find greater success, faster and with less drama.

Therefore, in the pages of this book I've incorporated the lessons and stories of real estate investors from the BiggerPockets community in an effort to help you gain the greatest perspective. Together, as a community, let's help each other find financial freedom through real estate investing.

What Do You Want?

Let me ask you a very basic question: What do you want?

Go ahead, say it out loud. Money? A new house? To fire your boss, quit your job, and work for yourself? How about a better retirement? More wealth for your kids? A summer in Europe? Longer sleep? Whatever it is, yell it out! (Unless you are sitting in a Starbucks right now, in which case, you probably shouldn't yell. But I'd like a tall extra-hot peppermint hot chocolate, please.)

Let me share with you one of my all-time favorite quotes. Michael Jordan (yes, *that* Michael Jordan) once said, "Some people want it to happen. Some wish it would happen. Others make it happen."

Which kind of person are you?

Now, there is nothing wrong with wanting things in life. Don't feel silly about identifying material things you want when you answer that question. Having goals is great—but it's not enough. You need action, too. You will need to get off your butt and change your world yourself, because no one else will do it for you. My goal in writing this book is to not only give you theory and hope but to also give you the tools and knowledge you need to reach your goals. You already know that real estate can change your life. Now it's time to learn how to make that happen. It's time to take action.

- Are you committed to taking action?
- Are you committed to dedicating your spare time?
- Are you committed to replacing daydreams with strategies?
- Are you committed to investing your money?

I hope you answered "yes" to all of these questions. And don't worry if you don't actually have the money, the spare time, or the knowledge just yet. If you are committed to giving this a try, I'll help you get there. Remember, you are not doing this for me; you are doing it for *you*.

As you work through this book, I encourage you to not only read but also internalize every concept. Don't simply pass your eyes over the words without understanding the concepts being explained. Reread sections if you need to. Ask other experienced investors about the topics. Share the lessons you're learning with your significant other as you digest them. Question everything I say, and do whatever is necessary to have it make sense in your own mind. Take your time.

About Me

"If you do this, Brandon, you're going to go broke, be homeless, and ruin your life. Please reconsider. "

This was not the response I was hoping for when I finally told my parents I wasn't going to go to law school, despite months of studying and a strong score on the law school entrance exam. Instead, I had set my sights on becoming a real estate investor.

I had been raised in a "go to school, get a great job with a great company, and be responsible" household. I can't fault my parents for this mentality—after all, this was how they themselves had been raised. My parents are incredible people who simply wanted the best for me, but I needed to do things differently. The path I had in mind was neither better nor worse—just different.

My entrepreneurial itch led me to the fascinating world of real estate investing, and specifically to rental properties. The idea of using my creativity in place of cash to build passive income exhilarated me. However, my ambitions hit an almost immediate roadblock with my parents' warning of catastrophic failure. My tenants wouldn't pay, they feared. I would have to deal with evictions. I would lose all my money, lose my properties, end up on the street, start dealing meth, and, for good measure, probably end up killing someone in a bar fight.

All because I wanted to be a real estate investor.

At that point, I was forced to face my future head-on. Do I abandon my newly discovered dreams and come back to earth? Should I suck it up, stop complaining, and go to law school? After all, my parents had a point. A good law education pretty much guaranteed a good job. A good job meant stability. Real estate, on the other hand, didn't seem very stable. *What if* my tenants wouldn't pay? *What if* I had to deal with evictions? How could I survive?

Before giving up and accepting what seemed to be my fate, I turned to the only source I knew at the time to ask: Google, which brought me to this brand-new website called BiggerPockets. Suddenly, a switch flipped in my brain. There on the screen were other aspiring (and practicing) investors with the same questions and concerns.

More importantly, there were answers.

My entrepreneurial ambitions didn't necessarily mean I would end up a meth dealer wanted for murder. My quest for knowledge brought me to www.BiggerPockets.com, for which I now blog, design, write, teach, network, and have grown into the role of VP of Creative Content.

In short, I had discovered that all my questions had *answers*. There was hope. "Financial freedom" was not just a buzzword late-night charlatans used to sell their programs. Financial freedom was a real thing, enjoyed by millions of people around the world. And I wanted it with every ounce of my being!

So I quit my job, walked away from my law school applications, and jumped into full-time real estate investing, acquiring dozens of rental units over the next decade, moved to Maui where I have done a couple of house flips, and established a real estate investment fund called Open Door Capital that invests in large mobile home parks across the U.S.

And, now I am financially free. Because of my real estate investments, I'm able to live the kind of life *I* choose, not one given to me. As I continue to earn more money, I can pour that extra income into additional investments. My current investments are allowing me to buy more investments, a concept known as "exponential growth"—and it's awesome! Thanks to my rental properties, I am creating a fulfilling and rewarding future for myself, my wife, and our future children.

Most real estate authors and gurus tend to be reluctant about sharing information about their personal investments, but I say screw that! As of this writing, I have around 600 units, spread out over a dozen or so properties (including single family, multifamily, and now a growing collection of mobile home parks). In the beginning, I worked hard to acquire small deals, and now I try to pick up a few new big ones each year. My wife and I hire property managers to take care of our units so we don't have to deal with the day-to-day stress of landlording, making our investments a lot more passive.

To help us keep our life sane and manageable, we collaborate with some invaluable individuals, including an assistant/finance manager, numerous contractors, and other professionals. We travel a lot, but in a modest way. We buy nice stuff, but we don't overdo it. We hang out with our friends and family every chance we can. And we absolutely enjoy life to the fullest. Real estate has been a major contributor to our lifestyle design. Furthermore, I am not done with my journey. I am not writing this book from the position of "back in the day, this is how it was done." I am writing it in real time, as I live the very life I'm describing. As I said before, this is a journey you and I are on together, and I still have more to learn. I'll make mistakes, screw up, get frustrated, and feel discouraged. I don't yet have it all together.

I hope that this book will be different than others on the market *because* of this.

I can't tell you how many books I've read by has-been investors who no longer invest and are teaching tactics that no longer work because the game has changed. I'm happy for them that they achieved financial freedom and were able to retire, but that's not me.

I only want to teach what I actually *do*.

ABOUT THIS BOOK

This book will likely ruin your life, as great books tend to do.

It will challenge the way you look at life, finances, and real estate. It will lead you to envision a different life for yourself, one not suggested by your parents, society, your alma mater, or the media. It will encourage you to step out and create a whole new path for yourself, one that *you* construct out of thin air. It will introduce you to numerous ideas, paths, strategies, and concepts for achieving financial freedom through rental properties. It will give you answers to questions you never knew to ask, and likely leave you with a few more questions I didn't think to answer (but don't worry, that's not a bad thing).

My goal with this book is to create the single greatest guide on rental property investing ever written. Trust me, I've read hundreds! In each chapter, I will explore one specific step in rental property investing, explaining it in depth and helping you understand how to navigate every stage of the process.

Whether you are just getting started or already own hundreds of units, I hope this book will help you make more income, retire sooner, unlock more free time, amass more units, or achieve whatever other goals you might have. Yes, this is an ambitious undertaking, but I am up for the challenge. Are you?

Finally, I believe one pass through this book will not be enough. I include so many lessons, tips, stories, and details that you'll likely remember only 20 percent of what you read. Do you want to be only 20 percent prepared to take on your first (or next) rental property investment? I didn't think so! I therefore encourage you to read this entire book not just once but multiple times. You'll never look back at your life and say, "I sure wish I hadn't spent so much time preparing for my future." As good ole Abe Lincoln reportedly remarked, "Give me six hours to chop down a tree, and I will spend the first four sharpening the axe."

It's time to sharpen your axe. I'll see you in Chapter 1.

Your friend,

Brandon Turner

Chapter One
WHY I LOVE RENTAL PROPERTIES

"My mission in life is not merely to survive, but to thrive; and to do so with some passion, some compassion, some humor, and some style."

—MAYA ANGELOU

My eyes were glued to the nine simple words I held between my shaking fingers in that dark all-you-can-eat Chinese buffet restaurant.

Surely it was a coincidence; it had to be, right?

Or perhaps someone was playing an extremely elaborate prank on us. No, that would be impossible. This *really* just happened.

It was a hot summer afternoon, several days after my high school graduation. My best friend Matt and I had decided to venture down to our favorite restaurant, a hole-in-the-wall Chinese buffet restaurant on the outskirts of Minneapolis, to grab an early dinner. We talked about life, girls, our college plans, our crazy friends, the latest small-town gossip, and all the other pressing issues that two 18-year-old guys in the Midwest typically discuss over sweet and sour chicken, fried rice, wontons, Jell-O, and unlimited soda refills.

As our conversation began to wind down, the tall, middle-aged waitress came to collect the dirty plates and drop off our check. Neither of us reached for the bill, though; instead, we reached for the two fortune cookies that lay atop the overturned invoice on the table.

"Brandon," Matt asked, "as we grow up, do you want to live an ordinary life or an extraordinary one?"

As I held my fortune cookie, still in its wrapper, I thought about his question for a moment. I was an ordinary kid in an ordinary town, with ordinary grades, an ordinary job, and an ordinary outlook on life. Things seemed pretty good to me, so as I peeled the clear plastic wrapper off my fortune cookie, I looked Matt in the eye and replied, "I'll take an ordinary life. I'm happy with that."

In reality, I didn't believe I could ever achieve something more than ordinary, so why kid myself? I could handle ordinary. I deserved ordinary. I was destined for ordinary.

I cracked my fortune cookie in half and carefully retrieved the white strip of paper nestled inside. Printed in red ink were nine words I will never forget: *"There is no such thing as an ordinary life."*

Why Do I Love Rental Properties So Much?

It's no secret that I love rental properties.

Sure, flipping and wholesaling properties might be fun. Notes and tax liens might have fewer tenants. The stock market might be more popular. But rental properties are my true business love.

Let me explain why.

Ability to Purchase with Leverage

Rental properties are great because you can borrow the bank's or someone else's money to increase the potential return. This is known as leverage. In other words, you don't need to have 100 percent of a property's purchase price on hand to be able to buy it. I'll explain this more in depth later in this chapter, but for now, I'll say this: Rental properties allow me to buy large properties for far less cash than I might need to purchase stocks or other investments.

Ability to Hustle for Greater Returns

Not only can I leverage my cash, but I can also leverage my time and abilities to make magic happen in this game—something difficult to do with other investments. In other words: I can hustle. If I want to do the work needed to rehab a property, I can do that. If I want to leverage my networking skills to raise money, I can do that instead. If I want to leverage my knowledge and time to find better deals that provide an even greater return, I can do that. Rental property investing gives me the ability to hustle for my future.

Ability to Manage My Investment Directly

I'll fully admit I'm a bit of a control freak, and that drives me toward rental properties in a powerful way. With a rental property, I am directly responsible for the outcome of my investment. It is up to me to analyze a property before I buy it; it's up to me to ensure the property is in good condition to rent; it's up to me to ensure the property is running at peak performance. I don't have to depend on some board of directors in New York City for my life's direction. I can manage my investments directly and personally.

People Always Need a Place to Live

The real estate market will go up and down, but the beauty of rental properties is that demand will never end. People always need a place to live, so unlike investing in the latest tech trend or in your brother's start-up, real estate is an investment that will last. Furthermore, because increasing student loans are making qualifying for a mortgage more difficult, and our culture increasingly values mobility, the demand for rental properties will only grow over time.

It's Worked for Millions of People Before Me

Perhaps one of the greatest benefits to rental property investing is the proof of concept handed down by millions of successful investors before us. Since the dawn of human civilization, landlords have built wealth by owning and leasing out residential property. Today is no different. According to a joint survey produced by BiggerPockets and Memphis Invest in 2012, "One out of eight, or 28.1 million Americans, either consider themselves to be residential real estate investors or own residential investment properties today."[1]

---

1   http://www.biggerpockets.com/news/pr/BP-MI-NewsRelease9-20-12.pdf

Fairly Stable and Predictable

Yes, events such as the market collapse in 2007 do happen, but rental property owners who were investing for long-term gains did not suffer like those who were trying to be "fancy." (Or as my good friend and fellow landlord Jordan says, "punk drunk on greed.") Furthermore, I would argue that the 2007 real estate crash *was* predictable for those who were paying attention, because one of the defining characteristics of the real estate market is the boom-and-bust cycle that never goes away. Once an investor learns to identify this cycle, the old adage of "buy low, sell high" becomes much easier to achieve.

Incredible Variety

Rental properties also offer an incredible amount of variety within the asset class. I can invest in single-family houses, small multifamily properties, large multifamily apartments, office buildings, high end, low end, Section 8, transient, and any of a number of other options. Then, within each of those classes, I can find larger properties, smaller properties, ones that are newer, older, taller, shorter, ugly, beautiful, and so on. The possibilities are endless. As President Donald Trump once said, "It's tangible, it's solid, it's beautiful. It's artistic, from my standpoint, and I just love real estate."

Simple and Straightforward

Although I'll never claim that working with rental properties is easy, I do maintain that investing in rental property is fairly simple and straightforward. Sure, it involves more than just buying a piece of property and placing renters in it, but the strategies for success are not overly difficult to learn or master. To help, a tremendous amount has been written on the topic by those who have mastered it. Books (such as this one), podcasts, videos, blogs, forums, networking groups, mentorships, and more can be found to help you learn nearly everything you will ever need to know.

In addition, knowledgeable people are available to help. Several months ago, I ran into a situation I didn't know how to handle (a tenant that smokes accidentally lit part of the outside of her house on fire yet claimed she hadn't). I reached out to other investors on the BiggerPockets Forums and received some excellent advice on how to proceed—and it didn't cost me a thing.

I Can Buy Below Market Value

I was raised by a "garage sale mom" who taught me the value of always haggling for the best deal. As a result, one of my favorite reasons for investing in rental properties is my ability to find properties that I can buy below market value. In other words, I can shop for a great deal! Finding properties that are worth $100,000 that I can buy for $80,000 truly excites me and is an integral part of how I've been able to build wealth so quickly over the past eight years. And I will definitely cover this strategy in more depth later in this book.

Insider Trading Is Legal

In the Wall Street world, there is a concept known as "insider trading," which is when an investor makes a profit on a stock because he or she had access to some secret bit of information that helped him or her buy or sell at the right time. This practice is not just discouraged in the stock market, it is also illegal and can even land you in jail (just ask Martha Stewart). However, as a rental property investor, I can leverage any secret knowledge I can find to benefit my investments. If I know that a new light rail is moving into a neighborhood, I can jump in and swoop up properties before word gets out. If I hear that a major industry is leaving an area, I can get out of that area before the market declines. And unlike in the stock market, this is 100 percent legal and encouraged in the rental property realm.

Multiple Ways to Profit

One of the greatest benefits of rental property investing, especially compared with other real estate niches and strategies, is the opportunity to capitalize on all four of real estate's major profit sources. This point is so important that I believe it deserves its own section, which follows next.

Not Having to Be Present to Make Money

Finally, I love the idea that I can make money without physically needing to be present. That's called a "JOB," and I want to avoid that. However, understand that real estate is not generally a 100 percent passive activity, but over time the systems you create can help you outsource most of the landlording process. The dollars will roll in whether you get out of bed in the morning or not.

The Four Wealth Generators

When I first decided to become a real estate investor, my inclination was to become a full-time house flipper. I love the idea of taking a property in disrepair and making it shine. However, I quickly realized that when I was flipping houses, I was building a job rather than an investment. Although I could make good money when I sold a property, I was capitalizing on only *one* source of wealth generation, and when I stopped working, the money stopped flowing. Then I discovered another investing niche that took advantage of not just one but of *four* different sources of wealth generation: rental properties. Those four sources are appreciation, cash flow, tax savings, and loan paydown. Let me explain each one in more detail.

1. Appreciation

When I was in high school, my dad bought himself a gorgeous 1969 Chevy Camaro with a convertible top, leather interior, and roaring engine. Lucky for me, he is a generous guy and had no problem letting his 17-year-old son drive the car around on special occasions, including a couple of proms. He held on to that car for about five years and sold it soon after I graduated, for roughly $5,000 more than he paid for it. In other words, unlike the cars most of us drive every day, this car actually went *up* in value, as classic cars tend to do. In a way, my dad enjoyed the use of a classic American muscle car for free for five years, thanks to appreciation.

Now, by appreciation, I don't mean *enjoying* the car (though, yes, we did appreciate it that way, too). I'm talking about appreciation in the sense of positive financial investment. By its simplest definition, appreciation is an increase in the value of an asset over time.

- A muscle car worth $15,000 in 1999 might be worth $20,000 in 2004.
- A nice wine might be worth $45 the day it was bottled but $455 a few years later.
- A house worth $100,000 in 1990 might be worth $500,000 today because of appreciation.

There are actually two kinds of appreciation in real estate: natural and forced.

- **Natural appreciation** is the natural tendency for prices to rise over time. This kind of appreciation is tied to several factors, including inflation, scarcity, and good ole American greed. When the house your parents purchased in 1955 could be sold 40 years later for ten times its original value, this is natural appreciation.

- **Forced appreciation** is also mentioned often in the investment space, and it's the concept of improving a property so the property's value becomes greater. For example, turning a two-bedroom home into a three-bedroom home can increase its value immediately. Adding a second bathroom can likewise increase its value immediately. Increasing the amount of profit a property can earn, especially a large multifamily property, can increase its value immediately. Each of these tactics involve forced appreciation.

As I mentioned earlier, when I flip a house, I capitalize on only *one* kind of wealth generation, which is appreciation (primarily forced appreciation). Rental properties capitalize on all four.

Great wealth *has* been built through appreciation, of course. I know numerous homeowners who bought a simple home in California 20 years ago and are now millionaires because of that one purchase. Appreciation is a powerful tool and something investors should seriously consider.

However, as great a generator as appreciation may be, it does have a dark side. In the early 2000s, the real estate market across the country was "appreciating" like crazy. People bought terrible properties and made a killing just on the appreciation. They began losing sight of the math behind an investment and simply bought whatever they could because they could always sell it for more later. "Who cares if the property loses money every month?" they thought. "I'll just sell it in a few years and make so much more!"

This "greater fool theory" of investing eventually caught America with its pants down.

Prices stopped climbing, unemployment grew, and individuals suddenly realized that they were no longer holding on to investments but rather playing in the world's largest game of legalized gambling—and they had just lost. This plunged the world into the greatest recession most of us had ever seen and caused more than four million completed foreclosures.[2]

There's no denying the incredible role appreciation has played in investors' lives, but there's also no denying the risk involved in relying

---

2 https://www.corelogic.com/research/foreclosure-report/national-foreclosure-report-10-year.pdf

on appreciation to make a profit. I recommend that, instead, investors view appreciation as icing on the cake, a bonus that will assist in the investment but is not the basis of that investment. Investing in locations where appreciation is likely is a wise move, but I don't recommend investing in a bad or marginal deal in hopes that appreciation will bail you out. This is known as "speculating," and it isn't much better than getting in your car, driving to Vegas, and betting all your money at the poker table.

Will prices continue to climb because of inflation, scarcity, and greed?

I have no doubt they will. Appreciation will make millionaires (and billionaires) out of certain people reading this book, but your deal analysis should not assume it. Treat appreciation for what it is: a possible reward for an investment done right.

Let's move on to the second wealth generator in real estate: cash flow.

2. Cash Flow

In layman's terms, cash flow is the amount of income left in your business after all the bills have been paid; this amount is often expressed as a monthly dollar amount. In the real estate rental business, cash flow is the income left after paying out expenses that affect the property, such as mortgage, taxes, insurance, vacancies, repairs, capital expenditures, and utilities. Therefore, to truly understand your cash flow, you must truly understand your income and expenses, and this is where most people struggle. After all, we are not magicians, so how do we accurately predict the future cash flow of a property we don't yet own?

Although predicting the cash flow of your investment with 100 percent certainty is impossible, you *can* generate a fairly close estimate by looking at both historical data and industry-averaged data. Cash flow is perhaps the most important wealth generator for rental property investors. Appreciation is nice, but most investors, including me, are looking for a solid, stable return on investment, which is achieved through steady cash flow. I want to see that the property is generating revenue today (or as soon as possible after it is purchased). I don't want to buy for a "what if" scenario; I want to buy for a "this *is*" reality. Cash flow is the lifeblood of any rental property investor. Keep the cash flow pumping, and you'll keep growing. Break even on cash flow or lose money on cash flow, and you are on a path to financial ruin.

I'll repeat myself one last time: Buy rental properties that offer cash flow today.

3. Tax Savings

The U.S. government likes real estate investors. We provide housing for the increasingly rent-minded population and ensure stability in the economy. As such, the government chooses to reward and encourage real estate investors through favorable tax treatment. Of course, I'm not a CPA, and you should always meet with one before making any major financial decisions, but let me assure you, I pay far less in taxes than most Americans, despite earning more income (both passive and active) than most.

Of course, this doesn't mean you should simply buy any property just because of the tax benefits. Tax benefits will never make a bad deal good, but they can make a good deal even better.

4. Loan Paydown

The fourth and final wealth generator is known as the loan paydown, which, in simple terms, is this: You can automate part of your wealth building by simply obtaining a loan on your rental property and using the income from your tenants to pay that loan down each and every month.

If you'll recall, I remarked earlier that a property's cash flow is its total income minus its total expenses. One of these expenses is the entire mortgage payment, though in reality, a mortgage payment has two separate parts:

1. Principal
2. Interest

The principal is the actual balance of the loan being paid down, while the interest is the profit the lender makes, based on the interest rate you agreed to pay when you secured the loan. For example, you might have a mortgage payment that is $500 a month, and part of that payment amount (the principal) goes to pay down the loan, while the rest (the interest) goes to pay the interest. For most U.S. loans, the portion of interest versus principal is defined by a term we know as "amortization." At the beginning of a loan, most of the borrower's monthly payment goes toward interest, but as the loan matures, the payment concentration shifts, so that most of the payment eventually goes toward principal. That means your payment might be $500 per month for 30 years, and during month one, you'll pay $400 just in interest and only $100 toward the principal. In month two, however, this shifts to $399 in interest and $101 toward the principal. This trend continues until the 30 years have passed, at which point 100 percent of your final payment goes toward the principal.

To best determine exactly how much of your monthly payment is applied to principal and how much to interest at different times during the loan payback period, use an online amortization calculator such as the one found here: www.amortization-calc.com.

Let's return to the matter at heart: how loan paydown can be a wealth generator. As I mentioned earlier, you can build wealth simply by using the rental income from your tenant(s) to pay down your property's mortgage. It's a somewhat automatic way of building wealth, because it happens naturally. I like to joke that I could work a minimum-wage job for the rest of my life and never save a penny, and I would still retire a millionaire because my current property mortgages are being paid down by my tenants each and every month.

Now, I'm not suggesting that you go out and purchase a property that is a bad deal but breaks even in hopes of building wealth that way. Instead, I'm simply explaining how the loan paydown can be a wealth generator for a rental property investor. Keep in mind, though, that this particular wealth generator does not apply if you pay all cash for a property, because in that case, there is no loan to be paid off over time. However, without a loan, you get to keep a higher percentage of the property's rental income, so the cash flow would likely be greater.

I think this leads us to a very valuable question: How much money does one need to get started? Should a person obtain a loan? Should an aspiring investor pay all cash? What about down payments?

How Much Money Does One Need to Invest in Rental Properties?

In the history of the world, perhaps nothing has killed more real estate ambitions than the belief that one does not have enough money to get started.

In fact, I speak with people all the time who don't realize that investing in real estate without having the full, 100 percent purchase price of a property is totally possible. They look at a $100,000 property and try to do the math in their head, thinking, "Well, if I saved $100 per month from my job, I could start investing 83 years from now. But that's never going to happen, so I guess investing in real estate is only for the privileged rich."

Not so! Enter *leverage*.

Leverage is a financial term that simply means applying a small amount of force to achieve far greater results. With real estate, leverage usually comes in the form of a loan. Although such a loan could come from a number of different sources, the practice is quite similar. A small down payment is supplied by the real estate investor, a lender provides the remaining balance of the property's purchase price, and the investor pays that lender a small amount each month until the loan is paid off.

For example, I might consider that same $100,000 property but get a bank to lend me 80 percent of the purchase price. They would supply $80,000 via a loan, and I would need to come up with just the $20,000 down payment (plus closing costs, which I'll cover in a moment).

Let me repeat using this approach: I only need to save up $20,000 to buy the property, instead of the entire $100,000 purchase price. Yes, I will need to pay the bank a certain amount each month for many years, but if I've done my math correctly, I'll ultimately make far more income each month than I'll spend on that loan payment. Granted, saving $100 a month, as I mentioned in my earlier example, to save up a $20,000 down payment would still take many years, but other strategies are available for using even more leverage or finding lower-priced properties. I'll cover these strategies in a later chapter of this book.

Yes, this is pretty basic stuff, but you might be surprised how many new investors fail to realize that this is how the game is played.

Leverage, of course, can be both a blessing and a curse. The more leverage you use, the greater the risk you may be taking. For example, if you paid 100 percent cash for a property, you wouldn't have a loan payment due each month, so a three-month vacancy on your property wouldn't hurt as much. Or if you bought a house with just 5 percent down, and the value of that property dropped by 20 percent, you would then be "underwater" on your loan, meaning that you'd owe more money on the house than its worth. This, in turn, limits your future options and can make selling, refinancing, or doing pretty much anything else with the property very difficult. In fact, leveraging was largely the core cause of the housing collapse and glut of foreclosures in the market in 2007 and 2008.

Homeowner Hank purchased a home for $100,000 using 100 percent financing, putting down $0 on the property. When the value of that property later dropped to $80,000 and Homeowner Hank lost his job, he couldn't sell the property because he owed far more than what he could get for it. The bank needed $100,000 to be satisfied, but the most Hank could recover by selling the property was $80,000. As a result, Homeowner Hank—like millions of others—simply allowed the bank to foreclose on and take the house.

Was leverage to blame? Should we pay 100 percent for rental properties? What is the magic number?

I'd like to reframe these questions and force you to think about things in a slightly different light. Rather than discussing how much money to put down for a property, I want to encourage you to think, "How secure can I be?" There are ways of increasing your security when you use leverage, so let me cover the two main points.

First, a property's down payment is not as important as the deal you get. To illustrate this, let me ask you a simple question of "which of the following is riskier:"

- You purchase a house for $100,000 and put 30 percent down, thus obtaining a $70,000 loan;
- I buy an identical house for $70,000 with 0 percent down, thus obtaining a $70,000 loan.

Who is at more risk? Even though our loan amounts are identical, I would argue that *you* are at the greater risk because you have more cash invested. I just did the upfront work required to pay $70,000, and you did not. I leveraged my creativity in place of a down payment.

Secondly, when investing in rental properties, knowledge can help decrease the risk involved with leverage. The better you understand the market, your investment, and how to manage that investment, the lower your risk that something will go wrong. For example, if you do the math correctly before you buy an investment property and know that you must account for the property sitting empty a certain percentage of the year, then that vacancy, when it occurs, will not have as negative an effect on your bottom line. It's just part of the business. Your knowledge can help secure your investment(s) against the things that *will* go wrong. For this reason, you'll spend an entire chapter of this book learning how to analyze a real estate investment.

Perhaps you can now see why I can't give a simple answer to the question "How much money does one need to invest in rental properties?" However, I don't want you to finish reading this section without having a good number in your head, so let me offer two of the most common scenarios.

- **House Hacking.** If you plan to purchase and live in a small multifamily property of two to four units, you could obtain a bank loan for as low as 3.5 percent down through the FHA loan program. This approach, known as "house hacking," is a great strategy for individuals who are just starting out with real estate and have limited cash and experience. However, to qualify, you are required to live in the property for at least one year.
- **Conventional Loan.** A conventional loan is a loan that conforms to some strict government guidelines. Most banks want a minimum of a 20 percent down payment for rental properties. A number of banks will allow less, in some cases as low as 10 percent, while other banks will require more, such as 25 percent or even 30 percent. Each bank has its own requirements, but as of the writing of this book, obtaining financing for roughly 20 percent down should be possible, as long as you qualify for such a loan, which we'll discuss later. Many of the examples in this book will use conventional 20 percent down payments as the norm for planning and strategizing for the future, as this approach is the most common. Understand, however, that the dollar amount or down payment percentage is not as important as the concepts working below the surface. No matter how much money you have, keep reading.

If you want to read more of what I know about investing with creativity, check out my previous book, *The Book on Investing in Real Estate with No (and Low) Money Down*, which is available anywhere books are sold.

I have no problem with people who want to use 100 percent cash for their real estate purchases, completely avoiding any kind of loan. I am a big fan of the personal finance advice of Dave Ramsey, who is a staunch advocate for always paying 100 percent cash for any investment property. However, I also recognize that for many people, including me, waiting to invest until all the cash needed has been saved up would require decades of sitting on the sidelines.

If you decide to invest using all cash, I encourage you to pretend that you are *not* doing so when you are shopping for deals. Having excess money on hand when you're shopping is dangerous, whether you are at Nordstrom, the supermarket, or looking for rental properties. Being able to pay all cash allows people to be "soft" on the math and pay too much for a property because writing a check is much easier than finding a great deal. Know your numbers, scrutinize each property carefully, and be sure the property you're targeting will provide a solid return on investment. Remember, price does not equal value. As Warren Buffet said, "Price is what you pay, value is what you get."

What About Reserves?

The past several pages have focused primarily on the down payment needed to invest in rental properties. However, there is another purpose for your cash, and that is for reserves.

As the saying goes, "It's better to dig a well before you are thirsty." The fact is, when investing in rental properties, things are going to go wrong. You'll have good months, bad months, and average months—and you'll never know which one you will get. This is why having cash reserves to cover any problems you might face is so imperative. Buying a rental property and being forced in the first month to evict a tenant and invest thousands of dollars in repairs would be terrible, but this kind of thing could, in fact, happen.

The amount of cash you should have in reserves depends on a number of factors, most notably the number of properties you own, the condition/ age of those properties, the anticipated cost of fixing the properties (would you do the work yourself?), saving for larger future big-ticket expenses, and your management abilities. However, I would encourage you to start with six months of expenses for each unit you have. For example, if you own a single-family home that costs you $800 per month in expenses, I would recommend having $4,800 in reserve savings for that property. As you obtain more and more properties, you may be able to decrease this amount some, but it serves as a good starting point.

So, how much money should you have to get started? This will depend on your plan, which I'll cover more in the next chapter, but the simple answer is this: enough to cover your down payment and reserves.

Now, I don't want to be accused of making rental property investments sound too glamorous, so let's address some of the downsides.

Top Five Difficulties of Rental Property Investing

As I've mentioned numerous times already, I love rental property investing. It's my passion, my hobby, my career, my baby.

However, it's not always fun, and I want any potential investor to know both the positives and negatives before jumping in. Obviously, I don't want to discourage you, but I'd rather have you know the tune before starting the dance. The following list outlines some of the primary difficulties, dangers, and annoyances of being a rental property investor. I will also include some thoughts on how to overcome these issues.

1. Building Wealth Takes Time

"What? You mean rental property investing is not a get-rich-quick activity? I want my money back!"

Yes, incredible wealth has been built by those who own rental properties. However, that wealth has never been built overnight. Instead, generating wealth through real estate is about taking consistent action over a long period of time. The keywords there are "consistent action" and "long period of time." Are you prepared to get in this game for the long haul? Are you ready for the ups *and* the downs that will come with your rental properties? If so, proceed.

2. It Can Be All-Consuming

Rental property investing has a tendency to take over your life, as any passion can. My wife and I sit down for dinner each night and struggle to *not* talk about our rentals. When I lie in bed at night, I have to force myself to not think about all the moving parts. Even when I'm watching an episode of *Friends*, I find myself thinking, "Hmmm, I wonder how much that apartment would actually rent for . . ."

Then there are vacations. Landlording doesn't offer a two-week, paid vacation each year. There is no "vacation auto reply" feature you can engage to deal with maintenance emergencies while you're away. Problems do happen—any time, any day, any year. A broken pipe does not respect your personal time. However, your business will run the way you set it up to run. If you appoint yourself the "fixer of pipes," then, yes, you may run into problems. However, if you run your business like an owner instead, you can then outsource most problems and enjoy the occasional vacation.

3. You Have to Deal with Difficult People

As a rental property owner, you are not an island. You must be involved with—*gasp!*—other people. One of the things that has gotten me "down" in the past decade of being a landlord is being required to deal with people who aren't necessarily easy to get along with.

From contractors to deadbeat tenants to bankers and other challenging individuals, sometimes you will have to associate with difficult people in difficult situations. You may need to fire a contractor who doesn't show up on time. You may need to let your property manager go when he or she can't fill a vacancy fast enough. You might have to hear the same sob story about why the rent was late for the 100th time. You will probably have to evict a tenant.

Understand, however, that you *can* limit your exposure to difficult people by managing effectively. By doing your due diligence up front to find a great contractor or property manager, you will reduce the probability that you will later need to fire that person. By screening your tenants exceptionally well, you'll be able to weed out the ones who will cause you the most damage. By outsourcing tasks you don't want to do (such as answering phones and showing vacant units, as I have done), you can decrease your interaction with difficult people and situations.

4. It Involves Paperwork and Bookkeeping

Here's something no one told me when I was getting into the rental property game: There is *a lot* of paperwork to keep track of. From leases to forms to taxes to insurance, a good portion of an investor's time is spent just keeping the paperwork side of the business organized. I probably receive 50 pieces of mail each week that somehow involve my rental properties, and each one needs to be opened, read, dealt with, and filed. Luckily, my wife is a master at handling this side of the business and keeps our life organized, because without her, I'd be an unorganized mess.

Furthermore, when investing in rental properties, you absolutely must keep accurate bookkeeping and accounting records, which can be challenging. QuickBooks is not an easy software to learn, and if you stick to using spreadsheets, be prepared to juggle a lot of them. Receipts need to be logged and filed, contractors must be paid and those charges recorded, and, come spring, your taxes will begin to take on a life of their own as your rental portfolio grows.

5. You Can Lose Your Investment

Lastly, let's be honest: Rental properties *are* an investment, and as the basic definition of investments would imply, you could end up losing. Not every rental property owner is successful. In fact, I would argue that most "mom and pop" landlords lose money because they don't run an effective rental property business. However, there are ways of decreasing your risk and increasing your chances for success, and by reading this book and improving your knowledge, you are already employing one such way.

There are likely other downsides to rental property investing that I didn't cover in this section, and you'll hear about them the more time you spend around landlords. (We're a vocal bunch!) However, none of these problems are insurmountable. With the right education, networking, and systems in place, you'll do great.

But I Don't Want to Fix Toilets at 2 a.m.!

When talking to people about becoming a rental property investor, the most common excuse I hear is "But I don't want to fix toilets at two in the morning!"

Really?

Let me just clear up this myth right now. The only landlords fixing toilets at two in the morning are those who are not managing their properties effectively. They are running their business like a hobby rather than a business. Only once in my decade of investing in real estate have I woken up in the middle of the night to handle an emergency, and, lo and behold, it wasn't actually an emergency.

Yes, things happen in the middle of the night, but 99.9 percent of them can be fixed during business hours, and for the .1 percent of instances when you *do* face a middle-of-the-night emergency, there are people who can be called (usually a plumber). I don't wake up at two in the morning to fix toilets, and you shouldn't have to, either. As I've said several times so far: You have the power to set up your business the way you want it, so don't create a business where the 2 a.m. toilet fix is even a possibility.

The 2 a.m. toilet story that everyone seems to talk about is not something that really ever happens, but it *is* an excuse that millions of broke people have used to stay broke. Saying, "But I don't want to fix toilets at 2 a.m.!" is much easier than saying, "I don't want to invest my time and energy into an opportunity that will help me gain financial independence."

Which kind of person are you?

Why Do So Many Rental Property Owners Fail?

They started investing in real estate 30 years ago, with so much hope for their future.

A rental house here, a duplex there, and soon they had a rental portfolio that would make anyone proud. They actively managed their properties and worked to make sure they were operating at peak efficiency. Then, several years ago, the husband and wife both retired from their day jobs and eased into retirement—funded by their rental income and social security.

This year, they are filing bankruptcy and losing a majority of their properties to foreclosure.

Sadly, this is not a made-up example; this is the story of one of my friend's parents, and they are not alone. In fact, 95 percent of the units I've purchased have been foreclosures that belonged to landlords who failed and lost their properties to the bank. Most of these people, I would guess, will never again be active in real estate investing. They worked hard for years to build a financial future for themselves, only to see it come tragically crashing down around them, dashing any hopes for lasting wealth creation.

This begs the question: why?

If real estate is as good an investment as investors make it out to be, why do so many real estate investors fail?

Perhaps more importantly, how do you avoid this possibility in your own life?

This question has been swimming around in my mind for some time now. Each week on the *BiggerPockets Podcast,* I ask our guest, "What is it that sets successful investors apart from those who fail?" The answers are as diverse as the personalities of the guests with whom we've spoken. So what is it?

I'm intrigued by this idea and scared that I may end up the same way. After all, as Mark Cuban famously said, *"Everyone's* a genius in a bull market." Is that what real estate is? Do some people simply get lucky, while others don't?

Let's look at some of the possible reasons rental property investors go broke and explore the things you can do to protect yourself.

Too Much Risk?

First, let's talk about the elephant in the room: risk.

Risk is inherent in every investment there is. After all, you know the phrase "more risk, more reward."

However, there is obviously a tipping point at which the risk becomes too great, as my friend's parents discovered. Perhaps it's overleveraging properties by obtaining too many "low-down" deals that weren't deals after all, or maybe it's trying to buy too many properties too fast. Maybe it's constant refinancing of the properties, pulling out all the equity and investing it in more and more deals. Whatever the reason for the bankruptcy, the risk clearly became too great, and these investors lost.

As rock 'n' roller Nick Cave sang, "If you're gonna dine with them cannibals, sooner or later, darling, you're gonna get eaten."

How might someone prevent this? Avoid risk altogether? Invest only in 100 percent safe deals?

Of course not. Risk is required for entrepreneurs, but learning to navigate that risk will define your success.

Like a team of white-water rafters braving the wild waves, you can't always see what the future holds, where the rocks hide just below the surface, or when the next waterfall will appear. However, by having the right people in the boat with you, keeping an eye out for potential dangers, working to avoid potential problem areas, and wearing the proper life jacket, you can avoid a premature "death."

I caution anyone reading this chapter, including me, to think of risk as a dangerous but powerful tool—and to never forget that this tool cuts both ways.

Not Enough Education?

Far too many people jump into buying real estate before understanding what they are doing. They simply decide that real estate is the right path for them and start purchasing properties. There is a big difference between being busy and being effective, and this is the case with a lot of real estate investors; they believe that because they are buying properties, they are going to succeed. Never mind that they bought the wrong property in the wrong area with the wrong financing.

The solution to this problem is proper education.

I'm not talking about the "get rich quick," late-night television kind of education. I'm talking about taking the time needed to build an educational foundation that can support your investing future. Furthermore, I encourage you to continue learning through library books, meetups, and other low-cost resources. You don't need to spend tens of thousands of dollars for an education. Information has been democratized, so you simply need to reach out and grab it. No one can do it for you!

Not Enough Analysis?

When I first began investing in real estate, I thought I knew what I was doing, but I made some big mistakes because I didn't do a careful enough analysis. Had I continued on that path, I would have been in the same boat as my friend's parents.

You see, so many people buy properties without doing the right math. As I often say, "Without the right math going into an investment, you'll never get the right profit coming out of it."

The future is impossible to know, but with solid analysis, it's much easier to predict. We'll talk a lot more about analysis throughout this book, and I would encourage you to look at these sections with the reverence the topic deserves. Bad math makes for bad investments!

Are You Working on Your Business or in Your Business?

Is real estate your investment or your hobby?

I believe one of the greatest reasons investors fail is that they don't treat their business like a *business*.

- They never develop systems to help them as they grow.
- They treat their tenants like friends.
- They don't create clear policies for finding good tenants.
- They simply approach investing like a church picnic, and it shows.

If you want to avoid failing, treat your rental property business the same way a CEO would look at any other business, because that is what it is. Monitor your business's health, hire the right people to do the right jobs, and continually find ways to improve your bottom line to create a long-lasting business.

So Why Do They Fail?

A real estate investor may fail for a variety of reasons. However, in my limited time on this planet, I've seen the four mistakes I just listed played out time and time again in the lives of those who ultimately failed in their investments. It breaks my heart to see someone so excited about what real estate could do only to lose it all in a foreclosure or bankruptcy.

Don't be that person.

If you want to avoid losing all the hard work you are putting in (or all the hard work you are about to put in), pay attention to the following four points:

- Understand that risk is a powerful but dangerous tool, so tread cautiously.
- Build a solid educational foundation for yourself before getting in too deep.
- Don't skimp on the math. Always understand the numbers for any property you buy.
- Work *on* your business, not *in* it. Treat your investments like a business—which they *are*.

Quitting (or Not Quitting) Your Job Through Rental Properties

Let's be honest: We all dream of quitting our jobs, whether next week, next year, or in the next decade. And real estate is appealing because of the financial freedom it can offer through rental properties. But when is the right time to quit? Do you need to leave your job soon to become a successful real estate investor? What if you love your job?

Should You Quit?

Do you love your current job? My guess is that if you are reading this book, you probably don't. According to *Forbes*,[3] nearly two-thirds of Americans are not happy at work. I know I've been there. I once worked for a large national bank and hated it. I loved the bank and loved my coworkers, but I hated the job itself—the pressure to sell, the pressure to please, and the pressure to perform. *Ugh.* I don't like pressure. So I quit my job and went full-time into real estate investing. It wasn't always easy, but it was much better than working at the bank. Later, after I had stabilized much of my rental portfolio and had enough passive income to pay the bills, I actually went back *into* the work world, but for different reasons. I no longer *had* to work; I was *choosing* to work to help build BiggerPockets with people I love and respect.

Allow me to share some thoughts on how *you* can quit your miserable

---

3 http://www.forbes.com/sites/susanadams/2012/05/18/new-survey-majority-of-employees-dissatisfied/

(or not so miserable) job and embark on a career in real estate investing, whether you plan to quit in 20 days or 20 years. Remember, it won't be easy. Rental property investing is not a get-rich-quick strategy. It takes commitment, persistence, and maybe even a little bit of luck.

However, before you put in your two-weeks' notice, we should get a few things straight.

1. Quitting Your Job Soon Through Rental Properties Will Be Tough

You can make money relatively quickly in real estate in a lot of ways, but rental property investing is not one of them. Wealth is built in the long run, and as a result, you'll probably not quit your job next week unless you already have a large amount of investment capital with which to start or you want to make rental property investing a job, which brings me to my second point.

2. Real Estate Investing Can Be a Job or an Investment. Which Do You Want?

A job is something that earns you money today to live on. You put in the hours, and cash is deposited into your checking account. An investment, however, is money earned from mostly passive sources. House flipping and real estate wholesaling, for example, are "jobs." Owning rentals is an investment (hopefully!).

Which one do you want?

This might seem to be a strange question, and there is no universal right or wrong answer, but I believe that thinking this one through all the way is fundamentally important. You see, there are a lot of other options if you don't love your current job. Going into full-time real estate investing should not be your only alternative to a bad job. Why? Because real estate investing for income *is* a job. Know that jerk from work you don't like and want to get away from? Yep, he'll be part of your real estate investing job, too, in some form. Know that pressure you feel at your job to perform? Yep, that will be there as well. The grass is not necessarily greener on the other side.

There is one essential truth that I harp on all the time: *Find what you love to do in life more than anything else, and do that for a career. If that means teaching high school math, teach high school math. If that means traveling the world, then find a job that lets you travel the world. And if that means investing in real estate for income, then invest in real estate for income.*

Now let me clarify something important here: I'm not suggesting that you should only invest in real estate if you love investing in real estate. I'm saying you should only invest in real estate *as a career* if you love investing in real estate. Do you see the subtle difference?

I believe everyone can—and should—include real estate investing as part of their strategy for retirement and wealth building. However, that doesn't always include doing it full-time and making a steady income from it. The beauty of owning rental properties is found in the flexibility to make the investment what you want, and if that, for you, means "passive," then you can make it (mostly) passive. I'll show you how throughout this book.

3. Even If You Can Quit, Should You?

The third point I want to make is this: Even if you *can* quit your job because of your real estate activities, *should* you? Because this book focuses specifically on rental property investing, I'm going to ignore the other ways of making money in real estate and get specific about rentals. To be able to quit your job and find "financial freedom" through rental properties, you have to be able to live off your cash flow. If your investment properties provide $3,000 per month in cash flow, and you need $3,000 per month to live, you might think that quitting your job is the next logical step.

This was my thought process when I quit my job the last time. I had enough cash flow from my rental properties to cover all my bills, so I quit. Then, when I sat down and spent some time working on my plan to build wealth, I realized a very important fact—I was eating my financial potential alive by destroying the greatest wealth-building device on earth: compound interest.

Compound interest is the profit earned by reinvesting profits. To quickly simplify this concept, I'll use a story. Let's pretend that your bank account has $1,000 in it. That account is special and automatically earns 10 percent interest every year, so at the end of the first year, it has $1,100 in it, meaning that you made yourself $100 (because 10 percent of $1,000 is $100). If it earns 10 percent interest again the next year, you will not have earned $100, but rather $110, because the 10 percent is now calculated on the $1,100 you had in the account at the beginning of that second year (10 percent of $1,100 = $110). In other words, your previous interest positioned you to earn additional interest. Following this pattern, after thirty years, that account would have more than $18,000 in it.

Now, compare that with a similar scenario: What would happen to that bank account if you withdrew the $100 in interest you earned the first year and hid it under your mattress? You'd still have $1,100 total after that year (the $1,000 in the bank plus the $100 under your mattress). But at the end of year two, you will have earned just $100 in interest, because the 10 percent is calculated only on the money in the bank account—the money under your mattress earns nothing. You could keep doing this every year for thirty years at 10 percent, and the most you'll ever make is $100 per year, or $3,000 in interest total, and you'll have $1,000 in the account at the end (if you add nothing else to it).

What's my point? Trust me, I'm getting somewhere, and if you can understand this entire concept, you can build an absurd amount of wealth in the coming years. Hang with me a little longer while I explain.

The graph in Figure 1 shows what your total net worth would be over thirty years using both of the scenarios I just outlined and with no additional money being deposited into the account. The curved line represents the "compound interest" scenario, in which the money is continually reinvested. The straight line represents the "simple interest" scenario, in which the profit is withdrawn and spent each year rather than reinvested.

Sure, at the beginning the two lines are almost indistinguishable. However, after a while, the compound interest line begins to take on a life of its own. This mathematical phenomenon is known as exponential growth, and it is exactly how wealth is built.

Let's now bring the focus back to real estate and your job. When you own a rental property and use all the profits from that investment to live on, you severely hurt your ability to build wealth through compound interest. Although you may still build wealth through the loan paydown, tax savings, and appreciation, *you can do better.* By reinvesting your cash flow *into* your business, you'll be able to earn additional interest on the previous interest, just as my example with the $1,000 bank account shows. Taking the cash flow and enjoying your profits may be tempting, but don't do so without first considering the long-term ramifications. Perhaps you don't want to build massive additional wealth. If that's the case, then by all means, live on your cash flow!

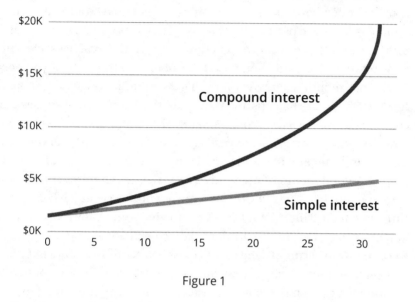

Compound Interest vs. Simple Interest
$1,000 @ 10% Interest Invested for Thirty Years

Figure 1

But if you are looking to grow your net worth exponentially, consider keeping your job or finding another way to make income.

When you invest for the future (largely with buy-and-hold investing), you are reinvesting your profits back into your business and thinking for the long term. You cannot simply rely on the money you earn from your investments to sustain you and pay your bills. You must have another source of income. This is why many rental property investors also flip houses or get into wholesaling. These options help them pay the bills and save up additional cash to support their rental property business.

4. How to Quit Your Job Through Rental Properties

Okay, so I just spent several pages trying to convince you to *not* quit your job, or at least to not live off your cash flow yet. However, I know some of you are further along this path or maybe don't want to build a massive rental property empire, so let me explore the idea of quitting your job *through* rental properties.

If you want to quit using rental property cash flow, common sense would dictate that you need a significant amount of cash flow coming in. There are two ways you can accomplish this: the "cash flow per door" method and the "return on investment" method. I'll explain both.

- **Cash Flow per Door.** One easy way to think about financial freedom from your job through rental properties is by looking at "cash flow per door." In other words, after all the bills are paid each month, how much money is left over per unit? Let's say you want to see a minimum of $100 per month, per unit in cash flow after all the expenses are paid. How many units would you need to have to quit your job? If you need $2,000 per month to survive, you'd need 20 units. (Be careful, though. Real estate always has ups and downs, with unforeseen expenses that could occur at any time, so make sure that if you are following this strategy, you have significant cash reserves.) Additionally, do you want just enough income to "survive?" How much income do you need to *thrive*? A good friend of mine advises investors that "your business should bring in at least 3X the income of your current job before you think about quitting. 1X for tax, 1X to survive, and 1X for reinvestment and unexpected events." I think his advice isn't too far off.
- **Return on Investment.** The more "math-minded" investors out there can get a lot more technical by looking at return on investment and the amount of cash invested. For example, let's say that you only buy rental properties that produce a 10 percent return on investment for your money; we'll also assume you want to "retire" with $100,000 per year in passive cash flow from your rental properties. You would then use these two figures to determine how much cash you'd need to invest. To do this, use the following simple formula:

  Annual Cash Flow / Interest Rate = Cash Invested
  $100,000 / .1 = Cash Invested
  $100,000 / .1 = $1,000,000

Therefore, at a 10 percent return on investment, you would need to invest $1,000,000 of your cash to achieve $100,000 in cash flow from your properties.

When I had less capital to invest, I generally used the "cash flow per door" method, simply because I was investing with creativity. After all, when I used $0 to buy a property, my return on investment was infinite, so the return on investment calculation didn't make much sense. As I grow my wealth and get into more and more boring traditional real estate investments, I'll likely shift my process to use the return on investment calculation to determine how much I need to retire. Depending on how much money you plan to use when getting started, you may want to use either option, or even both.

WRAPPING IT UP

If your goal is to quit your job, this book will help. If your goal is to pad your retirement, this book will help. If your goal is to build incredible wealth, this book will help. Whatever goal you have for your life, I believe rental properties can help you achieve it and attain the life you want to live.

I once sat in that dark all-you-can-eat Chinese buffet restaurant and read those nine words that changed my life: *There is no such thing as an ordinary life.* I truly believe this. Life itself is so extraordinary and unique that the only thing keeping people ordinary is themselves. This book is designed to help you break away from ordinary and achieve more. I want you to realize that an extraordinary life is not only *possible*, but it is also there for the taking. An "ordinary life" doesn't really exist, so it's time for you to take hold of your destiny and hang on for dear life. It's going to be a wild ride.

Chapter Two

THE FIVE KEYS TO RENTAL PROPERTY SUCCESS

"Success is not to be pursued; it is to be attracted by the person we become."

—JIM ROHN

Thomas Edison's teachers said he was too stupid to learn anything.

Beethoven handled the violin awkwardly, and his instructor once called him "hopeless as a composer."

Babe Ruth led the American League in strikeouts for five different seasons and was known as the "strikeout king."

Despite their past, these three would go down in the history books as incredibly successful individuals. They didn't let their past determine their future. They rose up and conquered their industry, leaving a mark that no one could ever erase.

You may not be the next Edison, Beethoven, or Babe Ruth, but you *do* have the ability to achieve incredible greatness yourself. Success is an action, and I believe you have what it takes to achieve it. This chapter is all about finding that success, despite what your past might be. You are about to learn the five keys to rental property success. Although acquiring rental properties involves many other steps as well, these five keys are essential and nonnegotiable if you want to find long-lasting success. Master these five, and you, too, will go down in history as a person of incredible success.

1. Think the Right Thoughts

The first and perhaps most important step in becoming a successful rental property investor is thinking the right thoughts. In other words, it's not an external action you need to take, but an internal mindset you need to create.

This mindset begins by flipping a switch in your head so that you say to yourself, "I *am* doing this," rather than, "I *want* to do this." You tell yourself, "I *will* do this," rather than, "I *can* do this." Your mind says, "I *won't* give up," rather than, "I *hope* I won't give up."

Let me illustrate this further using a common desire for most of the world: six-pack abs. You see, I want to have six-pack abs. I can get six-pack abs. And when I start to work toward those six-pack abs, I hope I won't give up on that journey. But you know what? I'm not getting six-pack abs with that mindset!

To take it a step further, I even know *how* to get six-pack abs. I know the exercises I need to do, the food I need to eat, and the lifestyle I need to follow. But I'm still not getting that six pack! Why? Because I'm not yet *committed.* I haven't yet flipped that switch in my head so that I tell myself, "I *am* getting six-pack abs, I *will* do this, and I *won't* give up." Deep inside my soul, I know I have not flipped that switch, committed myself, and started taking action. And as much as I don't want to admit it, I know that I have not yet committed to getting that six pack. It's just a dream, a desire.

Does this sound familiar to you? Have you "flipped the switch" of success in your mind? Have you made the commitment to yourself that you *will* become a rental property investor, come hell or high water?

If not, don't worry. I believe that by the end of this book, you will. First, here are a few tips for moving in that direction.

A. Write Down Your Goals, and Read Them Out Loud Every Day

I got this tip from Grant Cardone, an investor with more than $350,000,000 in real estate assets whom we interviewed on the *BiggerPockets Podcast* (episode 108). He's been reading his goals out loud to himself every morning and every night for 30 years, and he also reads them when he's feeling down. In addition, in his book, *The 10X Rule: The Only Difference Between Success and Failure*, Cardone encourages his readers to take whatever goal they might have, multiply it by ten, change their plan/mindset to reflect that new goal, and then take massive action to accomplish their revised objective.

For example, one of my goals was to achieve one hundred rental units, and my mind worked toward that goal. I could buy a fourplex here, a single-family house there, a small apartment building there ...it was all very *attainable*. After applying the 10X Rule to my goals, though, I'm now aiming for 1,000 units. My mindset is very different. I no longer think in terms of "a single-family house here." That will never get me to 1,000 units! I have to think bigger. As Napoleon Hill states in *Think and Grow Rich*, "Whatever the mind can conceive and believe, it can achieve." Your mind will naturally work to solve the problem or goal you've set before it. Raise your goal, think differently, and 10X your life.

B. Realize That You Are Who You Associate With

As entrepreneur Jim Rohn said, "You are the average of the five people you spend the most time with." Think about the five people with whom you occupy your day—you are likely very similar. Why is this? One big word: homeostasis.

Homeostasis is a scientific term that essentially means that things like to stay constant and level. The human body is a homeostatic biological machine that wants to stay at 98.6 degrees. Your home's thermostat is a homeostatic device that wants to keep the house temperature at a comfortable 72 degrees. Your car's cruise control is a homeostatic feature that keeps your freeway commute moving at a steady 74 mph while you drive to work.

Your social life is a homeostatic entity that desires to keep everyone on the same level, usually subconsciously. As you start to grow your wealth or your level of success, your friends will naturally feel the pull of homeostasis and, with no maliciousness intended, attempt to pull you back to their level. They won't understand your newfound passion. However, if you instead hang around with five people far more successful than you, their homeostatic tendencies will kick in, and they'll naturally want to help you rise to their level of success.

Please understand that I'm not encouraging you to abandon all your friends. Money is, by far, *not* the most important thing in life, and the homeostatic phenomenon also applies to character, intelligence, passion, and other nonmonetary traits. I choose to spend time with people who make me a better person in *all* aspects of my life. I'm also not suggesting that you befriend successful people just to take advantage of their position and raise yourself up in the world. I'm simply encouraging you to be mindful of the people with whom you spend the most time and how they influence your worldview.

Try to spend time, each and every day, with other real estate investors. Their homeostatic tendencies will naturally lead them to want to help you achieve their level of success. When I first got into rental properties, I helped my best friend paint a house for his landlord. While painting, the landlord, Kyle, stopped by to check up on the work, and he and I got to talking. That conversation led to coffee later, which progressed to thousands of phone calls and one of the best friendships I have today. For the past eight or so years, Kyle and I have chatted about business at least once a week, sharing our stories, our problems, our tenant drama, our financing tips, and more. Kyle naturally wanted to bring me up to his level of success, and I graciously accepted.

Who do you know in your life with whom you could build a relationship? If you said "no one" and immediately shut your brain off, shame on you! There are tens of millions of real estate investors out there, and likely dozens right in your area. Get off your couch and go build some relationships! Local real estate clubs and landlord meetups are good places to find these individuals, as are referrals from your real estate agent or simply word of mouth.

C. Change Your "I Can't" to "How Can I?"

I love the concept of changing your mindset from one of "I can't" to "how can I?" This change of vocabulary is simple, yet profound. As Robert Kiyosaki explains in his book *Rich Dad Poor Dad*, responding to new ideas with "I can't" shuts your brain off and stops it from working for you. By changing your mindset from an immediate declaration of "no" to an immediate question of "how," you put your brain into overdrive to help you accomplish your goals.

- "I can't afford that property" becomes "How can I afford that property?"

- "I can't find a good deal" becomes "How can I find a good deal?"
- "I can't connect with the right partner" becomes "How can I connect with the right partner?"

In all these situations, suddenly you have a puzzle to solve, a journey to start. You'll begin to see solutions where before you saw only a blank wall. Your brain will learn to think creatively, and, over time, you'll find that nothing is impossible. Mom was right when she told you, "You can do anything you want if you just put your mind to it."

Change the way your mind thinks, and you'll change the way your mind operates.

2. Study the Right Source

Once you've "flipped the switch" in your head and are fully committed to a future that involves building wealth through real estate, it's time to take action. Before you make your first purchase, however, you need to gain some education. Therefore, the second key to success in rental property investing is to study the right source.

But what is the right source? And how do you study it?

What Should You Learn?

It's easy to get overwhelmed when you decide to take the plunge into real estate investing. There are literally hundreds of different paths you could take to achieve wealth through real estate, and, sadly, many people never decide on and commit to one path, and thus never get started. You've no doubt heard the term "analysis paralysis," which refers to when people spend so much time learning and analyzing, they never get around to actually *doing* anything.

The secret to overcoming analysis paralysis, I believe, is in focus.

When you are first getting started in the world of real estate, learning a little bit about a lot of things is important. However, as you progress, you will want to start focusing on a specific real estate strategy and avoid getting caught up in discussions on other strategies. Yes, flipping houses may sound fun, and wholesaling real estate may sound like a quick way to make a buck, but if you've committed to becoming a rental property investor, don't spend too much time thinking about these other paths. Every rule has its exceptions, of course, but don't get caught up chasing the next shiny object. Instead, when you hear about a different path someone took to achieve success, try to glean the mindset they took and apply it to the path *you* have chosen.

That you are reading this book on rental property investing is a good indication that this is the path you want to go down, which is great! But I believe you can refine your focus even more by narrowing down exactly what kind of rental property you want to buy. High end? Low end? Multifamily? Single family? I'll talk more about this later when the time comes to lay out your plan, but keep one word in mind as you move forward: focus.

Studying the Right Information

What is the "right" source for you to study? Where do you find the best real estate knowledge? Let's explore several of the most common learning methods you can use to obtain knowledge about the particular real estate niche you want to focus on. I'll start with one that I already know you are good at...

Books

Congratulations! You are already onto this one.

When I first got started investing in real estate, I fell in love with real estate books. The summer after I decided that real estate was going to be my future, I read more than one hundred real estate books, averaging almost one per day. I didn't pay for most of them because I simply went to my local library each week and reserved a handful of titles I wanted to read.

Books have a way of changing the way you think, because you are spending so much time inside an author's head. By reading *this* book, today, you are getting a glimpse inside my mind and learning how I think about real estate. It took me a decade to learn how to get where I am today, and you will learn everything I know about rental properties in the next few hours. Does that excite you as much as it does me?

I want to give you a list of my favorite real estate books, so you can head to your local library or hop onto www.amazon.com and pick up a few for yourself. But rather than taking up space in this book to do so, I'll simply invite you to go to www.biggerpockets.com/bestrealestatebooks to find my list of my twenty-one favorite real estate books, written by such authors as Gary Keller, Spencer Strauss, J Scott, Larry B. Loftis, Frank Gallinelli, and Ken McElroy.

The last thing I want to say about books before we move on is this: Don't just read. When you are first getting started, read as much as you can, but after a while, you will need to stop reading and start doing. You might brag to your friends that you read twenty books this month, but if you didn't learn anything or take action on the information in those books, what was the purpose? You would be better off reading just five books in a year and taking action on what you learned. With this book, set a goal for yourself of reading every word, maybe even twice, and then putting the lessons in it into action.

Podcasts

Podcasts are free, and you can listen to them while you drive, while you work, while you fold laundry. You can listen with your spouse, with your kids, or alone. You can even listen at double speed to fit more shows into your busy schedule.

Earlier in this book, I talked about the power of the people with whom you spend your time and the influence they can have on your success. Why not spend a few hours each week taking in a real estate podcast and learning from other investors? Start with the *Real Estate Rookie Podcast* or the *BiggerPockets Podcast* to get your first dose of investing tips and advice.

Podcasts have an incredible way of making you feel like you know the host or guest, as though you are actually sitting down with them for coffee. Every real estate meetup or event I attend, I hear that sentiment from dozens of people I've never met before; they tell me, "I feel like I know you!" And the funny thing is that, because they have listened to so many episodes of our show, I feel like I know them, too.

Keep in mind, if one show per week is not enough for you, there are dozens of real estate podcasts available, some better than others. Of course, the *BiggerPockets Podcast* is my favorite, but my other favorites are *The Real Estate Guys Radio Show* and *Just Start Real Estate* with Mike Simmons. If you look around, you may find others you enjoy also, and if you do, help the podcaster out by leaving him or her a rating and review.

Blogs

Anyone can start a blog and share their knowledge, which makes blog posts one of the best ways to gain real estate education without having to pay a penny. The internet has hundreds, if not thousands, of real estate investing blogs written by real-life, practicing real estate investors and covering practically every real estate niche and strategy.

Forums

Books are amazing sources of information, and blog posts can offer terrific insight, but both of these sources are "one directional." In other words, you only *receive* information. Engaging in a conversation with either one is difficult, if not impossible. For this aspect of your education, I recommend getting involved in an online real estate investing forum.

Forums are essentially online conversations around a particular topic. One person starts a "thread," or conversation, and anyone in the community can respond with a post to offer advice or knowledge, or to in any other way further engage in the discussion. Forums are great because when you are investing in rental properties, situations *will* arise that no book nor blog post has ever addressed. For these "what if" questions, being able to ask for input from others in the same position via a popular real estate investing forum, such as the BiggerPockets Forum, is really nice. And most forums are free to use.

Not only are forums great for asking questions, they are also a fantastic way to network. When you jump into a forum to engage in conversation (no matter what your experience level is), people see you and connect, just like in the real world. You can quickly establish yourself as someone who is serious about the business and find potential lenders, partners, deals, and other valuable resources and opportunities.

YouTube

Want to hear a secret?

YouTube has more than just cute cat videos! Shocking, I know. But with hundreds of thousands of hours of new content being uploaded to the site every day, YouTube is actually filled with a lot of great educational content that can help you grow as a rental property investor.

Keep in mind, I'm not just referring to videos on real estate investing. You can also find videos on business management, motivation, home repairs, and pretty much anything else you need to help you become a more successful real estate entrepreneur. Just don't get too sidetracked by all the cat videos. There are a lot of them!

What About Coaching Programs?

No doubt, you have seen expensive coaching and training programs advertised on late-night television or internet banner ads. Real estate gurus claim to be able to teach you to become filthy rich through real estate investing. Is this real? Can you really learn from these guys?

Let me first explain how this industry works. Typically, this kind of coaching or training involves several "layers," and as you peel away the layers, the education gets more and more expensive. Let me share the most common layers, so you'll be able to recognize them in the future.

1. **The Free Class.** You might come across an advertisement on the radio, on television, in your local newspaper, or on your favorite website— something like "Free Real Estate Seminar" at a local hotel or conference center. The marketing teams behind these gurus spend a lot of money to drive traffic to these free seminars, hoping to pack the room with wannabe real estate investors.

2. **The Hype.** In the seminar, the real estate guru creates massive hype around what real estate can do, showing photos of his properties, citing impressive numbers on how much profit he made, and claiming how easy it was. He tells stories of past students who have amassed a fortune from his investing tips. He pushes on all the right pain points about how hard being broke is, how you are not taking care of your family well enough, how you are missing out on life's luxuries. Then, he pitches hard for you to attend his weekend boot camp, usually for a small yet not insignificant chunk of money, between $200 and $500. After the pitch, he encourages the attendees to run to the back of the room to sign up—and many people do.

3. **The Boot Camp.** At the boot camp, the guru goes into more detail about what real estate can do, shares more numbers related to what he's done, and will probably spend a decent amount of time showing you a high-level overview of the kind of investing he is touting as "the best way to invest in real estate." He may talk about different strategies people use to build wealth in real estate. Some gurus are even known to spend a significant amount of time teaching those present how to negotiate, and, as a "test," encourage attendees to call up their credit card companies and get their credit card limits raised significantly. However, the guru's only real goal is to get you to sign up for the next level of training, which is typically a $20,000 to $50,000 in-depth coaching program with some live events built in.

I have no doubt that many (though not all) of these "real estate gurus" have good information to share. However, the problem lies not so much in the "what" as in the "how." These people are expert marketers and manipulators, and know how to touch on the right pain points and cause your emotions to lead you to make an expensive purchase. Their pitch logically makes a lot of sense: With just a $25,000 investment in your future, you'll end up making much more than that from the real estate training you'll learn. What's $25,000, $50,000, or even $100,000 when you'll be making millions of dollars from your real estate investing?

The problem, in my opinion, is twofold. First, I believe that the vast majority of those who attend these events will never actually use the information presented. And second, the information people learn from those programs could easily be learned elsewhere absolutely free!

Does coaching work? Sure, for some people. But I believe anyone who can succeed because they took a super expensive training program could have succeeded without that program as well. After all, the program is not what makes you successful. *You* make yourself successful. Real estate programs offer education, motivation, and accountability, which can all be obtained for *much* lower costs than what these salespeople charge. Rather than helping most people get ahead, these programs simply plunge many Americans further into debt and despair when they end up spending their life savings on coaching for an activity at which they will not succeed.

That said, do programs like this have a place? Yes, I believe so. Successful coaching has been demonstrated in almost every industry there is as far as getting people motivated and moving toward their goals. However, the people who get the largest benefit from coaching are those who have already found a significant level of success in whatever they are doing. They have proven themselves to be someone who takes action, is a self-starter, and is willing to work hard. And most importantly, they have money to spend—and it's not coming from a credit card.

To summarize, expensive coaching and training programs may have a place, but they are probably not appropriate for new investors. Real estate gurus have a terrible reputation for taking gullible and low-income people, and pitching them hard to pay for overpriced training that they are not ready for and that will only put them in a worse situation. In the end, these gurus provide no more than an organized version of what interested individuals can already get on their own: education, accountability, and motivation. If you want to save your money and still get all three of these benefits, get active on BiggerPockets and use your cash for your next big investment instead.

At this point, I've addressed both the need to think the right thoughts and the best ways to study the right subjects. Now, let's move on to the third key to success in rental property investing: picking the right plan.

3. Pick the Right Plan

> *"Would you tell me, please, which way I ought to go from here?"*
> *"That depends a good deal on where you want to get to," said the Cat.*
> *"I don't much care where," said Alice.*
> *"Then it doesn't matter which way you go."*

—LEWIS CARROLL, *ALICE'S ADVENTURES IN WONDERLAND*

Do you know where you want to go?

No, not physically. Do you know where you want your rental properties to take you? Do you know *when* you want to retire? Do you know *how* you are going to retire? Do you know what kind of rental properties you want to buy? Where you want to buy them? How you plan to put it all together?

These questions can all be answered by having a solid *plan*. Therefore, the third key to success in rental property investing is to create the right plan. Chapter 3 of this book will actually walk you through several distinct plans that others have created, but first, I want to talk about the basic theory behind having a plan.

Your Plan *Is Not* Your Business Plan

What?

Yes, I'm not talking about a formal document that you write "objective" at the top of and give to your banker. Although an official business plan might come in handy for you some day, I am talking about writing down your strategy for achieving financial freedom through rental properties. Yes, it should be written down, but *no*, you don't need to make it anything fancy. Your banker is not going to see this plan. I'm not going to see it. Your ninth grade English teacher will not see it. Most likely, the only people who will ever lay eyes on the document will be you and your spouse, significant other, business partner, or accountability partner. Sure, you can draft a business plan if you want, but what I'm referring to here is a written declaration of your deep-seated belief as to where you are headed.

I first wrote my plan down at 3 a.m., by hand, on an 8.5-by-14-inch piece of paper. Nine years later, I still have this document and refer to it often, and although I haven't followed it exactly (plans do change!), I have adhered to it as closely as possible.

Again, the kind of plan I'm referring to outlines your *vision* for where you want to go and how you plan to get there.

- What is the end goal? Where are you headed?
- What kind of strategy do you want to use?
- What won't you do? (e.g. I won't purchase condos, commercial real estate, etc.)
- What kind of properties do you want to buy?
- How often will you buy properties?
- How are you going to finance it all?

These questions are all part of your plan, which you will put together soon. You may not know all the answers to these questions yet, and that is okay. The goal of a plan is to get you thinking, learning, and strategizing.

Your Plan Can Change

That's right, your plan is not written in stone. It is fluid and may change over time. The purpose of a plan is not to outline every detail of your investing life, but rather to give you a road map for where you hope to travel. Your plan may begin with the idea of buying small, multifamily properties but may shift later to buying single-family homes, or apartments, or notes, or any of a hundred other strategies. Again, that's okay.

Like Alice in Wonderland, if you don't care where or how you end up, having a plan doesn't matter. But you are not Alice. You have goals, and you have a future to prepare for. You likely don't want to work the next fifty years and retire on social security, waiting for that small check to come in the mail each month before you can go buy bread. You want financial freedom—that is your goal. Am I wrong? If not, let's get started building your plan.

How Do I Start My Plan?

Begin your plan with the end in mind. This may seem pretty obvious, but so many people start planning their investment strategy by picking out a particular house, without even knowing whether that particular house is part of their plan or should be included in their plan. Just as a road trip begins with a destination in mind, so should your investment plan.

This takes us back to the idea of goal setting that I talked about earlier in this chapter. Where do you want to go? What are your long-term goals? Where do you see yourself in five years? Ten years? Twenty years?

There are numerous destinations people are trying to reach with their real estate investing, and each of these individuals is working a plan to get there. Take a moment and think about where you want to end up financially. Get specific! When do you want to get there? Get specific!

Write your goal/destination here (unless this is a library book! If so, write it down somewhere else):

_____

_____

_____

_____

Congratulations! You've just taken the first step in building your investment plan. Feels pretty good, doesn't it? Goals are incredibly important, but a goal without a plan is just a dream. We need to go further and help you get there. But first, let's talk about your "why."

What Is Your "Why"?

I want to challenge you to think even bigger than your goals. Goals are great, but they fall short because they are easy to change in difficult times. For example, you might set a goal to lose twenty pounds by Christmas, but a few weeks into your diet, you lose motivation and end up eating an entire chocolate cake.

Why? Because you were focused on the *goal*, not the *why*. **Why** do you want to achieve the goal you just wrote down? What is the purpose of doing so? Building wealth is great, but let me make one thing very clear:

You'll never see a hearse followed by a U-Haul, because you can't take it with you when you die! Material things are temporary, but experiences and the impact we have on others lasts forever. Acquiring assets just to acquire more assets is mostly pointless. There has to be a greater reason you want to achieve this. Take a moment and ponder your "why." What is your reason for wanting to build wealth, increase cash flow, or whatever other goals you might have?

- To spend more time with your kids or grandkids?
- So you can travel the world and collect life experiences?
- To help break the cycle of poverty in your family's lineage?
- So you can leave a terrible job?
- To ensure there is always food on the table for your family, even if you were to pass away?
- So you can wake up every morning and do what *you* want, not what someone else wants you to do?

Knowing your *why* will help you reach your goals. When attaining your goal becomes difficult, it is easy to say, "Well, I guess I don't need to build wealth. After all, rich people suck." But when your goal is "I want to attend every single sporting event and school play my kids are ever in, so I need the freedom to do that," suddenly those challenges become much easier to fight through.

Write *why* you want to build wealth through real estate here:

_____

_____

_____

_____

Let's now talk about the kind of vehicle you'll use to get there.

What Kind of Investment Property Should You Buy?

Do you plan to buy single-family homes? Small multifamily properties? Apartment complexes? Maybe all three? Maybe something else?

In Chapter 7, I'll cover the different kinds of rental properties you can buy, so you should probably finish this book before finishing your plan. But if you already have a clear idea of what you want to buy, you can write that here:

_____

_____

_____

_____

How Often Will You Buy?

Do you plan on buying one property in your first year? Two? Ten? What about in your second year? Or your third?

The goal of your plan is to help you envision what your future could look like based on certain things being true, so feel free to experiment here. What if you bought one house in year one, two in year two, three in year three, and so on? What if you bought one apartment complex every five years? What would that look like?

Again, this may change as you work your way through this book, but start by jotting down your thoughts on your buying frequency here:

_____

_____

_____

_____

How Will You Finance Your Deals?

Finally, knowing how you will finance your deals is a good idea. Do you make extra income from your job that you can dedicate a part of to buying deals? Or will you have to be more creative in financing those properties? This can be the most difficult part of the plan for many people, especially if they have not yet learned what those financing techniques are. (Don't worry, though; by the end of this book, you will.)

If you already know how you'll finance your properties, write that here:

_____

_____

_____

_____

What Should Your Plan Look Like?

As I mentioned earlier, I wrote my first investment plan on an 8.5-by-14-inch piece of computer paper because I happened to have it lying around. You can write yours on a piece of paper, type it up on a word processor, or draw it on your bedroom wall. The point is to write it down. I like using paper and pencil because this allows me to erase and move things around as I go.

To start, write the word "Today" at the top in big letters. Then at the bottom, write out your goal in big letters. The space in between is where you will write out your plan. Fill in that space with the vision you have.

In Chapter 3, I'll share four different plans with you that you can use as a guide for your own, editing, tweaking, or discarding as you like. But first, let's talk about the final two keys in rental property success.

4. Acquire the Right Asset

Step four in achieving success through rental properties is acquiring the right assets and avoiding liabilities. Simply put, liabilities are things that detract from your wealth, while assets help grow your wealth. Liabilities include things that take money from your pocket every month, such as car payments, rent, utility bills, and cell phone bills. Assets are things that help you grow wealth, such as real estate, stocks, and businesses. Therefore, if you want to build wealth, you need to start collecting more assets and decreasing your liabilities.

Of course, given that this is a book about rental property investing, I would argue that the greatest asset you can acquire is real estate. However, not all real estate is the *right* asset. A friend of mine once said, "You can go broke buying good deals," and he is right. Just because something seems like a good deal doesn't mean you should buy it. The right property must fit with your plan, your budget, and your ability to manage.

Throughout this book, I'll share numerous tips on how to find and acquire the perfect assets that fit your plan. For now, let's address step five, managing the right metrics.

5. Manage the Right Metrics

All the steps up to this point are for nothing if you can't manage the asset(s) you have purchased. Rental properties are different from most other asset classes because they must be continually maintained and managed. Unlike stocks, for which you can simply write a check and then ignore for years, rental properties require continual oversight.

Rental property investing is a lot like a tightrope walker trying to stay balanced on wire hundreds of feet above a crowded city intersection. One small slip, and all could be lost. The tightrope walker's primary job is to move forward while not falling off to the left or right. He simply needs to maintain his balance until he gets to the other side. When a gust of wind comes from the left, he leans to the right. When his foot begins to slip, his other foot keeps him steady.

When dealing with rentals, you'll encounter many "gusts of wind" that threaten to knock you off your tightrope. The way you manage will make the difference between staying on the wire or falling.

I use the phrase "manage the right metrics" not only because it rolls off the tongue nicely, but also because it describes exactly what a good rental property owner does. A metric is generally defined as "a standard for measuring or evaluating something." With respect to real estate, a metric would be how your property is performing. What did the cash flow look like last month? What kind of increase did you see in expenses over the previous twelve months? What has appreciation done to your property over the past decade? These metrics, and many others, will help you stay steady on the wire, balancing and counterbalancing until you reach the other side.

In Chapters 17 and 18 of this book, I'll specifically discuss managing the rentals you own, including both physical management (dealing with tenants) and business management (dealing with the numbers). Both are key to finding success through rental properties.

WRAPPING IT UP

Have you committed yourself to being successful?

Have you shifted the way your mind thinks, focusing on the "how can I?" question rather than the limiting "I can't" statement? Have you committed to investing the time needed to learn everything you need to know about real estate, building your educational foundation so no one can ever knock you over?

Have you committed to planning your future, setting goals, and working toward those goals consistently? Have you committed to finding only the best deals that fit your plan and to doing the work necessary to make your dream a reality? Have you committed to managing your investment to the utmost detail, watching every metric so you can continue to build and grow your wealth over the coming years?

I hope you have. Now, I want to actually show you a few real-life sample plans that you can adopt for your own future. Be careful though, the next chapter might just change your life forever.

Chapter Three
FOUR SAMPLE PLANS

"A goal without a plan is just a wish."

—ANTOINE DE SAINT-EXUPERY

Now that you know where you want to go, having a plan for how to get there is important. This chapter is all about developing a road map for your rental property future. After all, you would not pile the family in the car, back out of the driveway, and then drive across the country to visit Disneyland without a GPS or road map. Sure, you might make it all the way to your destination, but along the way, you'll hit numerous roadblocks and dead ends, make countless wrong turns, backtrack when you get lost, and arrive late, with a vehicle full of grumpy kids.

The same is true for your investing future. By knowing the general direction you want to go, you'll probably more or less reach your destination, but it'll likely take you much longer than anticipated and cause you a lot of stress in the process. Your goal should be to arrive at your destination with as little hassle and as much speed as possible. Your plan will be the catalyst to do just that.

In this chapter, I'll discuss several different plans that people use to achieve their goals through rental properties. My goal with this chapter is twofold:

1. To show you there are multiple ways of reaching your destination
2. To inspire you to create your own plan

Unlike most real estate gurus, I am not going to tell you that there is only one right way to invest in real estate. I will not say, "This is the path that will work for you." And you may not like this. Maybe you want a simple answer so you can just go do it. However, the truth is that there is no one right way, though there is probably a right way for *you*. I hope that by the end of this chapter you are ready to build your own road map and find that way.

Plan 1: How to Make $1,000,000 Through Rental Properties

The plan I am about to describe is very similar to the one I am taking in my life. The idea is simple: Buy incredible rental properties, save the cash flow, and reinvest that cash flow into even more properties. This is not a get-rich-quick plan. It plays out over seven to ten years—maybe more, maybe less. The timeline is not important, nor are the specific numbers. What matters is the underlying math, and I hope that after reading about this plan, you will better understand the kind of plan you will want to build for yourself.

Before I get to the plan for making $1,000,000 in net worth, let me clarify a few things:

- This is not the only way to make money in real estate, just one path that I like.
- This is not a guaranteed plan. This is an "if-then" plan. If A, then B, and if B, then C. Everything depends on those "ifs."
- This plan works based on ideal numbers. For example, I use a nice round "3 percent appreciation" number because that has been the U.S. historical average. However, real life is not likely going to appreciate by exactly 3 percent each year. Some years might be 1 percent, some might be 5 percent, and others might be -4 percent. Again, these are average ideals.

- The specific price per unit does not matter as much as the mathematical concepts I'm about to talk about. For example, if I say, "Buy a $100,000 house," half the readers of this book will instantly think, "Phhhh...I could never find a house that cheap," while the other half thinks, "Phhhh...I would never pay that much for a house." Real estate is relative to location, and that's okay! The mathematical concepts are what matter, far more than the specifics. You might find properties with values that are higher or lower, depending on your location.
- This is not legal advice. I'm not even telling you that this is the path you should definitely take. Again, this is just one plan that has worked.

Setting Your Buying Standards

The vast majority of properties out there are terrible investments and would end up costing you more than you'd make. Instead, you must adhere to certain standards for this plan to work. The following is an example of such standards:

- It must be a multifamily property (in this plan, we'll be buying fourplexes and 24-unit apartments).
- It must achieve cash flows of $200 per unit, per month after all expenses have been paid, including vacancy, maintenance, utilities, management, capital expenditures, taxes, and insurance, plus any other expenses the property may have.
- The property must be purchasable for a discount because you are great at finding deals in the market. For this sample plan, we'll be buying each property at 80 percent of what it's normally worth. For example, while the average buyer would pay $100,000, we'll pay $80,000.
- The property's value must be capable of being improved by 10 percent during the first year through "forced appreciation" (such as a paint job and landscaping).
- The property must appreciate at 3 percent per year after year one.

You may be tempted to say that these standards are impossible to fulfill, but trust me, they are not. BiggerPockets is full of examples of investors who are following these very standards and succeeding. Perhaps the area you live in is different, but these locations do exist. I own properties just like this. However, you will have to think differently. For example, ask most average Americans whether buying a property for 80 percent of its value is possible, and they'll say, "No." Ask an experienced house flipper, and he or she will say, "Yes, but that's paying way too much." You see, a house flipper or real estate wholesaler typically has to purchase a property for far less than 80 percent of the value for their plan to work. It all comes down to mindset. Are you someone who says, "It can't be done!" or someone who asks "How can it be done?"

Buying Your First Property

Using these standards, we find a fourplex that needs a little help. Perhaps it's a bank repo that smells like a hundred cats, or a for-sale-by-owner (FSBO) property owned by someone who can't quite take care of it. I'm not talking about a disaster—just a place that needs some cosmetic assistance.

The property is listed at $100,000, but we are able to buy it for $80,000. For simplicity's sake, we'll say that the seller will pay our closing costs, which means we are required to put down $16,000 for a 20 percent down payment. In addition, we will spend $4,000 on minor repairs and improvements to satisfy the standard of 10 percent appreciation during the first year.

Year One

Here is a summary of our portfolio after year one:
- Our loan is for $63,500 (approximately).
- Our value is at $110,000 (10 percent appreciation during year one).
- Our cash flow saved (from cash flow) is $10,000. (Okay, technically $9,600. I like easy math.)
- Our total equity is $46,500.
- Our total net worth is $56,500.

Now, I just want to quickly remind you that this kind of property doesn't exist on every street corner. Is finding these properties difficult? Yes! Is finding these properties hard if you only need to find one such property every two years across the entire United States? Well, it's definitely not impossible.

Year Two

Nothing changes during year two. During this year, you simply manage your property incredibly effectively. Cut expenses as much as possible; raise the rent as much as possible. Run a well-oiled machine. By the end of year two, our portfolio looks like this:

- Our loan is for $63,000 (approximately).
- Our value is at $113,300 (3 percent appreciation during year two).
- Our total cash flow saved is $20,000.
- Our total equity is $50,300.
- Our total net worth is $70,300.

Year Three

At the start of year three, we will buy our second fourplex, using the $20,000 we have saved from the cash flow. (That's right, we're not going to put any more of our hard-earned cash into this plan.)

This next property will be exactly like our first—identical, with the same numbers, same price, and same cash flow. (Remember, this is an "ideal" scenario just to represent how this works in the real world. Maybe you'll buy a fiveplex, a triplex, or four separate houses. The underlying math is what is important.) We now have two income streams going: Fourplex A and Fourplex B. For the sake of time, here are our combined figures for the end of year three:

- Our combined loans are $126,000.
- Our combined value is $227,000.
- Our annual combined cash flow saved is $20,000.
- Our total equity is $101,000.
- Our total net worth is $121,000.

Year Four

At the end of year four, we will simply "rinse and repeat" once again. You guessed it—another fourplex, same numbers. We now have three streams of income going: Fourplex A, Fourplex B, and Fourplex C. The totals for the end of year four are as follows:

- Our combined loans are $177,000.
- Our combined value is $350,500.
- Our annual combined cash flow saved is $30,000 ($10,000 from each property).
- Our total equity is $173,500.
- Our total net worth is $203,500.

Year Five

At the end of year four/the beginning of year five, we will make our first "trade-up." If you are familiar with the board game Monopoly, you'll recognize this strategy. In Monopoly terms, we're essentially going to trade our houses for hotels. In this example, however, we will trade our three fourplexes for one apartment building. As you saw at the end of year four, we have accumulated approximately $203,500 in equity, but we can't use all of this cash; the trade-up has certain costs associated with it (such as agent fees and closing costs) that need to be covered.

We will use a 1031 tax exchange to defer taxes to a later date (I'll explain the power of the 1031 tax exchange deferral in Chapter 19), but we still need to pay closing costs and for an agent to sell the properties. After all expenses have been paid out, we will have approximately $175,000 remaining to invest in our next property. As you can probably guess, we will use this as a 20 percent down payment on our next investment, allowing us to pay up to $875,000 for a property.

We will buy our new property using the same "standards" as our first three properties. These were (as a quick reminder):
- Multifamily property
- Cash flows of $200 per unit, per month after all expenses have been paid
- Property must be purchasable for 80 percent of its value
- Property must be capable of being improved by 10 percent during the first year through "forced appreciation"
- Property must appreciate at 3 percent per year after year one

After some careful searching, we find an apartment building worth $1,000,000, but we are able to buy it for $800,000. Our 20 percent down payment ($160,000) makes the loan amount $640,000, and leaves us with approximately $13,000 for closing costs, reserves, and some repairs.

At the end of year five, our portfolio looks like this:
- Our loan is for $625,000.
- Our value is $1,100,000 (10 percent during year one).
- Our cash flow saved is $57,600 (24 units × $200 × 12 months).
- Our total equity is $475,000.
- Our total net worth is $532,600.

Year Six

No changes or purchases are made during year six. We just relax and collect the cash flow, saving every penny for our next trade-up. Again, this is a time to manage effectively and save cash. At the end of year six, our portfolio looks like this:

- Our loan is $610,000 (approximately).
- Our value is $1,133,000 (3 percent during year two).
- Our cash flow saved is $115,200 (24 units × $200 × 24 months).
- Our total equity is $523,000.
- Our total net worth is $638,200.

Year Seven

Year seven is another year of rest—if you can call it that! We simply manage effectively and save all the cash we can. At the end of year seven, our portfolio looks like this:

- Our loan is $595,000 (approximately).
- Our value is $1,167,000 (3 percent growth over the previous year).
- Our cash flow saved is $172,800 (24 units × $200 × 36 months).
- Our total equity in the property is $572,000.
- Our total net worth is $744,800, including the cash flow saved.

Perhaps you want to simply live off the cash flow from this point on. This scenario is generating a respectable $57,000 in passive income each year, which is approximately what the average American household earns. However, the total net worth is only three-quarters of a million dollars. One final trade-up would be needed to reach that final million-dollar figure. Perhaps this could happen right away during year seven or perhaps not for several years. The key is to work with the market, to learn to ride it like a wave. For example purposes, let's sell now and trade up.

End of Year Seven/Start of Year Eight

We take all the equity and cash we have (approximately $744,800) and subtract the sales expenses (we'll say $94,800) to give us a nice round final profit of $650,000 to use for our final down payment.

Our final purchase will be a 75-unit apartment community listed for sale at $3,400,000, but we are able to purchase it for just $2,750,000 (20 percent off because the same rules apply). We'll use the down payment of

$650,000 (making the seller pay closing costs) for a total mortgage amount of $2,100,000. At this final stage of our "million-dollar journey"—the end of year seven or the start of year eight—our portfolio looks like this:

- Our loan is $2,100,000.
- Our value is $3,400,000.
- Our cash flow saved is $0 (but will be $15,000 per month going forward).
- Our total equity is $1,300,000.
- Our total net worth is $1,300,000.

We did it! One million dollars ($1.3 million, actually), with only five purchases in seven (maybe eight) full years of investing.

Is This Possible?

Remember, this is an ideal situation with nice round numbers. Many people have moved much faster, while others have moved much slower in their investment journey. The purpose of this exercise was simply to give you a "big picture" idea of how the approach works and to provide a good illustration of what I call "trading up." This journey could take ten years, or it could take twenty. It depends on a number of factors, many of which are outside your control (such as inflation, the market, the economy). However, this represents a possible road map. If this were your road map, it would be much easier to stay on track and avoid the shiny-object syndrome so many of us face. This plan sets standards that, if obtained, would give us the outcome we desire.

Let's now look at the second plan in this chapter, which focuses on single-family homes.

Plan 2: Building Wealth Through Single-Family Homes

In this plan, we'll look at the concept of building wealth through the purchase and holding of single-family homes. While in the previous example, we started with a goal of achieving $1,000,000 in net worth, this time, our goal is to make an extra $5,000 per month in cash flow from rental properties. This might be perfect for someone looking to quit their job, supplement their retirement, or just create more passive income with which to travel more and live a more luxurious life.

For this plan, let's pretend we are currently making $60,000 a year after taxes from our day job, which works out to $5,000 per month. We have $10,000 in savings and have "flipped the switch" in our head that says, "Yes! I'm going to do what it takes!" Therefore, the first part of this plan will be to set aside 20 percent of our income for investment purposes. Yes, cutting 20 percent out of our life is not always easy, but sacrifice is often needed. As a result, we will live on only $48,000 per year and put $12,000 per year toward our investments.

Year One

During year one, we are simply going to save money and learn. We'll read a lot of real estate books, ask a lot of questions, hang out in the BiggerPockets Forums for a few minutes every day, listen to podcasts on our daily commute, and simply grow our knowledge base. We'll also save $1,000 per month from our job. At the end of year one, we have $12,000 saved, plus the $10,000 we started with, giving us $22,000 with which to begin our journey at the start of year two.

For those who say that $1,000 per month is impossible to save, perhaps consider finding a way to earn an extra $1,000 per month instead. The same principle applies.

Year Two

The first property we will purchase is a three-bedroom, two-bath 1970s home located in a blue-collar neighborhood. The home is a bank foreclosure listed at $100,000. However, because of a smoke smell permeating the home, the property has been sitting on the market for several months. We come along, and after doing an in-depth analysis, we decide that we can pay $80,000 for the home. We offer this price and ask the seller to pay the majority of the closing costs. After some brief negotiation, they accept.

Take a look at Figure 2, the breakdown on this property's numbers, produced by the BiggerPockets Rental Property Calculator (www.bigger-pockets.com/analysis). As you can see, with this property, we are planning on making approximately $370 per month in cash flow. At the end of the year, we may have to pay some taxes on this, so we're going to set aside about $70 a month for that purpose, and use a clean $300 per month as our cash flow number on this property. Keep in mind, this is after all the expenses have been paid or set aside for, including property management, vacancy, repairs, maintenance, capital expenditures, taxes, insurance, and utilities. A person could theoretically have an extra $100 per month added to this cash flow by managing the property themselves, but I like to include management in here, because we are still working a job while putting this plan in place. Therefore, we are now able to save $300 per month extra because of this property.

Purchase Price:	$80,000.00		
Purchase Closing Costs:	$1,500.00	Monthly Income:	$1,150.00
Estimated Repairs:	$4,500.00	Monthly Expense:	(−)$779.40
Total Project Cost:	$86,000.00	Monthly Cashflow:	$370.60
After Repair Value:	$100,000.00	Pro Forma Cap Rate:	9.97%
		NOI:	$8,570.00
Down Payment:	$16,000.00	Total Cash Needed:	$22,640.00
Loan Amount:	$64,000.00	Cash on Cash ROI:	19.64%
Loan Points:	$640.00	Purchase Cap Rate:	10.71%
Loan Fees:			
Amorized Over:	30 years		
Loan Interset Rate:	5.00%		
Monthyl P&J:	$343.57		

Total Cash Needed by Borrower:	$22,640.00

Total Operating Expenses:	$435.83
Mortgage Expenses:	$343.57
■ Vacancy:	$46.00
■ CapEx:	$57.50
▦ Management:	$115.00
▦ Property Taxes:	$104.83
▨ Repairs:	$57.50
▨ Insurance:	$55.00
▨ P&I:	$343.57

Figure 2

Also, from this point forward, each year we will add $100 per month in savings from our personal income, because we get an annual raise from work and have decided to save a portion of this for our future as well. Therefore, during year one, we saved $1,000 per month; during year two, we will save $1,100 per month; in year three, we'll save $1,200 per month; and so on.

We add the $300 per month from the property to the now $1,100 we saved from our income each month, which means we are now saving $1,400 per month for all of year two. At the end of year two, therefore, we have $18,800 saved in total—enough to purchase another property.

Year Three
For simplicity, we will purchase a second rental property this year using the exact same numbers as we did the first time. In other words, we will spend $16,000 on the down payment and achieve, after all expenses have been paid, $300 per month in cash flow. We can now add that to the $300 we are saving from our first rental property and the $1,200 we are saving from our job for a total monthly savings of $1,800. At the end of year three, then, we have $21,600 to use for another purchase.

Year Four
Again, for simplicity, we will purchase a third rental property this year using the exact same numbers as we did for the first two. In other words, we will spend $16,000 on the down payment and achieve, after all expenses have been paid, $300 per month in cash flow. We can now add that to the $300 we are saving from our first rental property, the $300 we are saving from our second rental property, and the $1,300 we are saving from our job for a total monthly savings of $2,200. At the end of year four, therefore, we have $26,400 to use for another purchase.

Year Five
Once again, we will repeat this exact same process to buy a fourth rental property, using the money we have saved as our down payment. Although the down payment is only $16,000, we have $26,400 to use, which means we have some more cash to put into repairs, reserves, or any other costs.

We'll purchase this property using the exact same numbers as we used for the others, and we will once again increase the amount of cash we are saving from our job. Therefore, at the end of year five, we will be saving $2,600 per month and own four rental properties.

Years Six Through Eleven
As you can see, we are following a very simple pattern here of buying one house per year and saving our income. However, starting in year seven, some interesting things start to happen. We are able to save so

much money at this point that we can buy not one but two rentals in year seven. By the end of year six, we are saving $1,500 per month from our job and $1,500 per month from the five rentals we now own for a total of $3,000 per month. This translates to $36,000 per year, enough for the down payments on two properties instead of just one.

This is when real estate starts to get fun, because we get to see the effects of compound interest kicking our investments into high gear. Check out the following graph, which shows this pattern of using total saved cash flow to buy rentals. In fact, every year after year seven, we'd be able to increase the number of rental properties we can buy. We'll buy two properties in year seven, two in year eight, three in year nine, four in year ten, and five in year eleven.

	YEAR 6	YEAR 7	YEAR 8	YEAR 9	YEAR 10	YEAR 11
Properties Purchased	1	2	2	3	4	5
Rentals Owned	5	7	9	12	16	21
Job Savings	$1,500	$1,600	$1,700	$1,800	$1,900	$2,000
Total Cash Flow	$1,500	$2,100	$2,700	$3,600	$4,800	$6,300
Total Saved	$36,000	$44,400	$52,800	$64,800	$80,400	$99,600

Clearly, the total cash flow we are receiving each month is increasing very rapidly. In fact, after we purchase the five properties in year eleven, we are receiving $6,300 per month in cash flow. Our goal, if you'll recall, was just to make an extra $5,000 per month, and already we have surpassed that!

At this point, there are a few things we could do:

1. Continue working our day job and buying more properties
2. Continue working our day job and begin paying off all the properties
3. Quit our job and become a full-time real estate investor
4. Retire and lay on a beach

It's up to you. The exciting thing is that we achieved our goal: $5,000 per month in passive income from the rentals we owned.

If this plan didn't seem cool enough as it is, keep in mind that we did not even take into consideration the fact that rental income tends to climb over time, so that $300 per month in cash flow from the first few properties would likely become much more, resulting in even greater total numbers. The plan also doesn't factor in the equity you would be building through the loan paydown or through appreciation.

Again, this plan is a very simplified representation of what *could* happen if you choose to follow this particular rental strategy. Understand, however, that real life is never as neat and clean as it looks on paper. For example, consider the following scenarios:

- What if you got laid off from your job and couldn't buy for a year?
- What if you didn't get a raise at work?
- What happens when the bank stops lending?
- What if interest rates rise dramatically?

These are all real-life situations that could happen to you along your plan, so don't freak out when they do. Life will never look like it does on paper, and that's okay. The point of a plan is not to map out exactly where you're headed, but to give you a North Star to follow.

Let's look at another plan, one often well-suited for younger investors and those just starting out: the house hack.

Plan 3: House Hacking

The third plan I want to discuss in this chapter is the idea of the "house hack."

House hacking is the idea of combining your investment property with your personal residence. Although it is possible to do with just a single-family house (by doing a "live-in flip"), the phrase is more often used to describe the practice of buying a small multifamily property (a duplex, triplex, or fourplex), living in one unit, and renting the other units out.

My first rental property was a small duplex that I bought for $89,000. The property needed some "sweat equity," which my wife and I spent a few weeks doing, and then we rented the property out. Although we had stumbled across this "house hacking" strategy accidentally, we quickly realized the power of this method when the mortgage payment of approximately $630 per month was fully paid by the tenants in the other unit who were paying $650 for rent. In other words, the tenants were allowing my wife and I to live for free, before operating expenses.

House hacking has several distinct benefits that make it an especially terrific investment for first-time investors:

- **Low (or No) Down Payment Financing.** When you plan to live in a property for at least one year, financing becomes much more friendly for the borrower. For example, an FHA loan allows for just a 3.5 percent down payment and the USDA (United States Department of Agriculture) loan allows for $0 down if you are buying in a rural area. Traditional 20-percent-down loans also work in this pricing structure and can do even more for your wealth-building plans.
- **On-the-Job Training.** House hacking is a great introduction to the world of landlording. You buy the property, and suddenly you are a landlord—so you'll learn very quickly what to do and what not to do.
- **Close Monitoring of Your Investment.** When you live in your investment property, keeping an eye on the property and making sure it's running at peak performance is easy. It's unlikely that the lawn will get overgrown, the tenants will deal drugs from the house, or maintenance will go unreported for months.
- **Saved Expenses.** Because you live at the property, you can manage the other tenants yourself very easily and don't have to worry about paying a property manager who will do substandard work.

The following plan that you and I are about to walk through follows a serial house hacker. We'll pursue the house-hacking strategy for numerous properties to reach our goal. In this case, let's set a goal of simply "living for free," so we can save money and pursue other investments in the future.

The Plan

To start the first year, we will buy a triplex. We'll start small because it's our first property, though we could start with a two- or a four-unit property. Triplexes in this area run between $210,000 and $230,000, depending on the condition. However, we are smart shoppers and can get a great deal on a foreclosed triplex for $180,000, and each side will rent for $950 per month. (As before, pay more attention to the concept here than the actual numbers; every area is different.) To get this $180,000 mortgage, we'll put just 3.5 percent down through an FHA loan.

After the purchase, we'll invest a few thousand dollars and a few hundred hours making it look fantastic—new paint, cleaning, etc.

At this point, if the property were 100 percent rented out to tenants, it would bring in a total of $2,850 per month, but because we'll be living in one of the three units, we can only expect approximately $1,900 per month in income.

For expenses, we can expect a mortgage—including taxes, insurance, and mortgage insurance—of $1,200 per month. We also know the water bill, which the landlord is responsible for paying, runs roughly $130 per month, plus the other utilities or trash ($230 total). We'll set aside 5 percent of the total gross rent ($2,850) for the vacancy, 5 percent for repairs, and 5 percent for future capital expenditures (CapEx, the big-ticket items that need to be replaced every so often) of about $142.50 each (because $2,850 × .05 = $142.50).

At this point, our expenses look like this:

Mortgage:	$1,200
Utilities:	$230
Vacancy:	$142.50
Repairs:	$142.50
CapEx:	$142.50
Total Expenses:	$1,857.50

If you'll recall, our total monthly income on this property with the other two units rented out was $1,900, so our cash flow is as follows:

$1,900 − $1,857.50 = $42.50

Now, we are not only living for free, but we are also making a small sum of money each month for doing so! Notice that in the expenses we just listed, we did *not* include property management. I generally advise that people include property management in their analysis, because they won't always be able to manage their property themselves. This includes house hacking, because you will not be living in one of the units forever either.

Therefore, whenever you analyze a "house hacking" potential deal, you should analyze the deal two different ways: while in the process of house hacking and after you move out. After all, if the deal only makes sense because you'd be living there, then it really closes off your options for moving someday. You must buy with the end in mind, so let's run the numbers on this property as if you are no longer living there. To do this, I'll double the cost of the vacancy and repairs (up to 10 percent each) and add in an 11 percent expense for property management.

Total income: $2,850

Total expenses are as follows:

Mortgage:	$1,200
Utilities:	$230
Vacancy (10%):	$285
Repairs (10%):	$285
CapEx (5%):	$142.50
Management (11%):	$285
Total Expenses:	**$2,427.50**

Total Income – Total Expenses = **Total Cash Flow**

$2,850 – $2,427.50 = **$422.50**

As we've discovered, even after moving out of this property, we could reasonably expect to get around $422.50 per month in cash flow. For putting just 3.5 percent down, that sounds like a pretty great deal to me. What do you think?

Plan 4: How to Make $100,000 Per Year Using the BRRRR Strategy

Some people work so hard to make money in real estate. They flip dozens of homes, deal with hundreds of tenants, and are always trying to put out a fire somewhere. Sounds exhausting, doesn't it? But what if I told you that within five years, you could be making $100,000 annually from just two real estate transactions per year? Sound too good to be true?

Today I want to teach you about the BRRRR strategy and the power it can have in your real estate investing. I'll also be walking you through a step-by-step plan for making $100,000 per year using this powerful investing plan.

What Is BRRRR?

BRRRR is an acronym for a popular investment strategy that, until now, hadn't been given a name. So I decided to name it! BRRRR stands for:

- Buy
- Rehab
- Rent
- Refinance
- Repeat

In other words, it's the strategy that involves buying fixer-upper rental properties, repairing them, renting them out to great tenants, refinancing them to get your money back, and then repeating the process. This can be a powerful strategy because it allows you to acquire numerous properties without running out of capital to invest.

Let's break the strategy down and look at each step.

Buy

The first step in the process is to buy a great deal. Not just any deal—a *great* one. Great location and great neighborhood, but a fixer-upper house.

BRRRR investing is very similar to house flipping; in fact, it *is* house flipping, but rather than selling the house, you rent it out after fixing it up. But the same principles that go into house flipping are needed here.

For example, a popular rule of thumb used by many house flippers is the 70 percent rule. This rule states that the most a flipper should pay for a property is 70 percent of the after-repair value (ARV, what the house is worth after it has been fixed up) less rehab costs. A house that has an ARV of $150,000 and needs $30,000 worth of rehab could be bought for $75,000, because:

$150,000 × .7 = $105,000
$105,000 − $30,000 = $75,000

Think that's impossible to achieve? Just ask most successful house flippers, and they'll tell you that their entire business model is built on similar margins. Stop saying, "I can't do this," and start asking, "How can I do this?"

It may require direct mail. It may require Craigslist. It may require driving for dollars. It's going to take some hustle. But if house flippers can do it, so can you.

To finance this first purchase, you'll not likely be able to use a traditional lender. Most lenders are unwilling to loan money on a fixer-upper. This means you'll probably have to look at options such as hard money, private money, cash, home equity, and the other creative strategies.

Rehab

The next phase in the BRRRR strategy is to fix the property up. However, because this property will be rented out for a period of time rather than flipped, the materials you use should reflect that reality.

For example, I'm working on a BRRRR property right now (I just purchased it last week and am in the middle of the rehab part now). When my crew tore up the carpet, we discovered beautiful hardwood floors underneath. Although this seems great, I'm actually *not* going to refinish them—yet. To refinish them would cost me around $3 per square foot, or $3,000 total. Then, when I go to sell the property someday, I'd probably have to refinish them *again* because of the heavy tenant usage. And that's *if* I can refinish them again (you can only refinish floors so many times before they are sanded too deep). Instead I'm going to use laminate wood floor throughout the entire home. This will protect the original floors for around $2 per square foot and will look amazing. Before I sell it someday, I'll just remove the laminate and finish the floors then to sell for top dollar.

The key to rehabbing a BRRRR property is to make the property as "tenant-proof" as possible, using materials that will last a long time and won't need to be redone later. Also, rehabbing with the goal of getting the highest ARV and rent possible is important. For example, if you can turn a two-bedroom home into a three-bedroom home, do it! This can add hundreds of dollars per month in cash flow and thousands in equity.

Of course, you could do all the work yourself if you wanted, or you could hire it out. That's up to you and depends on your skills, availability, and desire. DIY can save you a lot of money, increasing the odds that you'll find a deal with numbers that work. But it will also take a lot of weekends and evenings.

Rent

Next, it's time to rent the property out to reliable, responsible tenants. Luckily, you just bought a property located in a great location and rehabbed it to look brand new. Finding incredible tenants to rent the house shouldn't be hard.

Furthermore, because the property was rehabbed at the start, your repairs and capital expenditures (roof, siding, paint, etc.) should be fairly low for the next few years. Everything has already been fixed. Of course, you'll still need to budget for repairs and maintenance, but these should be much less than you thought.

To rent the property out, you might choose to hire a property manager, but because you already rehabbed the property and are renting to high-class tenants, managing a BRRRR deal shouldn't be too difficult. I recommend saving the money and doing it yourself.

I'm going to say something a little controversial now: The goal of the BRRRR strategy is *not* to make a ton of cash flow. I know, I know—that goes against almost everything I've been preaching thus far. But I'm not saying to buy something that *won't* cash flow. Long-term negative cash flow is not acceptable, ever. However, if I'm only making a little bit of cash flow, that might be okay with the BRRRR strategy, because the power of this strategy is in the long "flip"—the equity built. I'll explain this more in a bit.

Refinance

Earlier, I talked a little about how you were going to finance the property and mentioned that getting a conventional mortgage on a fixer-upper is tough. However, conventional mortgages are ideal—low interest, long term, easy. So the fourth step in the BRRRR strategy is to refinance into a nice conventional mortgage after the property has been fixed up. Even better, by refinancing, you have the possibility of getting all your money back.

Of course, you don't need to refinance the property to get your money back. Perhaps you make great income from a job and can afford to let your down payment/rehab money stay in the property. This will likely help you get better cash flow, and maybe you'll get a better return on investment (ROI) than you'd get elsewhere. However, if you are like me, you probably want your money back so you can do it again and again. Let's talk about how to do that.

In other words, let's go back to those numbers we used earlier. We found a property that had an ARV of $150,000. We purchased it for $75,000 and put $30,000 into the rehab. At this point, we have $105,000 into the purchase.

Most lenders will allow you to refinance a property for 70 percent of the ARV—in other words, they will do a 70 percent loan-to-value (LTV) loan on the property. Well, it just so happens that 70 percent of $150,000 is $105,000, so we could theoretically get back 100 percent of our invested capital.

That's right, we're going to refinance this property with a low-interest, 30-year fixed mortgage for $105,000. This will pay back whatever source of funds we used for the original purchase and rehab. In this example, the only money out of pocket will be the closing costs.

After the refinance, you should have a completely stabilized rental property that shoots off a little bit of cash flow each month and has roughly 30 percent equity just sitting there. Plus, you'll have all your money back, so it's time for the next step.

Repeat

The final R in the BRRRR strategy is to repeat the process. It worked once, and we got all our money back, so why not do it again? And again? And again?

Sure, at some point, the bank will stop refinancing the properties for you. And maybe you'll need to find another solution, such as a portfolio lender or a partnership. But it *can* be done.

With each deal you repeat, you are gaining 30 percent equity at the end of the day and getting your cash back in your pocket.

How to Make $100,000 Per Year with BRRRR

Now that we've covered the five steps of the BRRRR strategy, let's look at an example of how someone could make $100,000 per year using it.

Historically, prices of real estate have climbed approximately 3 percent per year on average. Yes, some years are better and some worse, but over time, this has been true. For our example here, though, let's be a bit more conservative and assume 2 percent per year.

Using this figure, let's say we bought a property today with an ARV of $150,000 but paid just $75,000 for it, then rehabbed it with $30,000 and refinanced it for $105,000. Then we rented the property out. At a 2 percent increase per year, this property could be worth $165,000 in five years. At the same time, the loan during those five years would have been paid down, so the balance would be just $96,000.

In other words, after five years, we would have $69,000 in equity. Of course, if we went to sell the property, it would likely need another coat of paint and maybe some other minor fixes. Plus, we'd have to pay the real estate agent about $10,000 as commission. And then we'd pay a few thousand in other sales closing costs. So that $69,000 in equity would look a lot more like $50,000 in profit at the end of the day.

Therefore, to make $100,000 per year using the BRRRR strategy, you simply need to buy two deals each year, and then begin selling two each year starting in year five. As long as these numbers work, you'll never have more than ten properties, and after five short years, you'll be making six figures—by just doing two purchases and two sales per year.

The Biggest Drawback of the BRRRR Strategy

At this point, you are probably thinking, "This sounds great. What's the catch?" As with all investments, you need to be aware of a few drawbacks. One you may have already wondered about: What if you can't refinance?

If you are unable to refinance the property to get your money back out, you are forced to kind of stop in your tracks. Therefore, I recommend visiting a few local banks and making sure you are a good enough borrower before you ever purchase the first deal. Of course, if after the rehab you are unable to refinance the property, you could always wait until the first-year lease is over with the tenants, kick them out, and sell the property. Having multiple exit strategies is always a great thing, and it's one of the perks of the BRRRR strategy.

Other drawbacks exist as well. What if the tenant destroys the house? What if you can't find a good enough deal? What if you can't finance the original purchase?

These are legitimate questions, but the cool thing is this: There are answers! These are the kinds of questions asked every day in the Bigger-Pockets Forums, so if you are not engaging there, you are missing out on one of the most powerful tools you have at your disposal.

WRAPPING IT UP

The BRRRR strategy has many moving parts, but if you work it right, it can be a powerful ally in helping you build some serious wealth.

Following this strategy can help you combine the equity growth of flipping with the tax benefits, cash flow, and appreciation of rental properties, maximizing your profit at the end of the day.

Chapter Four
THE TEN MEMBERS OF YOUR REAL ESTATE TEAM

"Talent wins games, but teamwork and intelligence win championships."

—MICHAEL JORDAN

"Man, this is the closest I've ever been to dying."

Although he uttered these words at the end of the ninth round, Muhammad Ali would go on to fight five more rounds against his rival Joe Frazier on that blistering hot October morning in 1975. With temperatures at an estimated 120 degrees inside the arena, 27,000 pairs of spectator eyes remained glued on the two fighters, as Ali and Frazier danced around the ring, looking for the next blow that would disable the other man. Their faces bruised and swollen, and with sweat pouring into their eyes, each man landed punch after punch on the other without any sign of relenting. Associated Press boxing reporter Ed Schuyler later said of the fight, "I'm sure I never saw a fight where two guys took as much punishment as those two did that day."

Finally, just before the bell rang to start the fifteenth round, Frazier's coach ended the fight, and Ali was declared winner of the "Thrilla in

Manila"—which became one of the most talked about fights of all time.

Even though Ali's bruised face was the one plastered all over the newspapers, he was not the only winner that day. Ali may have been named one of the greatest fighters of all time, but without his *team*, he would have never made it to that overheated arena in the Philippines. From his boxing coach Angelo Dundee to his trainer/speechwriter Drew Bundini Brown to his ringside physician Ferdie Pacheco to his cornerman Jabir Herbert Muhammad and many others, Ali used an entire entourage of individuals to secure victory time and time again.

A solid team can help turn an average fighter into a world champion and can help turn you from a new investor into a successful real estate mogul. But what does a "team" mean when talking about real estate? How does one build this team?

Your real estate team is a collection of people alongside whom you will work to make your real estate ambitions a reality. I am not talking about hiring employees, though an employee could be considered part of your team. I am referring to the professionals with whom you surround yourself and who each play an important role in finding, financing, and managing your rental portfolio.

People get kind of weird about the word "team," thinking of such groups as more formal than they probably need to be. A team is just made up of people you can depend on, and your teammates don't even need to know they are part of this team. You don't need a team name, a uniform, or matching socks. You just need reliable people. As with any sport, you are only as good as the members of your team, so work hard up front to build a solid roster of professionals. In this chapter, I outline ten different team members you should begin building relationships with, starting today.

These are the teammates who will help you win your own Thrilla in Manila.

1. Spouse

Perhaps the most important member of your team is your very own spouse (or serious romantic partner). It doesn't even matter whether or not they care about real estate: Your spouse/significant other has a huge impact on your mental state, ambitions, free time, money, future, and every other aspect of your life. Your spouse will likely become your confidant, your sounding board, and your cheerleader as you get into this game of real estate. A spouse who is opposed to your mission can be a serious hindrance to you reaching your goals, so having your spouse "on your team" and not being an outsider is imperative.

But what happens if you reach the conclusion that real estate investing will be your ticket to financial freedom before your significant other does? In other words, what if your spouse doesn't support your real estate goals or dreams?

This is one of the most common questions I am asked on Bigger-Pockets and a problem nearly every real estate investor must overcome (because it's unlikely that both people will fall in love with real estate at the same time). For those who have not yet been bitten by the real estate bug, real estate investing will likely appear no different than selling selling multi-leveled marketing schemes like Pampered Chef, or one of the 50 other moneymaking ideas you've had in the past decade. So how do you convince your spouse that your motives are pure and that this time is different?

The following are five tips to help you do just that, based on the things I had to do at the beginning of my real estate journey.

1. **Focus on Your Education.** The first way to show your significant other that you are serious about this business and to help them also see the light is by becoming an expert. Be able to answer every question they might ask you. Learn everything you possibly can about what you want to do before trying to convince them to come along on your journey. Read tons of real estate books, listen to a ton of podcasts, hang out in the BiggerPockets Forums, and attend local real estate networking events. Show your significant other that this is not just a fad in your life—this *is* your life!

2. **Start Slow.** When you begin to tell your significant other about real estate investing, you'll likely be very excited and want to share every-thing you've learned. In your excitement and zeal, you can very easily overwhelm your spouse with theories, facts, figures, concepts, math, and properties. Rather than convincing them, you'll just drive them further away as they see a huge, complicated world that requires far more effort to understand than they want to put forth.

   Instead, start slow, and keep things simple. An easy-to-under-stand concept, such as the idea that passive income could replace a 9-to-5 job, might be easier to digest than the concept of the awesome wealth-building potential of a 1031 tax-deferred exchange. (I'll cover that in Chapter 19.) The Roman Colosseum wasn't built in a day but was constructed bit by bit; in the same way, you'll need to build your partner's knowledge.

3. **Encourage Them to Learn.** In addition, you can always encourage your partner to read or listen to the same educational material that got you hooked. When I first started, I remember asking my wife to read *Rich Dad Poor Dad,* because it changed my thinking in such a profound way. I simply let Heather know how important this was for me and asked her to try it out. It took a bit of prodding, but eventually she did read the book, and it helped put her on the same wavelength as me. Books have a unique ability to do this.

   Another great way to get your spouse to learn without them needing to work is by listening to a real estate podcast or an audiobook together in the car while driving somewhere. Sure, your partner might zone out, but audio has a way of penetrating the mind on both a conscious and subconscious level, and transforming how a person thinks. Nearly every week, I get an email from a listener telling me about how the podcast finally made things "click" for their significant other. It can do the same for you.

4. **Share the Why.** We talked a lot about goal setting in Chapter 2, and one of the points I stressed was understanding the "why" behind your goal. Having a goal of making $1,000,000 or retiring at 40 years old is great, but goals are rather useless without the *why*. The why guides you through difficult times and keeps you focused on the stuff that really matters. The same is true when trying to convince your spouse—let them know the why. Which of the following sounds more convincing?
   - A. Honey, I want to invest in real estate so we can make millions. or
   - B. Honey, I want to show up for every football game, school play, and music recital our kids are ever in. With our current jobs, we'll miss out on so much. This is why I want to use real estate to build passive income.

5. **Include Them.** Finally, find ways that your significant other can get involved (if they want to). They don't need to know everything you know, but maybe they'd love to help out in one way or another to feel "included" and "on your team." For example, my wife doesn't sit down

and analyze every property with me, but she enjoys dealing with the books and keeping us organized (something I do not excel at). In this way, she is able to provide incredible support to *our* vision, and we are able to work together to find even more success.

Understand that your spouse does not need to participate with you in your real estate ambitions for you to succeed. However, it's helpful if your spouse is at least supportive of your goals and not fighting against you.

Finally—and this is just my personal opinion—your marriage is worth far more than your wealth. I recently read a business book that advised readers to leave their spouse if their financial goals did not align. How tragic! To summarize a lesson from one of the most well-known people to ever walk this earth (Jesus), "What good is it to gain the entire world but forfeit your soul?" Keep your ambitions in check on your journey to build financial freedom. Otherwise, you may gain the freedom you desire but find it incredibly lonely at the top.

2. Mentor/Accountability Partner

The next person you should have on your team is a mentor or accountability partner. This is the person you can turn to when things get tough or you need some motivation to continue. Of course, succeeding without a mentor or accountability partner is entirely possible, but having someone there you can talk to and who can keep you moving in the right direction is exceptionally helpful when building a real estate empire.

Now, when I say "mentor," a lot of folks instantly think of a paid coach, someone who advertises their services for educational training. This is not what I'm talking about at all. I'm referring to a *real* mentor, someone who is in your local area, also invests in real estate, and is willing to share their stories, lessons, failures, and successes with you.

For me, this person was Kyle, who I mentioned previously in this book. Kyle was my best friend's landlord, whom I met while helping my friend paint a house. I had just purchased my first rental property and was excited about the future of real estate in my life, so of course, I had a lot of questions for Kyle. How did he get started? Did he know any good contractors? How did he find good tenants? Where were the good or bad areas to buy? As we talked, Kyle could see that I was passionate and excited about real estate, which I believe helped encourage him as well.

We ended up having coffee on several occasions over the next few months, and I soaked up as much information as I could. I also started doing small maintenance tasks for him, cleaning properties after a tenant vacancy, dropping off legal notices for tenants, picking up supplies for construction projects, screening potential tenants for him, showing units when he couldn't, watching over his properties while he was on vacation, and whatever else I could do to provide value in the relationship.

Through my developing friendship with Kyle, I was able to learn an extensive amount about our local market, attract private lending from someone he knew, and get introduced to a lawyer I still use today. We even worked together on a number of projects. Kyle has been hugely influential in my success thus far and has become one of my best friends in the process.

Do you see the value in having this person on your "team"?

How do you find this person? It's not necessarily easy, but it also isn't as hard as you might think. With 19 million real estate investors in America and only 43,000 zip codes, that works out to about 442 real estate investors per zip code. You only need to find one or two who will work. Sometimes, new investors get a little weird about finding a mentor and end up approaching their potential mentor in a manner similar to how I asked my high school crush to the prom. Please do not approach an experienced person and ask, "Will you be my mentor?" Doing so is like asking a person to marry you on your first date. As I explained earlier, you are not forming some exclusive club here; you are building relationships, and relationships happen organically, yet purposefully. Here are a few ways you can find local investors with whom to build relationships:

1. **Position yourself where landlords hang out.** If you have a local real estate club or landlord association, I recommend attending their meetings and striking up conversations with as many folks as you can. Be wary of anyone who is selling any kind of mentorship or product, though. You want to find *real-life* landlords to develop relationships with.

2. **Ask your family and friends who are renting.** Who is their landlord? Does that person have a lot of properties? What are they like? Can they introduce you? As I mentioned earlier, this is how I found my mentor, Kyle.

3. **Ask a real estate agent.** Great real estate agents love to be a connector of people. As a result, if you want to find a prolific landlord in your area, simply ask an experienced real estate agent if they would

introduce you to some of the local players.

4. **Hang out on BiggerPockets.** Finally, remember that millions of land-lords come through the halls of BiggerPockets each year, and many spend a good amount of time in our forums. I encourage you to consider BiggerPockets, as a whole, your *digital* mentor as you embark on your real estate journey. You see, a mentor provides real-time feedback, tips, stories, and a willing ear to listen, and this is exactly what you will find on BiggerPockets. Seek to become the enthusiastic learner that mentors *love* to help, and do so every day in the forums. Ask questions, send colleague requests, and form solid, lifelong relationships with those in the community.

Now, how do you get this person to become your mentor? Let me ask you this: Who is the most recent friend you've made in your life? When you met this person for the first time, did you walk up to them and ask, "Will you be my friend?" Of course not! You developed that friendship via numerous conversations and encounters. The same thing applies when building a mentorship. I once had a BiggerPockets member ask me to be his mentor (mistake number one), and then ask that I drive two hours to go talk to him since he didn't want to drive to my town (mistake number two). Do you think I ended up working with this person? Not a chance. Another friend of mine recently received an email from someone that stated, "I've selected you to be my mentor. When can we meet?" No, no, no! Come on, people! Use some common sense when looking for a mentor.

Once you meet someone with whom you'd like to build a relationship, rather than uncomfortably asking that person to commit to being your mentor, why not just ask them to grab a cup of coffee or some lunch? Or ask if they'll show you their most recent property. Or offer to help them fix up a unit for free. Or ask them what kind of property they are looking for, and then go out and find it for them. The point is this: Build a relationship by offering value. Give more than you get. Offer more than you ask. Be a friend first and a real estate entrepreneur second. By following these simple steps, you'll build some lifelong relationships that will help you achieve your real estate goals.

3. Real Estate Agent

The next member you must find for your team is a *great* real estate agent.

Even if you plan to use other, more unconventional methods to find your deals, having a solid working relationship with a real estate agent as you build your rental portfolio is still good. A great real estate agent can help you better understand the real estate market, including which areas and property types are selling or renting well. A great agent can help you find comparable sales data (aka "comps"), so you can know the value of any property you go to look at. A good agent can help you bid on HUD (U.S. Department of Housing and Urban Development) properties, bank repos, and other properties listed on the MLS (Multiple Listing Service), as well as set you up with automatic alerts so you'll be notified the moment a new property that matches your qualifications hits the MLS.

How much does a real estate agent cost?

Well, if you are looking to use them to buy property, nothing! In a typical transaction, the real estate agent is paid by the seller, which means using an agent will be free for you. For this reason, working with an agent is a no-brainer when you're looking for properties to buy. However, when you go to sell a property, you will need to decide whether using an agent is the right thing to do (it probably is) and factor in the 6 percent or so that a seller must pay.

Keep in mind, a real estate agent is used to buy property that is listed on the MLS, not for unlisted properties. In other words, if you see a "for sale by owner" sign in front of a house, an agent may not get paid for helping you buy that house, unless the owner agrees to offer a commission (which they likely won't—hence the "for sale by owner" sign). If you find a deal through direct mail, you are most likely on your own for the offer, the negotiation, and the closing. (But don't worry, after finishing this book, you'll see that this is not such a tough process on your own.) So again, a real estate agent is an important person to have on your team whether you buy on the MLS or not, but the level at which you use them will depend on how you plan to acquire properties.

Notice that throughout this section, I've used the phrase "great real estate agent" numerous times. This is because all real estate agents are not created equal. In fact, I would go as far as to say *most* real estate agents are pretty terrible with regard to helping investors. If you are going to build a relationship with an agent, don't you think it would be wise to build one with an agent in the top tier? Me too. What makes a great agent?

• **Understands the Investor Mindset.** A great agent understands that a cute kitchen and a pretty tile design on the bathroom floor are *not* your primary concerns. If that is all your agent seems to talk about, run the other direction. You need an agent who understands the real estate investor's mindset and can help you achieve *your* goals, not theirs. They should understand the basics of return on investment, appreciation, making lowball offers, dealing with foreclosures, and what properties are currently renting for. You can find this out when interviewing your agent.

- **Responsive.** Real estate is becoming an increasingly fast-paced profession, and speed is often the number one determinant in getting a deal accepted. You therefore need an agent who is highly responsive and accessible through multiple means of communication. You should be able to reach them whenever you need to. I'm not saying the agent needs to work 24/7 for you, but if your agent shuts off their phone at 5 p.m. and avoids calls on weekends, you probably need to find another agent who is willing to be available when you are.

- **Hungry.** You need an agent who is ambitious and whose livelihood depends heavily on getting another deal. If they don't work, they don't eat. I've worked with agents in the past who have been in the game so long that they hardly have to work to make their commissions; the leads just casually come to them, and they casually work through the process. In other words, they aren't hungry. Avoid these agents and focus on the ones who are dedicated to finding you a great deal.

- **Has a Pulse on the Local Market.** Your agent should have a firm grasp on the current state of your local market. If there is a new Walmart going in, they should know about it. If there are zoning changes being discussed in the local city council, your agent should be aware of the proceedings. They should know where prices are rising, where they are falling, what areas are being revitalized, and what areas are becoming unfavorable.

- **Tech Savvy.** This should almost go without saying, but I'll say it anyway—your agent should be exceptionally tech savvy. They should know how to submit offers electronically to gain a competitive advantage over older, slower agents. They should allow you to sign documents via computer rather than with a pen. They should be able to use their smartphone on the fly to look up data about a property while visiting it. Although most agents today have a good grasp on technology, many are still stuck in the "old ways" and, as a result, are being left behind.

- **Has Investment Experience.** Although this is not a "make or break" characteristic, partnering with an agent who has personal real estate experience is helpful. After all, truly understanding the mind of an investor is hard if they haven't been there and done that themselves.

- **Offers One-on-One Support.** Some agents are so good at what they do that they have an entire team under them that gives them support, in which case, you may never actually talk to the agent directly, just to their assistants. In my personal opinion, I would avoid this kind of situation, if possible. You want to build a relationship with an agent, not with some big shot who will barely give you the time of day.
- **Well Connected.** A great agent should know people and be willing to connect you with them. If you need a contractor, they should have some good ideas about whom to call first. If you need a lender, they should have some personal favorites to recommend. If you are looking to connect with other local investors, they shouldn't keep their address book closed.
- **Honest and Displays Integrity.** Finally, working with an agent who has a reputation for being honest and true is imperative. There are many dishonest salespeople out there whose only goal is to get a paycheck. These are the kind of agents who will encourage you to buy a bad deal because it's good for them. An agent with integrity is one who puts your needs above their own, and understands that a slow dime is better than a fast nickel.

Here are three good ways I recommend to find a good agent:
1. Referrals
2. Referrals
3. Referrals

Don't hire an agent just because you saw their name on a park bench. Don't hire an agent just because your sister's boyfriend's parents' nephew is an agent—or even if your own mom is an agent. Get referrals from others, and find out who the best agents in your town are. Using the search tools at www.biggerpockets.com/meet to find agents in your area is a great start.

Finally, once you have the names of a few agents in your area, it's important to interview them carefully to make sure you are a good fit. Yes, I recommend actually setting up an appointment with them to sit down and talk. You'll be able to share your plans with them and ask them a series of questions to help you discover what kind of agent they are.

This meeting is also when the agent will size *you* up to decide whether they want to work with you, too. In reality, most agents don't like working with investors, especially new ones. Most agents have been burned by wannabe investors in the past, people who talked a big game but in the end were just another flash in the pan, fresh out of some guru boot camp. When agents think of investors, they often just think "big waste of time." This is your chance to prove them wrong by being prepared and having a solid plan in place for what you are looking for and how you plan to fund your deals.

Finally, I want to end this section with a warning: No matter how good an agent is, the buck always stops with you. Never rely on an agent to make decisions for you. Even the best agents tend to be highly optimistic about properties, and your job is to trust, but verify. Look at the data your agent provides and make your own decisions about a property, location, or market trends. An agent is one of the most valuable members of your real estate team, but they are not a substitute for poor planning or a shortcut to easy deals.

Should You Get Your Real Estate License?

A real estate license is not required to invest in real estate, of course, but many investors choose to get their license anyway. Should you? Let's take a look at the pros and cons of getting your license to help you determine whether this is the right path for you.

Pros
- **Direct Access to the MLS.** Perhaps the number one reason investors get their real estate license is to gain unlimited access to the MLS, so they no longer need to access all the listings through an agent. As I've mentioned numerous times already in this book, speed is key when trying to get a good deal in today's market, and being an agent can help you do this faster.
- **Property Access.** Having your real estate license gives you the ability to check out almost any home without needing another agent to open the door for you. This can make the property-searching process much easier, because you don't need to bend to anyone else's schedule.
- **Real Estate Relationships.** Being an agent can help you build relationships with other agents, as well as with lenders, appraisers, title

companies, and others in your local real estate industry.

- **Control the Deal.** When you have your license, there is no third party between you and the deal. Whether you are buying or selling, you are able to make decisions and control what happens to a much greater degree than when using an agent.
- **Commissions on Your Deals.** Being an agent can help you make (or save) money on your own deals. When you buy a home listed on the MLS, the commission is usually split 50/50 between the agent who brings the buyer and the agent who listed the deal. Therefore, when you buy a property yourself, and you have a license, you get to keep part of this 50 percent split for yourself, or use it toward your down payment or closing costs. (Your managing broker, with whom you will need to work for the first few years, will also get a chunk of *your* 50 percent commission, though. It's not all yours!) When you sell, you can either keep that money or use it as part of your negotiation strategy and give it to the buyer.
- **Commissions When You Work for Others.** Finally, once you have your license, you'll be able to help other individuals buy or sell properties, and you'll earn a commission each time they do. This can put a lot of extra money in your pocket, which you can then plow back into your investment strategy. You might even discover that being an agent is better than your current job and decide to quit that job.

Cons
- **Costs.** Getting your license is not free. You'll likely need to spend between $2,000 and $3,000 up front to get your license, plus several thousand per year after that to hold on to it. Of course, if you are making or saving more money than this by becoming an agent, this is not really an issue.
- **Education.** Becoming a real estate agent is not as easy as filling out a form. You must attend a significant amount of educational classes before you can get your license. In Washington State, where I live, the class is 90 hours long—more than two full weeks. Although you can take it at home on the computer, it's not a quick thing, no matter how you do it.
- **Disclosures.** As an agent, you will need to disclose that you have your license on all your paperwork, including direct mail, when dealing with motivated sellers. It's unlikely that this would be a problem (and in fact,

it could help bolster credibility), but sometimes, people just don't want to work with an agent. To be honest, I think this is a very minor issue and probably not an issue at all.

- **Paperwork.** An agent has a lot of paperwork to manage, which can add a degree of administrative hassle to the mix. I enjoy the fact that my agent handles everything for me and I just need to sign the occasional document.
- **Focus.** Finally, I am a strong believer in focusing on what you can do best and letting others do what they do best. This is the primary reason I do not currently have my license. My agent is the best agent in town, so why would I want to compete with him? I'll let him do what he does best, and I'll keep doing what I do best.

Should you get your license? The truth is that it probably wouldn't hurt. I've chosen not to have mine (currently), but there are many days that I wish I did. There is no universal "right or wrong" answer here, just a "best for you" answer that only you can know. You can succeed with a license; you can succeed without one.

4. Lender(s)

Unless you plan to pay all cash for your next property, you will likely need to build a relationship with a lender (or lenders) so you can get deals funded. Although I dedicate an entire chapter of this book to the world of real estate financing, I think touching on the lender here is important because they *are* part of your team—and a valuable member at that.

Lenders come in all shapes and sizes. For example, you could work with any of the following:

- A large national bank
- A small community bank or credit union
- A mortgage broker who helps you find financing from numerous different lenders
- A mortgage company
- A private or hard money lender with whom you build a relationship

As you continue reading the rest of this book, you'll begin to understand which of these five you should begin your journey with, but it doesn't hurt to start building relationships with all of them right now.

Whether you plan to start investing this week or not for three more years, start having conversations with bankers today. Find out what their requirements are. Ask them what kind of loan programs they have. Maybe even send them a Christmas card!

The truth about lending is this: Almost every lender can do pretty much the same thing. Loan programs do not differ that much from one lender to the next, but what *does* differ is the skill of the person behind the counter, typically the loan officer or banker. When I used to work as a loan officer, I would close significantly more loans than others in the bank, not because I was getting more leads, but because I was able to work those leads through the arduous process to have them come out the other side. It's important that you find a lender who is ambitious, creative, and hardworking. If you wait to add this person to your team until you have a deal, you are taking a risk that you'll end up with one of the bad ones, and you might even lose the deal.

5. Contractors and Handymen

Two weeks ago, I called six different contractors to come take a look at a small repair job on my personal house. Every single call went to an answering machine or voicemail. "Okay, understandable," I thought. "They are busy working. I'll leave a message."

In total, four of them called me back, and I scheduled four different appointments to get estimates. Of the four contractors with whom I had arranged appointments, two never even showed up.

Of the two remaining, one said he didn't know how to do the job. The other said he would call me back with an estimate in 24 hours. It's been a week, and now his phone is disconnected.

And I still need the repair job done.

For anyone who's ever tried to hire a contractor or handyman for their home or business, this story probably sounds a bit familiar. It's difficult!

Why is it so tough?

1. Contractors are not generally good business owners. This problem is part of the "E-myth" mentality, which dictates that just because someone can bake, that doesn't mean they can run a bakery. Just because someone can swing a hammer doesn't mean they can answer phone calls or show up on time.
2. Real estate investors are always looking for a good deal now, which

means we don't typically call the "big guys" (those who *are* good at running their business) because we know they'll be too expensive, are probably too big for small maintenance jobs, and will likely already be booked for the next three months.

What should an investor do? How can you add a good contractor or handyman to your team?

Finding an Incredible Contractor or Handyman

1. Be Proactive, Not Reactive

Have you ever heard the old phrase "The best time to look for a job is when you don't need one"? The same principle applies to contractors. If you are "reactive" in your search for a contractor, only waiting until something happens and you need to react to a situation, you are setting yourself up for problems. Instead, be *proactive*. Finding good contractors is a lifestyle, not a one-time event. Have a continually evolving list of people you could call for various problems, and continue to add people to this list, even when you don't need someone at the moment.

I ask nearly every person I meet in public if they have a good contractor, because I know that the success of my business hinges on the people I hire to take care of problems. The same will likely be true for your business, so be proactive and start looking for great contractors *today*.

2. Understand Price versus Cost

When you buy something, are you buying based on *price* or *cost*?

Confused? I was, too, but several days ago, I read something from the late Zig Ziglar in which he discussed the difference between price and cost, and, suddenly, I realized a huge error I'd been making in my investing business for the past decade. I've been hiring contractors based on price, not cost! Let me explain.

Price is the monetary amount you pay when you purchase something, but cost is the long-term monetary amount you pay over the life of a product or service. For example, the price of dishwasher A might be $400, and the price of dishwasher B might be $500, but if dishwasher A costs an extra $20 per month in energy to run, buying dishwasher B would be the smarter move.

You see, the difference between buying for cost and buying for price is subtle, but it can have a tremendous effect on your business. This principle also applies to hiring a contractor. Are you hiring on price or cost? If you are like me, price is probably the larger concern. But if you hire someone because their price is cheap, you might be setting yourself up for a lifetime of high cost on that repair.

When hiring a contractor, don't necessarily choose the cheapest option. You might think you are getting a great deal, but in the long run, you may end up spending *much* more. For two years of my investing business, I hired a local handyman to do most of my work because he had the lowest price. It's been two years since he stopped working for us, and not a week goes by that I don't find something he did wrong that I now have to pay to fix. If only I had hired based on cost instead of price.

As Mike F., an investor from Colorado said, "We learned long ago the old adage for construction has always rung true—pick any two: price, quality, service. You can't have all three."

3. Ask for Referrals

This is an obvious one, but it's so important, I can't skip it. One of the best ways to find good contractors is by simply asking others who they have used for similar work.

When people ask me who my best contractors are, I have no problem telling them, because I know it will help my contractor out *and* make me look good. I want my contractor to love working for me and to always put me at the top of his list, and giving him more work via referrals is a great way to do that. Don't be shy about asking other investors who they use.

Also ask your family and friends. As agent Jon Deavers said, "Good realtors work by referral to generate their own business, and part of that is by making good referrals to other professionals. You can bet if you have an experienced Realtor, he/she is going to refer someone that has completed work and made their previous clients happy."

4. Check References

Always check references.

Always.

This is especially true when dealing with contractors. Despite what you might think, even references supplied by the contractor will generally be honest with you, and you'll learn a lot. Ask to see examples of the kind of work you plan on having done.

Megan C., an investor from Texas, recently told me she always asks potential contractors for three referrals from the most recent jobs they've completed, and then calls those references to ask "if they showed up on time or when they said they would, did they complete the work, did they try to change the project cost mid-work or after it was done, and would you use them again."

Excellent advice!

5. The 6 a.m. Home Depot Trick

One of the more clever ideas I've ever heard for finding contractors came from house flipper J Scott (author of the best house-flipping book ever written, *The Book on Flipping Houses: How to Buy, Rehab, and Resell Residential Properties*).

J's suggestion was this: Go to Home Depot at 6 a.m. and meet the contractors who are there. These are the contractors who get up early and get their supplies *before* heading over to the job site. This is a strong indication that they know what they are doing and are not going to take advantage of you.

Although this is no silver bullet, but it can separate the ambitious contractors from those who sleep till noon or don't plan ahead well.

6. Ask Store Employees

Darren Sager, a real estate investor from New Jersey, suggests visiting supply stores (such as a plumbing supply store if you need plumbing or a lumber yard if you need something built) and asking the employees who work there who *they* would hire to work on their houses. These employees have a unique insight into the quality of materials that the contractors use, as well as into the experience level and management style of those who buy from them.

7. Place Craigslist Ads

Have you checked Craigslist for contractor ads? Or even better, have you placed an ad there yourself? I found one of the best handymen I have after we placed a free ad on Craigslist asking for local handymen who could do occasional tasks for our real estate investment company. We received several responses, hired each to do a small task, and quickly found a great guy we now use often for small tasks.

8. Make Them Compete

Sometimes, the best answer is not finding *one* contractor but *several* who can compete for your business, says Royce Jarrendt, a homebuilder from Virginia. Jarrendt says, "The best solution to finding a good contractor is finding three good contractors. It's way too easy to get cozy with what you think is a good situation with a contractor. Competition is what drives price and quality. All of my contractors know that I know other contractors, and because I am honest, respectful, and fair, they are willing to give me their best price, quality, and attention."

I know some investors call three to five contractors to do a bid and tell them all the same appointment time, both to minimize the hassle of meeting multiple contractors and to encourage lean bids.

9. Whom Do They Like to Follow?

Another idea is to ask good subcontractors whom they like to follow. In other words, which drywall person does the painter like to follow? Which framer does the plumber like to follow?

If you ask for referrals from other subcontractors, you can gain valuable insight from those who have to work where the last guy left off.

10. Be Clear About Your Expectations

With all this talk about finding a good contractor, there is also something to say about *your* responsibility in the relationship. Often a "bad" contractor only seems bad because they did not clearly understand the client's expectations at the start of a job. Martin Scherer, an investor from California, says to give contractors clear, detailed instructions of your needs: "Contractors are not mind readers. If you give contractors a clear list of expectations, you will find your task much easier."

Wrapping It Up: Finding Contractors

A great contractor or handyman can make your real estate investing life smooth sailing, but a difficult contractor can make you wish you had never bought a piece of real estate (and may keep you from buying any more).

Sure, finding good, reliable contractors can be difficult, but if there is only one thing you should remember after reading this book, this is it: *Finding contractors is a verb!* In other words, it's something that *you physically have to do* in your business, and something that never really ends.

You cannot sit by and wait for the ideal contractor to walk into your life. You must get out there and find them.

Now, I just spent a lot of time talking about the "big five" team members: your spouse, mentor, agent, lender, and contractor. The next five I will describe are also very important, but they require a bit less space to discuss. Each of the following can be best found through referrals from fellow investors, agents, or others in the real estate business. As with everything I've mentioned thus far, be sure to actively work to find the best team member possible. A team is only as strong as its weakest member, so don't skimp on any of these. Do the work needed to find great team members.

6. Bookkeeper

One of the things not often addressed in real estate books is bookkeeping, but this is one of the most important parts of an investor's job. Although you are entirely capable of doing your own books, you may want to hire a bookkeeper to keep track of income and expenses, and to get your finances tax-ready.

Bookkeepers keep an accurate record of the incoming credits and outgoing debits from your account, helping you keep constant tabs on how your business is performing. Each month, they reconcile the transactions they've recorded on paper (or on the computer) with the related bank account to make sure every penny is accounted for. Bookkeeping is largely akin to data entry but with some knowledge of *how* to enter that data.

A bookkeeper is *not* the same as a CPA (certified public accountant), and the same level of education and training is not needed; thus, the same kind of pay is not needed. Pricing for bookkeepers can be all over the board, depending on what you need done and the experience level of the bookkeeper, but, typically, good bookkeepers can be found in the $20 to $50 per hour range.

7. CPA

A CPA, short for certified public accountant, is a professional accountant who offers financial advice, creates financial reports, offers tax recommendations for your business, and prepares your personal and business tax returns. This is likely not the same person who does your bookkeeping, but rather someone who looks at the "big picture" of your business, and helps you plan and prepare for tax season. A great CPA is vital in your real estate investing business, and not just for investors with a lot of properties. I recommend finding a good CPA immediately, even if you have no properties yet, because a good CPA will help you choose the best tax-saving strategy for buying and holding your properties.

A great CPA can save you more money than they cost, but they are not cheap. Plan on spending between $100 and $300 per hour, depending on your location, for a qualified CPA. To prepare your tax returns, plan on spending much more than you would heading to your local grocery store to have some guy in a cubicle do them. Those tax preparers are simply not trained to offer the kind of advice and tax preparation needed by a real estate investor. I recommend finding a CPA who specializes in helping real estate entrepreneurs, and ideally a CPA who owns real estate. I've made the mistake of hiring just a local "general" CPA who cost me almost $10,000 in IRS fees. (Luckily, the IRS waived the penalty, because it was the CPA's fault. Thanks, IRS!)

8. Lawyer

As an attorney guest on the *BiggerPockets Podcast* recently told me, when you invest in real estate, it's not a matter of "if" you get sued but "when." The more wealth you build, the more properties you own, the larger your footprint on earth is, the greater chance you have of someone trying to take some of it away from you. This is why a good lawyer is incredibly valuable for your business.

A good lawyer will help make sure your lease and other forms are legally binding, as well as guide you on (and prepare) the best legal entity for holding your properties (which I'll cover in Chapter 14). They can help you evict a tenant who isn't paying, advise you on how to handle sticky situations, and, depending on your state, can help you actually buy or sell real estate. (Some states use an attorney, while others use a title company to transact real estate. I'll cover the specifics in Chapter 13.)

There are many types of attorneys out there, and the attorney who finalized your cousin's divorce or got your nephew out of his DUI is probably not the same attorney who will help you build your business. As with a CPA, having an attorney who either invests in real estate themselves or specializes in this kind of work is best. Be sure to interview your attorney to find out what they are good at and how much they charge, and, as always, ask for referrals.

Attorneys are one of the most expensive members of your team but one that you won't have to use too often. Attorney rates typically start at $200 per hour and can climb as high as $600 an hour, depending on experience and what they are doing for you. While these numbers can intimidate a lot of investors, understand that you will not likely be using your attorney for dozens of hours of work—usually just 15 minutes here, 30 minutes there, and so on.

9. Insurance Agent

If there is one thing I hate more than almost anything else in real estate, it's insurance. You see, one of the mistakes I've made in my investing career has been chasing the lowest insurance rate, switching companies every year to get a better deal. However, this created a logistical nightmare that I'm still digging myself out of. There were simply too many moving parts for me to control. It seems that not a week goes by that I don't have an insurance policy being cancelled or changed, or something being mailed to the wrong address. Just the other day, I found out that I've been paying for two different policies on the same property for years. Years!

All this would have been solved, or at least lessened, had I stuck with having one great insurance agent on my team. I recommend finding an insurance broker, rather than just an agent at a specific company. A broker can shop around at different companies for the best rate and coverage, and can switch your policy if necessary without having to take your business elsewhere. Today, I have a great agent who can shop numerous companies for the best policy and can change policies as needed while keeping all my paperwork in his office. Now when I get notice that a policy is changing, expiring, being cancelled, or whatever, he simply takes care of it for me.

Don't just get insurance, get an insurance agent on your team.

10. Property Manager

If you don't plan to manage your own property, you will need a property manager to look after your investment. Even if you do plan to manage yourself, building a relationship with a local property manager might not be a bad idea, because, let's face it, you didn't get into real estate to manage tenants for the rest of your life. At some point, you will probably want to transition to property management, so now is a good time to start planning.

A great property manager can mean the difference between success and failure for your investment. I hope you didn't just skim over that line. Just in case you did, I'm going to repeat it in all caps, bold, and italics: *A GREAT PROPERTY MANAGER CAN MEAN THE DIFFERENCE BETWEEN SUCCESS AND FAILURE FOR YOUR INVESTMENT.*

Let's talk about what a property manager does, what makes a good property manager, and how you can find one.

A property manager can manage a wide variety of tasks concerning your property, depending on the manager. Most commonly, a property manager will do the following:

- Advertise vacancies
- Take phone calls from potential tenants
- Show units to prospects
- Hand out and accept applications
- Screen tenants for rental, career, and criminal history
- Choose a tenant and sign a lease
- Accept maintenance phone calls and schedule needed appointments
- Prepare monthly reports concerning the property
- Supply the owner with a year-end summary
- Manage problems as they arise
- Stay in constant communication with the owner about problems
- Pay property bills (sometimes, depending on the manager and the bill)

A great property manager will do all of these tasks exceptionally well, keeping your property running at peak efficiency. Now for the bad news: If you are looking at this list and thinking, "Wow, they take all the hard work out of being a landlord! How do I sign up?" I need to caution you: Finding a manager who does all these tasks as well as you think they should be done can be very difficult. After all, the property is not their own, so it's tough to find someone who will go above and beyond like you might.

In addition, most property managers make a significant portion of their revenue on the turnover between tenants, so they are incentivized *not* to do a good job. I'm not saying that they purposefully would choose a bad tenant just to get the "turnover fee" again and again—because turnover does cost them a lot in time, advertising, and stress—but they may not try as hard as you would to keep a property operating at peak efficiency.

Property management fees differ depending on the size of the property and its location, usually ranging between 8 percent and 12 percent of the monthly rent, with 10 percent being the most common for single-family and small multifamily properties. Also, as I just mentioned, management companies have a "placement" fee that is typically equal to half of the first month's rent (or even the entire first month's rent) upon a lease signing. Some management companies also charge a "renewal fee" each year when the tenant renews their lease, but this is not as common. Again, this depends largely on your location, but be sure to interview multiple property managers in your quest to find a great one for your team.

You may or may not choose to use a property manager at this time, but it still does not hurt to have one on your team with whom you can begin building a relationship for more than just management reasons. A good property manager, even if they are not managing your properties, can be helpful in other ways. For example, they can be a great source of leads for your next property; after all, they know exactly how different properties are running and have a good indication as to the level of interest the owner has. They can also help you better understand the market, such as vacancy rates or current market rent.

I'll talk a lot more about property management in Chapters 17 and 18, but I wanted to give you a high-level overview of what a property manager does here so that you can begin formulating your thoughts in that direction. Let's wrap up this discussion on team members and start talking about the next leg of your investment journey (and one of the most important steps to get right): analyzing a deal.

Chapter Five
ANALYZING A RENTAL PROPERTY

"Nature is written in mathematical language."

—GALILEO GALILEI

When I was a kid, *Duck Tales* was one of my favorite television shows.

Each day after school, I'd watch the adventures of Huey, Dewey, and Louie as they fought off the Beagle Boys who wanted good ole Scrooge McDuck's hard-earned money. They always managed to thwart the efforts of the villains and save Scrooge's cash, and, as a reward, Scrooge McDuck and his three nephews would take a swim in his vault of money. Yes, you remember. They would jump off the diving board headfirst into mountains of gold coins. When I was a kid, nothing seemed more exciting to me than that.

How did Scrooge get so much money? To use his own words, by being "smarter than the smarties and tougher than the toughies."

Yes, this is only a cartoon, but I think there is a valuable lesson to be learned here. If you want to succeed and swim in your own river of cash, you need to be smarter than the rest. I believe the best way to do this is through a solid grasp of the numbers.

Math is not most people's favorite subject in school, but it may be the most important for a real estate investor. Understanding how your business makes money is imperative in helping it make more. This is why I harp so often on getting a firm understanding of the math involved when buying an investment property. I don't care if you are buying your first or 100th property, you need to understand and do the math.

That is my ultimate goal with this chapter: to help you learn to analyze a real estate deal so that you can make the best investment possible. After all, one of the most common phrases you'll hear over and over again in your investing career is this: You make your money when you buy. In other words, if you don't have the right math going into a deal, you'll never get the right profit coming out of it. You should know up front that your property will make money, and you do that by correctly analyzing the property. As Grant Cardone said, "If you don't know you made money on the day you bought it, that was a bad deal."

How to Analyze a Rental Property

I look at several primary factors when analyzing a rental property, but the two most important are as follows:

- Cash flow
- Appreciation

Cash flow is simply the money that's left after all the bills have been paid. Appreciation is the equity gained as the property value increases. As we discussed briefly in Chapter 1, there are not a lot of great ways to estimate future appreciation without a crystal ball, so I generally choose to focus on cash flow. After all, I am a buy-and-hold investor, and I assume any appreciation is "icing on the cake" rather than the goal.

What Is Cash Flow?

As I mentioned earlier, cash flow is the money left over after all the bills on a property have been paid. This is a simple enough definition, but it gets a lot of people in trouble. You see, technically, cash flow is defined this way:

Income – Expenses = Cash Flow

Okay, great. *However,* where people tend to screw things up is not knowing what is included under income and expenses. This distinction can get you into a lot of trouble, especially if you forget to list some of the expenses. Let's look at each one in detail, starting with income.

Calculating Income

A property's projected income may seem fairly easy to compute, but given that all the calculations for cash flow are based on this number and that the future success or failure of your investment is based on this, I hope you don't mind if we spend a few minutes talking about how to really nail this figure down.

The key to calculating income is knowing the fair market rent. The fair market rent is the price someone is willing to pay to use your property for a set period of time. Fair market rent is determined by the market and what the local average is for certain characteristics of the property, such as the following:

- Location of the property
- Number of bedrooms and bathrooms
- Amenities such as air conditioning, parking, and appliances
- Size of the property

Each of these items comes into play when you are deciding how much a property should rent for. It's your job, as a landlord, to accurately estimate the potential rent for any property you are analyzing. This is not always an easy task, but here are several tips for determining what your prospective property could rent for. The following eight tips were outlined perfectly by landlord Kevin Perk:

1. **Constantly scan your local papers.** I say "papers," plural, because many markets are served by more than one. For example, in my market, the daily paper does not really serve me well, but the weekly paper does. It may seem old school, but a lot of landlords and tenants are old school.
2. **Check out Craigslist often.** Many big and small landlords advertise their properties here, and you can get a lot more information than from the newspapers. This is a great resource for almost every part of the county. Plus, you can do keyword searches for your specific market and type of property.
3. **Check out your competitors' and local property management**

companies' websites. They will often have several listings near you and will show all of the amenities.

4. **Read local "For Rent" signs.** Call the number on the signs and act like a potential tenant. This is a great way to find out what properties in your area are going for.

5. **Talk with other landlords.** You can find them at your local REIA (Real Estate Investors Association) meetings. Rents are not a big secret, and if a landlord has been able to raise their rents, they are often almost boastful about it.

6. **When your unit goes vacant, try to bump up the rent. See if the market will bear the increased price.** If you do not get any takers in a week or so, start easing down on the price until the unit rents. You will eventually find the market rate.

7. **Too many applicants? Raise the rent.** Conversely, if you have multiple applicants on the first day of availability, your rent is likely too low. Renters flock to a deal. Back up, do a little research, and set the price higher.

8. **Check the MLS.** Many landlords and real estate agents now also list their available rentals on the local MLS. If you are an agent, you should check out this searchable database. If not, you may want to find one to help you.

Once you have a pretty good idea of what the property will rent for, you need to estimate the expenses of your rental property.

Estimating Rental Property Expenses

Expenses are deceptive.

If there is one thing that causes landlords to lose money each month and eventually go bankrupt, it's this: They underestimate expenses. On paper, their deal might look pretty good, but in reality, expenses add up very quickly. The low margins of profit to be made on rental properties can easily be cannibalized by unexpected expenses. Therefore, having a firm grasp on what those expenses might be is vital to your success.

Let me give you a *bad* example of calculating cash flow. You might say, "The mortgage is $800 per month, and the property will rent for $1,000 per month, so my cash flow would be $200 per month."

False.

You see, you forgot about a lot of other expenses, including these:

- Taxes
- Insurance
- Flood insurance (if needed)
- Vacancy
- Repairs
- Capital expenditures
- Water
- Sewer
- Garbage
- Gas
- Electricity
- HOA (home owner's association) fees (if applicable)
- Snow removal
- Lawn care
- Property management

Some of these items are easy to calculate, because you can simply call someone important to find out about the cost. For example, consider the following options:

- **Taxes.** Call your local county or look online at the county assessor's page.
- **Insurance.** Call your insurance salesman and ask for a quote.
- **Flood insurance.** Call your insurance salesman and ask for a quote.
- **Water.** Call your local water department.
- **Sewer.** Call your local water or sewer department.
- **Garbage.** Call your local trash provider.
- **Gas.** Call your local gas company.
- **Electricity.** Call your local electric company.
- **HOA fees.** Call the HOA president or hotline.
- **Snow removal.** Ask local landlords what they pay or call a snow removal company.
- **Lawn care.** Ask local landlords what they pay or call a lawn care company for a quote.

Keep in mind, not all of these will apply to every property (or tenants may pay their own expenses), and some properties will require more expenses than I've listed here. Don't get overwhelmed, though—the more properties you look at in your local area, the more you will understand what the normal expenses are.

The numbers we just listed are fairly easy to determine, but other numbers are more difficult, such as vacancy, repairs, capital expenditures, and property management. But just because these numbers are difficult to nail down doesn't mean we shouldn't include them. Instead, we need to use averages. And to do this, we look at those numbers as percentages and translate those percentages into dollar amounts.

Let's look at a few of the most common:

- **Vacancy.** Properties are usually not rented 100 percent of the time; tenants move on, and your property will likely sit vacant for extended periods of time. The length of time will depend on your local area and how good you are at filling those vacancies, so I can't give you an absolute number. If you are unsure, try talking with some local property management companies to see what their typical vacancy rate is.

  Once you know the typical vacancy rate, as a percentage, you can break that percentage down into a monetary amount. For example, if a property rents for $1,000 per month, and you believe the property will have a 5 percent vacancy rate, you simply multiply $1,000 by .05 to get $50. This is the amount you will want to include for your vacancy expense each month.

- **Repairs.** Repairs are difficult to estimate, because a lot of variables come into play. A house that is 90 years old will likely have significantly more repair costs than a house built last year. A recently rehabbed house will also likely have fewer repairs needed than a home untouched for decades. Therefore, when determining the cost of repairs, you will need to look at the property itself to decide how much you should allocate for repairs. Personally, I like to assume between 5 percent and 15 percent, depending on the condition and age of the property.

  Keep in mind, this is a percentage averaged out over a long period of time, so it doesn't mean that every month you can expect 5 percent to 15 percent of the rent to be spent on repairs. You may go six months without a single repair and then get hit with a $1,500 water leak. You just never know.

- **Capital Expenditures.** Also known as CapEx, capital expenditures are those expensive, "big-ticket" items that need to be replaced every so often, but not every month or year. This could include roofs, appliances, driveways, plumbing systems, or any other large item you should budget for. Many people ignore the CapEx in their analysis, which I feel is a mistake. After all, if you were to earn $100 per month in cash flow for ten years ($12,000) and then needed to put on a new roof for $12,000, what did you really accomplish in those ten years?

Like repairs, CapEx is difficult to estimate because it depends on the condition and age of your property. However, you can sit down and estimate how many years a roof will last, how many years an appliance will last, what the condition of your plumbing is, what a new driveway will cost, and so on—and then divide these out by the number of years.

To estimate the total CapEx you should set aside, start by listing every big-ticket item that might need to be replaced in the next 20 years. Use the following chart to get started, but understand that your area might have different expenses than these. (Special thanks go out to Ben Leybovich and Serge Shukat for illuminating this CapEx estimation process for me!)

The following chart lists thirteen of the major capital expenditures that a typical property has, then looks at the total replacement cost for that item and how long that item will likely last. This tells us how much per year we should be saving to replace that item. We can then break that figure down into a monthly price.

CAPITAL EXPENSE	TOTAL REPLACEMENT COST	LIFESPAN (YEARS)	COST PER YEAR	COST PER MONTH
Roof	$5,000	25	$200	$16.67
Water Heater	$600	10	$60	$5
All Appliances	$1,000	10	$100	$8.33
Driveway/ Parking Lot	$5,000	50	$100	$8.33
HVAC	$3,000	20	$150	$12.50
Flooring	$2,000	6	$333	$27.75
Plumbing	$3,000	30	$100	$8.33
Windows	$5,000	50	$100	$8.33
Paint	$2,500	5	$500	$41.67
Cabinets/ Counters	$3,000	20	$150	$12.50
Structure (foundation, framing)	$10,000	50	$200	$16.67
Components (garage door, etc.)	$1,000	10	$100	$8.33
Landscaping	$1,000	10	$100	$8.33
TOTAL	$42,100		$2,193	$182.75

According to this chart, then, we should be setting aside $182.75 per month for CapEx. However, there are limitations to estimating capital expenditures this way. This chart tends to assume that everything was brand new when the property was purchased, but what if the plumbing only has a few years left? What if the paint is peeling, so the property needs new paint next year? Although the average of $182.75 might be true over the long run, if, starting today, you only saved that much each month, and then you were hit with a $5,000 bill for a roof replacement next year, you wouldn't have enough cash set aside to cover it. Again, the $182.75 in this chart is just an example for one fictional property. Each item may cost more or less for you. You may have expenditures that I didn't list. The point of this chart is to merely show *how* to calculate CapEx for a property.

I have one final note about CapEx: Notice that the chart we presented wouldn't change much if the home were a $500,000 property or a $25,000 property. Sure, you might need to replace more windows or a bigger roof, but this differential is not as large as the cost difference between a $25,000 property and a $500,000 property. (In other words, just because a house worth $500,000 is 20 times more expensive than one that is $25,000, that doesn't mean a roof, windows, paint, or anything else will also be 20 times more expensive.) What this means is that CapEx is a much greater percentage of the income the lower the property value. On a home that rents for $2,000 per month, the CapEx of $200 per month is 10 percent of the income, but on a home that rents for $600 per month, the CapEx of $200 per month will be 30 percent of the rent. Just keep this in mind when you run an analysis on a property.

- **Property Management.** Property management companies typically charge a percentage of the rent, along with a fee, to rent out a unit. These numbers can vary based on area, but in my area, property managers charge 10 percent of the monthly rent and 50 percent of the first month's rent when a unit is turned over. Rather than spending the time to get the *exact* cost of the property management based on vacancy rate, I will generally just add 1 percent to whatever the monthly percentage is. In this case, the property manager charges 10 percent, so I'll call it 11 percent, assuming that extra 1 percent will cover the cost of their fee upon tenant turnover.

  Now what if you are going to manage yourself? You must still budget for management. Here's why: If you are successful (and you will be!), you cannot manage forever. There will come a day when you will have too many properties, and you'll need to start using property management. What happens if you never budgeted for it? That's right: You lose all your cash flow. So whether you plan to manage yourself or not, budget for a property manager.

Putting All the Numbers Together

At this point, you should have a list of all the expenses and income sources for your property.

For the rest of this chapter, let's look at a hypothetical scenario: 123 Main Street is for sale for $100,000. It is a three-bedroom home that would rent for $1,200 per month. Breaking down the numbers, we've determined the following monthly expenses:

- Taxes: $120/month
- Insurance: $55/month
- Flood insurance: None needed
- Vacancy: 5% or $50/month
- Repairs: 5% or $50/month
- Capital expenditures: $183/month
- Water: Tenant pays
- Sewer: Tenant pays
- Garbage: Tenant pays
- Gas: Tenant pays
- Electricity: Tenant pays
- HOA fees: None
- Snow removal: Tenant pays
- Lawn care: Tenant pays
- Property management: 11% or $132/month

We now know that our monthly expenses will average $590. This number is known as our "operating expenses." Keep this in mind—it will come in handy in just a moment.

We are not yet done determining our cash flow. There is still one major expense we have not included: the mortgage!

To determine the mortgage amount, simply use an online calculator to determine your monthly payment. In our example here, we know the total cost of the property is $100,000, so our loan amount will depend on how much of a down payment we put. Let's assume we put 20 percent down: $100,000 × .20 = $20,000. Therefore, our loan amount would be $80,000 (because $100,000 minus $20,000 is $80,000).

Now we simply enter $80,000 into the mortgage calculator to determine our mortgage payment. The calculator will also ask for an interest rate and loan period. To determine the interest rate, ask a local mortgage lender what current rates are for the kind of property you are attempting to buy. Most residential loans (one to four units) will allow you to go for 30 years, whereas most commercial property loans will allow 20 to 25 years. Plug those numbers into the calculator to determine your mortgage payment.

In this case, we'll use an interest rate of 5.5 percent and a loan period of 30 years to discover our monthly payment will be $454.23.

Finally, we have all the pieces needed to put together our cash flow analysis puzzle. We learned earlier that our total operating expense was $590 per month, and now we know our mortgage will be $454.23. Let's add them together:

$590 + $454.23 = $1,044.23.

Therefore, we can estimate that the total expenses on this property will be $1,044.23 per month.

Determining Cash Flow

Now, let's return to the definition of cash flow that we discussed earlier, which was this:

Income – Expenses = Cash Flow

We know the total income and we know the total expenses, so now we can determine our cash flow. To use our example, in this case, our property will rent for $1,200 per month. Therefore:

$1,200 – $1,044.23 = $155.77

On this sample property, our estimated cash flow will be $155.77 per month or $1,869.24 per year.

Is this a good deal? A cash flow of $155.77 might seem like a great deal, or it might seem terrible. For that, we need to look at the return on investment.

Cash-on-Cash Return on Investment

At this point, we know that our example property will give us about $155.77 per month in positive cash flow.

This seems to be a good thing, but is it really?

The best way to determine whether this is actually a good deal is by comparing it with something else. After all, this investment *did* cost you money to buy it, right? You spent $20,000 on the down payment, plus (let's say) another $5,000 on the closing costs and another $3,000 on rehab to get the property 100 percent rent-ready.

At this point, you have paid $28,000 of your own hard-earned cash to acquire the property. So is $155.77 per month a good deal on a $28,000 investment?

This is when the *cash-on-cash return on investment* comes in really handy. The cash-on-cash return on investment (often abbreviated as CoCROI) is a simple metric that tells us what kind of yield our money is making us based only on the cash flow (ignoring appreciation, tax benefits, and the loan paydown). The CoCROI is nice because it allows us to compare this investment against other investments, like the stock market or mutual funds, so let's do that.

CoCROI is simply the ratio between how much cash flow we received over a one-year period and how much money we invested. In other words:

CoCROI = Total Annual Cash Flow / Total Investment

Using our example, we get:

CoCROI = $1,869.24 / $28,000 = 6.7%

We have determined that this property should produce a CoCROI of 6.7 percent. Is this good? That's up to you to decide. According to Nerd-Wallet, the stock market has averaged around 10 percent return, so I like to think 6.7 percent is below average compared with that, and not likely something I would pursue. But keep in mind, this doesn't take into account the appreciation that will take place, the tax benefits you might receive, or the loan paydown that *is* taking place (after all, every month, the loan gets paid down a little more). The bottom line is: Only you can determine what a "good" return on investment is, because it will be based on your interpretation of what acceptable is. The question is this: Does the property and its return on investment fit within your plan? If so, you may want to pursue it!

What About the Rules of Thumb?

In the investing world, there are some "rules of thumb" to help people analyze properties a bit better. Colloquially, a "rule of thumb" is a principle with broad application that is not intended to be strictly accurate or reliable for every situation. It is an easily learned and easily applied procedure for approximately calculating or recalling some value, or for making some determination.

Notice two things about this definition:

1. Not intended to be strictly accurate
2. Easily learned and easily applied

I am hesitant to even include this section because of item one, but have decided to do so because of item two. You see, I might mention one of the following rules with numerous disclaimers and warnings, but some readers will still latch on to these rules as though I were handing down the Ten Commandments. Please understand that these are just quick guides, and although they are valuable for you to be familiar with, they do not carry immense weight in actually purchasing a property. Their main purpose is in helping you quickly identify *bad* properties so you don't waste time analyzing them. After all, when you are looking for a real estate deal, you will likely have hundreds to choose from. If you tried to analyze the income and expenses for each and every property that comes across your computer screen, you'd never leave your desk. Instead, the rules of thumb are a sort of "internal gauge" that will help you determine whether a property deserves further consideration.

But let me get to the two most common rules of thumb, and this will become more clear.

The 50 Percent Rule

Many people are terrible at estimating expenses on a potential deal. I just spent a significant chunk of this book showing you how to accurately estimate cash flow, but again, it would be a waste of your time to do this on each and every property you happen to come across. Therefore, another, much faster way to estimate cash flow is by using a technique known as the 50 percent rule. This rule of thumb states that a rental property's expenses tend to be about 50 percent of the income, not including the mortgage principal and interest (P&I) payment. The formula looks like this:

Cash Flow = (Total Income × .5) – Mortgage P&I

In other words, simply divide the income in half and subtract out the mortgage payment.

For example, you were scanning through www.zillow.com for properties and came across a duplex that piqued your interest. Knowing the rental rates in the area, you know that the property might rent for $600 per side, for a total income of $1,200 per month. You also see that the property is being sold for $120,000, so you do a quick calculation in your head and assume your mortgage payment (without taxes and insurance) would be approximately $550 per month (or simply use an online mortgage calculator to determine this number):

Therefore, according to the 50 percent rule:

Cash Flow = ($1,200 × .5) – $550
Cash Flow = ($600) – $550
Cash Flow = $50

In this example, using the 50 percent rule, you could expect $50 per month in cash flow.

How accurate is this?

It depends. You see, the expenses on this property could vary wildly. For example, the following are typically included in that 50 percent:

- Taxes
- Insurance
- Maintenance
- Repairs
- Vacancy
- CapEx
- Property management

But what if the taxes were much higher than normal on this property? What if the insurance was higher? Or what if the property was old and therefore needed lots of continual maintenance? You see, the 50 percent rule doesn't know the specifics of your property, so it could never be perfect. It is just a rule of thumb to help you quickly screen properties. Your property's operating expenses might be as low as 30 percent or as high as 70 percent—you won't know until you actually run the numbers. However, while you are looking at dozens of properties, the 50 percent rule can be a nice tool to quickly say, "No, no, no, no, maybe, no, maybe, no, no" on the properties you scroll through. Then you can take a deeper look at the "maybe" properties and ignore most of the "no" properties.

The 2 Percent Rule (the 2 Percent Test)

The 2 percent rule also helps you analyze a property for its cash flow potential, but in a different way than the 50 percent rule does. The 2 percent rule doesn't estimate *how much* cash flow you'll receive, but rather serves as a "pass-fail" test to flag properties that warrant further investigation.

The 2 percent rule is simply the ratio between rental income and purchase price. Meeting the 2 percent rule means that a property's monthly rental income must equal 2 percent of the purchase price or greater. The formula would look like this:

Monthly Rental Income / Purchase Price = X

If X > .02, then the 2 percent rule has been met.

If X < .02, then the 2 percent rule has not been met.

The 2 percent rule is really a terrible name for this process; it probably should be called the "2 percent test." Since I'm writing "the book" on rental property investing, I think I'll take this opportunity to officially change the name. Yes, that's right, you heard it here first. The 2 percent rule is now the 2 percent test!

Now, the value of 2 percent could easily be replaced with another number to test the strength of a deal. For example, many people look for "the 1 percent test," in which the monthly rental price is 1 percent of the purchase price or higher. You might hear people talk about the .5 percent test, the 1.5 percent test, the 3 percent test, and so on. It's all the same thing: the monthly rent over the purchase price.

What does this even mean? Why does 2 percent even matter? What do you win if you "pass the 2 percent test"? A new car? A 40-pound stuffed animal from the carnival? Hardly.

In fact, passing the 2 percent test doesn't really mean anything universally. The 2 percent test comes in handy once you know your local market. For example, in my local real estate market, I know that if I can find a property that gets close to 2 percent, it's probably going to cash flow well. I know that, because the rental income is so high compared with what typical expenses are, it should do pretty well. At the same time, I know that if something falls below 1.5 percent, it's probably not going to cash flow unless the tenant pays the majority of the bills. When I get down to 1 percent, I know for an almost absolute fact that it will not cash flow in my area.

Keep in mind this is *my area*. Yours might be different. Maybe you'll discover that 1 percent is plenty to get you enough cash flow to create a solid return on investment. The point is this: Don't get caught up on the idea that you have to hit some mythical 2 percent to have a good investment.

123 Main Street Analysis

Okay, enough with the talk *about* analyzing properties. Let's go ahead and analyze a deal together, from beginning to end. The following numbers are not made up—this is an actual deal that came across my desk today, and you are going to help me analyze it. (The address has been changed to protect the innocent.)

First, let me tell you a bit about 123 Main Street, as seen below in Figure 3.

123 Main Street—Metropolis
3 Bed—1.75 Bath—1,253 sq. ft.

Metropolis home with three bedrooms and one bath. A two car garage in the back with alley access.

Price	$77,900
Bedrooms:	3
Bathrooms:	1
Size:	1,253 sq. ft.
$/sq. ft.:	$62/sq. ft.
Type:	Single family house
Year built:	1968
Lot size:	7,200
Days on market:	21 days
Neighborhood:	Metropolis
MLS@:	747498
Status:	Active
Property tax:	$1,466.18

Figure 3

Step One: Figure Out Total Project Cost
The first step in analyzing this property is to find out our total project cost. In other words, how much is this property going to cost to buy, fix up, and get rented?

Four values typically help us determine the total project cost:

1. **Purchase Price.** This is pretty self-explanatory, but the purchase price is the actual amount you will pay for the property. This is *not* necessarily the asking price or what it's worth. This is what you will actually pay. In the case of 123 Main Street, I'll use a value of $75,000. (They are asking $77,000, but it's been on the market for twenty-one days, so I think they'll go down a little.)

2. **Purchase Closing Costs.** The purchase closing costs are all the costs associated with the purchase transaction. Included might be loan points, loan origination fees, prepaid insurance, prepaid property taxes, title and escrow fees, recording fees, attorney charges, and other fees custom to your area. In my experience, these purchase closing costs usually average around $1,500 for a $100,000 property, *plus* any fees added by your lender. In the case of 123 Main Street, it's fairly inexpensive, but I know that I would likely be obtaining a loan, so I'm going to use $2,500 as my purchase closing costs.

3. **Pre-Rent Holding Costs.** In other words, how much will I need to pay monthly for this property before I can get it rented? Enough for two months? One month? Because you won't likely have a renter the first day you buy it (especially if it needs a lot of repairs), you should be sure to account for any holding costs. These costs will likely be the mortgage, taxes, insurance, and utilities. For this property, I think it could be rented within two months, so I'm going to use a nice round number of $1,200 here.

4. **Estimated Repairs.** How much work does this property need before it's rent-ready? Although I dedicate an entire chapter to this question later in this book, let's do a quick preliminary analysis of the repairs needed. At this point, you may not have even been to the property, so you might need to make some assumptions. Once you've walked through the property, you'll be able to refine those assumptions to be much more accurate. Then, after the inspection and bids from contractors, you'll be able to get even more specific. To help estimate the rehab budget, I recommend filling out the following form with your best estimates. These are the twenty-four main categories of repairs you'll likely face when estimating the repairs. As you can see in this chart, Figure 4, I'll use $17,250 as our total repairs needed.

Interior Repairs

Demo	$250	HVAC	$2500
Sheetrock	$200	Cabinets	$200
Plumbing	$300	Appliances	$1200
Carpentry	$0	Doors	$600
Electrical	$500	Flooring	$2400
Painting	$3500	Insulation	$0

Exterior Repairs

Roof	$100	Landscaping	$500
Concrete	$0	Painting	$2500
Gutters	$0	Septic	$0
Garage	$500	Deck	$0
Siding	$5000	Foundation	$0
Windows	$3600	Other	$2000
		Total repairs	$17,250

Figure 4

At this point, we have everything we need to estimate the total cost of the project:

Purchase Price:	$75,000
+ Purchase Closing Costs:	$2,500
+ Pre-Rent Holding Costs:	$1,200
+ Estimated Repairs:	$17,250
= Total Cost of Project:	**$95,950**

At this point, we can see the total amount we'll have in this property and can compare this with other homes selling in the area. After all, a fixer-upper like this house doesn't make sense if all the other homes that are already fixed up cost around the same price (why go through the hassle of a rehab if you aren't getting something for your work?). In this case, however, I can see numerous examples of similar fixed-up properties selling in the $110,000 to $130,000 range, so I actually expect the ARV (after repair value) for this property to be approximately $120,000. So far, so good.

Step Two: Figure Out the Financing and Total Cost Out of Pocket

Next, we want to determine how much the financing on this property will cost us each month. If you plan to pay 100 percent cash for the property, then you can skip this step. However, if you plan to use a loan, we'll need to know how much it's going to cost each month. I'll dedicate an entire chapter to financing later in this book, so don't worry too much about the specifics right now. Instead, let's just look at the underlying math.

Typically, a bank will require a 20 percent down payment on a rental property like this, with some banks requiring 25 percent. In addition, they will likely not cover the repairs, pre-rent holding costs, or the closing costs. Instead, they will base that 20 percent or 25 percent on the purchase price alone. In this case, the purchase price we are analyzing for is $75,000, so a 20 percent down payment would mean our loan is for 80 percent of the purchase price.

Down Payment: $75,000 × .2 = $15,000
Loan: $75,000 × .8 = $60,000

Our loan from the bank will therefore be for $60,000, and we will need to pay $15,000 for a down payment.

Now, to determine the total amount of cash we'll need to have to make this deal a reality, we simply need to subtract the loan amount from the total project cost.

Total Project Cost – Loan Amount = Total Cash Needed

In the case of 123 Main Street, we know that the total project cost is $95,950, so:

$95,950 – $60,000 = $35,950

Therefore, to buy this property with a 20 percent down payment loan, and to cover repairing the property, closing costs, and pre-rent holding costs, we'll need approximately $35,950 in cash.

Before you start with Negative Nancy thoughts like "I don't have $35,950!" continue reading. There are numerous ways to finance real estate, including a lot of creative methods that don't require a full 20 percent down payment. There are also ways you can include the repairs in the cost of your loan. I'll talk more about these strategies in Chapter 13, or pick up a copy of my other book *The Book on Investing in Real Estate with No (and Low) Money Down*.

Step Three: Calculate the Monthly Mortgage Payment

To calculate the monthly mortgage payment, you'll need to use a mortgage calculator; the calculation is impossible to do in your head but exceptionally easy to do online through one of millions of online mortgage calculators. To calculate the mortgage, you'll need three numbers:

1. Loan amount
2. Loan period (length)
3. Interest rate

The loan amount we have already determined, so we just need to know the length and the rate. Although mortgages come in all shapes and sizes, 30 years is the most common, though some people do choose 15. For our purposes, we'll choose 30. As for the rate, it changes daily and depends on numerous factors, so your best bet is to call a few local banks and ask them where current rates are for non-owner-occupied properties. Those rates hover around 5 percent, so that's the number we'll use.

Now we simply need to plug our values into the mortgage calculator to determine our mortgage payment. Some mortgage calculators allow you to include annual taxes and insurance with the payment, but we will include those items later in our discussion on expenses, so we'll leave them blank here.

As you can see in Figure 5, our expected mortgage payment will be $322.09.

Mortgage Payment Calculator

Loan Amount	Loan Period (years)	Interest Rate
$ 60000	30	5 %

Annual Taxes	Annual Insurance
$	$

Calculate Monthly Payment

Calculator Results

Total Monthly Payment:	$322.09
Monthly Principal + Interest (P&I):	$322.09
Monthly Taxes:	—
Monthly Insurance:	—

Figure 5

Step Four: Determine Total Income

What do you think our 123 Main Street property will rent for?

That's kind of a silly question, isn't it? After all, you know nothing about the area. Remember, trying to determine the fair market rent depends on numerous factors, including location and characteristics of the property.

A quick scan of Craigslist and the local newspaper for this area shows us that prices for three-bedroom homes in this neighborhood are renting for between $975 and $1,350 per month. The higher end of that spectrum seems to be nicer homes that have been rehabbed, whereas the lower end seems to be more in line with houses that need a ton of work. Since 123 Main Street will be rehabbed, you can expect it to get near the top of that range, but we also don't want to price it too high in our estimates. Let's shoot for a $1,200-per-month price for fair market rent.

With this property, there are no obvious extra ways to make more money—no laundry machines, no storage buildings, etc. Therefore, we can move on.

Total Monthly Income: $1,200

Step Five: Determine Total Expenses

Next, we need to nail down the expenses for 123 Main Street. To do this, let's take another look at that list of all possible expenses and determine which ones we might need to pay as the landlord.

EXPENSE	APPLICABLE?	MONTHLY COST
Mortgage	Yes	$322.09
Taxes	Yes	$122.18
Insurance	Yes	$56
Flood Insurance	No	
Vacancy	Yes	5% or $60
Repairs	Yes	5% or $60
Capital Expenditures	Yes	$150
Water	No	
Sewer	No	
Garbage	No	
Gas	No	
Electricity	No	
HOA Fees	No	
Snow Removal	No	
Lawn Care	No	
Property Management	Yes	11% or $132
Other	No	
Total		$902.27

According to our graph, we can estimate $902.27 per month in expenses for 123 Main Street. Of course, we would also want to check to make sure there were no other special expenses unique to this location or this house, but we've done that homework and are comfortable with this number.

Our total expenses: $902.27

Step Six: Evaluate the Deal

We now have all the numbers needed to make a decision on this property.

Total Monthly Income:	$1,200
Total Monthly Expenses:	$902.27

To determine our cash flow, we subtract the expenses from the income:

$1,200 − $902.27 = $297.73

Therefore, we can estimate that, per month, 123 Main Street will produce approximately $297.73 in cash flow, on average, over time. To get the annual cash flow, we simply multiply this number by 12:

$297.73 × 12 = $3,572.76

Now we want to determine what kind of ROI this cash flow represents. To do this, we simply need to divide the annual cash flow by the total invested capital.

Annual Cash Flow / Total Invested Capital = CoCROI

We determined back in step two that the total invested capital on this project would be $35,950. We've also estimated the annual cash flow to be $3,572.76. Therefore:

$3,572.76 / $35,950 = 9.93% CoCROI

In this example, we could estimate that this property, with this cash invested, should return around 9.93 percent on our money. Remember, however, that this does not take into account the fact that the loan is being paid down each month, that the home has some incredible equity built in (since we did a slight rehab on it), and that there may be other tax benefits to go with it, or that would at least minimize the tax we would need to pay on the property.

Let's take this one step further and try to determine our overall return (the ROI we'll see when we combine the cash flow, equity growth, and loan paydown over time). A 9.93 percent CoCROI might be a good number to know, but let's quickly compute the overall return on this property, assuming a few things.

First, let's assume that we'll hold this property for five years and then sell.

Let's also assume that appreciation will increase the value of the property 2 percent per year over those five years. In step one we determined that the property was worth $120,000. Therefore:

START	$120,000
End of Year 1	$122,400
End of Year 2	$124,848
End of Year 3	$127,345
End of Year 4	$129,892
End of Year 5	$132,490

At the end of year five, our property is worth $132,490. Of course, if we were to sell it, doing so would cost us some money. Again, we'll need to make a few assumptions. We know real estate agents will charge around 6 percent (roughly $8,000), and the other closing costs will likely run around $4,000. Plus, we'll probably need to do some cleaning up of the property, such as a new paint job, so let's add another $5,000 there. Our total sales expenses, at this point, would be $17,000.

Next, we simply need to determine how much the mortgage balance would be at the end of five years. Our initial mortgage, if you'll recall, was $60,000. However, we know that in five years, that loan will have been paid down some. To determine just how much, we need to use an amortization calculator, which you can find easily online on a site such as www.amortization-calc.com. By doing this, I can see that at the end of year five, we'll owe $55,004.72 on the loan.

We now have all the puzzle pieces needed to determine our overall return. To do this, we will want to find out exactly how much profit we made over those five years. This profit is spread across two categories: cash flow and equity. Let's look at equity first. The equity is the profit we'll get if we sell, not including any money we've paid for a down payment.

To determine this, we simply start with the sales price and deduct everything that has ever been paid for the property, including sales expenses, the loan payoff, and the total invested capital. For 123 Main Street, these figures are as follows:

Sales Price:	$132,490.00
Sales Expenses:	$17,000.00
Loan Payoff:	$55,004.72
Total Invested Capital:	$35,950.00
Profit:	$24,535.28

Therefore, when we go to sell the property, we will have made a profit of $24,535.28. However, we are not quite done. We've also made some good cash flow over the previous five full years. A few moments ago, we estimated that this property would produce $3,572.76 in cash flow each year. Knowing that we held on to the property for five full years, we can multiply the annual cash flow by five to get our total received cash flow:

$3,572.76 \times 5 = $17,863.80$

We've made $17,863.80 in cash flow over those five years and another $24,535.28 in equity over the same time frame, for a total of $42,399.08. But we are still not quite done. What does this actually mean?

Remember, the total return is the ROI we'll see when we combine the cash flow, equity growth, and loan paydown over time. It's similar to cash-on-cash return, but it includes all the profit made, not just the cash flow.

To determine our total return, we need to use the following formula:

$$\frac{\textbf{(Total Profit / Total Invested Capital)}}{\textbf{Time (in years)}}$$

If this is confusing for you, let me try to explain in words what we are doing. Essentially, we are doing the same ROI calculation we've done in the past, just taking profit divided by investment. However, because we are spreading this out over a number of years, we need to divide by that figure to likewise spread the investment out over a number of years. Let's do this with 123 Main Street:

$$\frac{(\$42,399.08 \,/\, \$35,950)}{5}$$

$$\frac{1.1475}{5}$$

Total return = 22.9%

We determined earlier that our total CoCROI on this property would be 9.93 percent, and now we can see that if our rehab caused the value to increase to $120,000, appreciation carried the value up 2 percent per year, and we sold for full value in five years, after expenses we might expect a 22.9 percent overall ROI, on average, each year for the next five years. However, we've made a number of assumptions that could or could not be true. What if appreciation carried the property's value up 5 percent per year? What if we received *no* appreciation? What if we held on for ten years? Twenty years?

The point of this exercise is not to show you exactly what you will receive from a property, but to help you learn *how* to calculate these numbers. If you want to get even more specific, you can pull out the IRR (Internal Rate of Return) or MIRR (Modified Internal Rate of Return), but those discussions are far beyond the scope of this book.

Once you have a firm grasp of *why* the numbers work the way they do, and you are able to do these calculations by hand, I encourage you to check out the rental property calculator at www.biggerpockets.com/analysis to help you save a lot of time crunching these numbers. Everything we just went over can be done in a few minutes on the calculator, and numbers can easily be adjusted and changed as needed. For example, if you wanted to know what would happen with a rehab budget of $30,000 instead of $17,250, you can simply edit the report and run the numbers again, rather than starting over at the beginning and going through the whole process. Online calculators can help you out tremendously and save you a lot of time once you understand the basics of how they work.

WRAPPING IT UP

At this point, you can likely run the numbers on any potential deal just like a pro. If not, don't worry—you'll get better in time. I encourage you to start analyzing deals every single day, both for practice (practice makes perfect!) and because real estate investing is a game of odds. The more deals you analyze, the more offers you can make, and the more deals you'll get accepted.

Think about it: If you analyze two properties every day, at the end of a month, you will have analyzed 60 different deals. Let's just assume that 10 percent of those deals, after analysis, looked promising enough to pursue and make offers on. That leaves you with six properties you can make an offer on each month. Of those six, how many of those offers will get accepted? Perhaps one? I think one out of six offers is very reasonable. Therefore, if you analyzed just two deals per day, made offers on 10 percent of them, and had just 16.66 percent of those offers accepted, you could buy a new property every month.

People often complain to me that they can't buy a deal, and I usually ask them, "How many offers have you made this week?" or "How many deals have you analyzed today?" The answer is usually zero. If you are looking to do more deals, start by analyzing more properties. It really is as simple as that.

Of course, what if you start analyzing a lot of deals and *no* deals look promising? What if 100 percent of the properties for sale in your area are too expensive and don't look good after analysis? This is an increasing problem these days, one that is especially prevalent in expensive areas. If you find yourself in a city where home prices easily climb above $300,000, you might have tremendous difficulty finding any deal that will work. How should you invest in real estate when you live in such an area? Let's find out.

Chapter Six

INVESTING WHILE LIVING IN AN EXPENSIVE AREA

"Opportunities don't happen. You create them."

—CHRIS GROSSER

"I'll be right over to take some photos," my agent said to the woman on the phone, who was calling to list her property for sale while I sat in my agent's office, "and I'm actually sitting here with one of my biggest clients. Do you mind if I bring him over to look at your property?"

I followed my agent to the woman's house. I knew the location well, because I owned another house on the street already. I was actively looking for a house to flip, and this neighborhood could work well.

After my agent signed a couple of documents with the woman, the property owner gave us both a tour of the home. "I just need to get out of this town," she complained. "My family has all recently moved to California, and this house is keeping me here. I just don't have the money to repair it."

I made her an offer that day, which she readily accepted: $16,000. Yes, that's right: $16,000. The house wasn't in terrible shape, but it did need a good deal of work to get it up to rentable standards. But for many of you reading this book right now, you are thinking, "Just $16,000 for a house? That's insane."

Yes, it is. That was the lowest-priced home I have ever purchased. To brag a little more, my 24-unit apartment complex only cost me $565,000. Also crazy, right? I mean, in some areas of the country, you can barely buy the lowest-end home for what I paid for my apartment complex. Is that the secret to my success? I'm just "lucky" enough to live in an area where prices are cheap?

It's a perfectly valid question. Sure, I am located in a very low-priced area, and I know that there are some areas where prices are astronomically high. Many major metropolitan areas, such as New York; Los Angeles, California; Denver, Colorado; Seattle, Washington; and Washington, D.C., have prices well above the national average. If you live in such an area, this chapter is for you. I want to share a few thoughts I have concerning high-priced locations and how you can still invest while living in such a place.

Are You Looking for Homes on Sale?

How much do you pay for a gallon of milk?

Three dollars? Four dollars? Five dollars? These are all prices I see when I shop for milk, but I never spend more than $2.50. How is it possible that I can get milk for $2.50 a gallon while others are paying up to double that? It's because I'm actively looking for a deal. My $2.50 a gallon for milk is not normal; it's a sale.

In the same way, the property prices I talk about are not normal. No one lists a home for $16,000 like the one I mentioned earlier, even in my area. Often, seasoned investors like me talk about the cheap prices we are getting to make a point (as I'm doing in this very section of this book), but remember that those prices are not retail prices. That home was actually listed at more than $30,000 (still a low price, I know), but I knew the seller was motivated, and I could solve her problem quickly.

Are you actively seeking a deal?

When you pull up your list of nearby homes for sale, are you simply looking at the average sale price and trying to compare that with the $16,000 deal I got? If so, you will be very disappointed. The average price for a home in my area is more than ten times as expensive than what I offered. I've seen only a few properties that cheap, and most have *major* problems. The $16,000 deal was a special deal. The apartment complex for half a million dollars was also special. *I only buy special deals.* They are not once-in-a-lifetime opportunities, but they are also not everyday deals.

To find a good deal, you should look at 100 homes, offer on ten, and get only one offer accepted. This means that just 1 percent of the deals that look promising actually are.

What does this mean for your business?

It means you need to look at a lot of properties. You can speed up the time by having very defined standards that you follow, but in the end, you are simply going to need to look at a lot of properties and try to find a great deal.

Next, let's talk about relativity. And no, we're not going to talk about Einstein.

Is the Price Relative?

Let's go back to that analogy about milk. I have a bit of a riddle for you:

When would it be the same for my budget to pay $5.00 for milk as it would to pay $2.50?

The answer, of course, is if I made twice as much money. In other words, if I suddenly made double my income but spent double the amount on milk, the percentage of my income I'm spending on milk wouldn't change.

This is also true in real estate. A home that sells for $100,000 in one area may produce $1,000 per month in rent. However, that same style house in another area may sell for $300,000, but the rent may be $3,000 per month. *It's all relative!* So before you instantly assume you live in an area that is too expensive to invest in, decide first whether the math still works. Many times, it will!

Often, certain investments are working in your town, but they are just not working at your financial level. In other words, the numbers work, but they are so high that the barrier to entry is keeping you out. If so, there are creative methods you can use to get involved. For example, forming a partnership, raising private money, or engaging in real estate wholesaling can allow you to still be involved.

I understand, of course, that in some areas, a home selling for $300,000 still may only rent for $1,000 per month. I understand that, in some areas, the relativity between rent and price is out of whack. Sometimes, properties are just not worth buying.

What then?

What Is Working in Your Area?

Perhaps your goal is to buy and hold single-family homes in Manhattan. I'm sorry, but that's probably not going to work out real well for you. Each location is optimal at certain things, but not at everything. If the math doesn't seem to work on a certain type of investment in your area, perhaps it's time to consider what *is* working.

- Would wholesaling commercial properties be a better use of your time?
- What about multifamily properties?
- How about condo conversions?
- What about fast-food triple-net leases?
- Have you considered subsidized low-income housing?

Before blacklisting your entire town, make sure you take time to investigate exactly what your town is good at. Perhaps you'll discover a highly profitable investing strategy that your "expensive town" is excellent at.

There are dozens of different ways to invest in rental properties; you might just need to find the right niche.

To find what is working in your town, simply connect with investors who are actively engaged in your market. What are they investing in? How are they making a profit? Discover the secret to their success, and you'll find the path to yours.

Have You Checked the Outskirts?

How much do Starbucks employees make in downtown New York City?

My guess is not a whole lot more than they make in my small rural town. My point is this: The large percentage of society who make less than $15 an hour and work in expensive cities still need to live somewhere near their place of work. Baristas are not making six figures, yet they still manage to work in expensive areas. How?

In nearly every expensive city, there are pockets of low-priced properties.

Don't get me wrong, I'm not advocating slumlording or investing in a dangerous area of town. Those areas have problems and extra expenses of their own. Location is still key in any real estate investment. I'm referring to the middle-class neighborhoods on the outskirts and in the suburbs. Generally, these areas are found 20 to 40 miles outside the city center, in smaller towns and communities. Speak with a good real estate agent about these areas or connect with local successful investors to find out where they are investing. Find the best location with the lowest prices, and focus your efforts there.

If still you find that there are no decent locations nearby that you can invest in, perhaps it's time to look outside your area and consider long-distance investing.

Long-Distance Rental Property Investing

We've talked about ways of making real estate investing work in your area, but what about simply investing somewhere else, in an area that *does* make sense? Is that a terrible idea?

Not necessarily. However, investing at a long distance can prove difficult if not done correctly. When you are first learning the ropes behind real estate investing, you will quickly learn that there are a lot of ropes. Sometimes, those ropes get tangled and need to be untangled, and investing from a long distance can make the untangling process difficult.

That said, if investing outside of your area makes the most sense to you, there are strategies that will work. In this next section, I'll outline three different strategies people use to invest in real estate from a long distance.

1. DIY

The first method I call the "DIY" approach, because you will "do it yourself." This is the method I probably wouldn't recommend to the average person just getting started, because trying to do anything by yourself is tough. However, many people do invest at a distance on their own and are able to do so quite well.

The first step in DIY long-distance investing is to establish your ideal location and truly understand that city. It helps to look somewhere where you have some sort of connection. For example, I grew up in Minnesota until my college sweetheart took me west, so today, I would not be opposed to investing back in my homeland. I understand all the different towns, the main drivers of industry, and the areas to avoid, and I have connections to people there.

Secondly, when investing at a distance with the DIY method, I highly recommend using an excellent property manager. I'll cover the topic of using property managers much more in depth in Chapter 17, but don't assume that it will be easy to manage a property from thousands of miles away without a property manager. Yes, you could look up the phone number of a plumber or handyman to take care of repairs, but who will check to make sure the work was done right? Who will make sure the tenant is abiding by their lease? Who will show a vacant unit to prospective tenants? Who will make sure the home is physically being taken care of? I'm not saying it's impossible to invest in real estate at a distance without a property manager, but it would not be my first choice.

Perhaps the most difficult aspect of DIY long-distance investing is being able to buy the right property. After all, if you don't live near the location, it can be exceptionally hard to know the true value of a home by the little pictures and description you see on the internet. Getting a true feel for the location without being there is tough! Therefore, if you plan to go this route, I recommend you spend a lot of time researching the location (as I'll explore in Chapter 8), and then actually take a trip there to see it firsthand. Drive the streets. Talk to local business owners. Speak with local real estate agents. Seek to truly understand as much as you can about the area and determine the best place to invest in that community. A $300 plane ticket is far less expensive than buying a bad deal.

No matter how much research you do, you'll still never understand the area to the same depth that a local resident might. For that reason, you may want to consider forgoing the DIY method and using a long-distance partner.

2. Using a Long-Distance Partner

A second technique some people use when investing at a distance is partnering with someone who currently lives in a good location and using that person to be the "boots on the ground." The right partner will understand the local area and have keen insight into the good and bad areas. They can also check out properties, meet contractors, show vacant units, do property maintenance, and keep tabs on it over the years.

Partners, of course, bring challenges of their own. In a partnership, each party has their own agenda, personality, and way of doing business.

A partner, especially one located far away from you, must be completely trustworthy, and trust can be tough to build. However, if you can overcome these challenges, a long-distance partnership can help you get a foothold in a location you don't know very well.

Now, to give you some additional insight into this strategy of using a partner to invest at a distance, I want to introduce you to a friend of mine, Mehran Kamari, who uses a partner to invest at a distance because he lives in an expensive area. The bolded text below were my questions to Mehran, followed by his answers.

Mehran, where do you currently live? I live in sunny Southern California (Woodland Hills).

Why don't you invest in your area? My current real estate goal is to replace my W-2 income with stable cash flow. I feel without getting very "creative," it's difficult to achieve this goal in my local market. Everything is so expensive, and the price-rent ratios are not great at all. I also don't like the landlord-tenant laws here. California is a lot more tenant-friendly than many other states.

Where do you invest? Right now, I invest in the Midwest, with an emphasis on Milwaukee, Wisconsin.

How did you pick an area to invest in? It's important to decide on your investing goals, so you can pick a market that aligns with them. Looking for stable cash flow, I naturally gravitated toward the Midwest markets. There are less volatile swings in property values and lower barriers to entry. In contrast to the SoCal market, the price-rent ratios in some of these Midwest markets are amazing. I felt in these parts, my limited funds could go further than in SoCal. My main market now, Milwaukee, is pretty landlord-friendly, too!

What are some of the challenges you've faced? One challenge I've had is with a bad property manager on my first deal in Indianapolis, Indiana. I made the purchase without first developing relationships with a team on the ground. I relied solely on the property manager (PM) that was already managing the property for the previous owner. Things started out smooth, but she quickly turned into the PM from hell. I started getting reports and rents a month or two late, eventually ending up not receiving them at all. I procrastinated on firing her, and it has cost me thousands of dollars now. I've learned that management can make or break any deal. As an out-of-state investor, almost everything relies on your person on the ground; they are basically an extension of you. I can't stress how important it is to not tolerate poor performance from your PM.

What has worked really well for you? On my second deal, I tried a different approach. I partnered with a local investor in Milwaukee, Dawn Anastasi, instead of just going the basic property management route. I didn't know it at the time, but this turned out to be a game changer. This strategy is great because our interests are aligned and we're both financially vested in our deals. It's a different story when you're working with someone that can focus on your projects rather than 500 other properties they're managing. I don't just feel like another number on a spreadsheet; we're partners. I wouldn't make another out-of-state purchase without this arrangement in place. In fact, it's worked so well that I've had no reservations in making acquisitions. I now own/co-own more than 20 properties, and things are going great!

Okay, so that was a quick email conversation I had with Mehran Kamari, which I thought was important to include here because his strategy is definitely something you could adapt if you find yourself in an expensive market like Mehran did. But now, let's move on and talk about a third strategy for investing at a distance, especially if you are looking to invest in smaller single-family homes: turnkey investing.

What Is Turnkey?
Turnkey investing is a loosely defined investment strategy in which the investor buys, rehabs, and has a property managed through a third party, usually from a long distance away. Their goal is to make the entire real estate investment process as simple as possible, so all you need to do is "turn the key" (get it?).

There are hundreds of turnkey providers in America (and across the world), and no two companies are exactly alike. Some will buy, rehab, rent, and *then* sell a property to you, the investor. Others will simply help you find the property and let you do most of the heavy lifting on the rehab side (if there is any rehab to do), then manage the property for you. Again, each company runs their operation a little differently, so if you decide to go with a turnkey company, it's important that you do some in-depth research on exactly what that turnkey company will and will not do.

The Benefits of Turnkey Investing
Turnkey investing has several distinct advantages over doing it all yourself.

- **Service at a Distance:** The first and most obvious benefit to turnkey investing is the ability to invest in a good real estate market without needing to live there. Being a landlord is not always easy, and trying to be one from thousands of miles away can be even tougher. Many people who live on the East or West Coast of the United States, as well as many who live outside the country, rely on turnkey companies (usually in the Midwest, where cash flow tends to be higher) to invest in great markets.
- **Market Insight.** A good turnkey company knows its market with far more precision than an outsider would. You might be able to do some research on a particular area and check out the school ratings, crime reports, and price ranges, but a turnkey provider will know the *heart* of an area. They will know *why* people prefer one area over another. They'll know why this block is worse than that block. They'll know the reputations behind certain neighborhoods, properties, and businesses. They'll have an ear to the ground about societal changes that could affect the local economy. It is very difficult for an outsider to gain this perspective because it is normally reserved only for long-time locals, which a good turnkey provider should be.
- **Professional Staff.** Turnkey providers, because they are property management companies, will generally either have in-house staff or work closely with vendors to make sure your property is taken care of. They have someone who will answer the phone, someone who will fix a running toilet, someone who can sign a lease with a new tenant. When you invest on your own, you have to either do all these roles yourself *or* find someone to do them in a market you may not know.
- **Marketing Machine.** Many turnkey providers buy, sell, and rent dozens or even hundreds of homes per month. For this reason, they are required to consistently drive leads to all parts of their marketing machine. They might use billboards, radio ads, newspaper ads, and other avenues to direct both motivated sellers and tenants to their

business. As a result, they may find better deals than you could—and get tenants faster.

- **Management Experience.** Let's face it, most people are not good managers. Turnkey providers, on the other hand, are usually experienced in dealing with tenants and contractors. Their experience helps them make the right decisions more often.
- **Simplicity.** Finally, although each turnkey company operates a little differently, they all have the same goal: to make the investment property easier for you. When you invest in real estate by yourself, you are forced to handle all the moving parts yourself, which can be overwhelming. A turnkey company attempts to simplify the process so that, ideally, you will only need to write and receive checks.

The Downsides of Turnkey Investing

At this point, you are probably thinking to yourself, "Wow, turnkey sounds pretty ideal. Why wouldn't everyone do this?" There are some potential downsides to turnkey investing that you should know before you jump in, so let me walk you through three big ones:

- **Financial.** A turnkey company is a business that *needs* to make money, and they do this through several methods. First, turnkey companies often buy property at a discount and then sell it to you, the out-of-state owner, for a higher amount, essentially "flipping" the property to you for a decent profit. Then, the turnkey provider usually makes a monthly income by managing the property for you. It makes sense that you would pay a premium for the ease of service you get. You can't usually have your cake and eat it, too! That said, remember that turnkey companies *do* have a marketing machine running 24/7, and as such, are generally able to find incredible deals in their market, so even if they do make a profit when they sell to you, you might still be buying "below average" and getting a great deal.
- **Analytical.** Perhaps the largest complaint I hear about turnkey companies is their inability to correctly analyze a property. They conveniently underestimate (or completely ignore) many important expenses, such as maintenance, repairs, vacancy, and CapEx. Perhaps the turnkey companies do this on purpose, or maybe not. The point is that if you are going to buy a property, *you* need to do the math. Never outsource the analysis to a third party.
- **Ethical.** Perhaps the greatest risk you take when choosing to invest in

real estate through a turnkey company is the level of trust you must place in this provider. After all, you are relying on their knowledge and expertise to choose a location, choose a property, choose a tenant, and manage that tenant. That's a lot of trust you are placing in someone who gets paid whether or not the investment is good. It would be fairly easy for a turnkey provider to take advantage of out-of-state investors by encouraging them to buy bad properties in bad locations. In fact, I've heard many horror stories of investors who buy a property through a turnkey provider only to discover that it was a "pig with lipstick" that immediately began costing the investor a lot of money in repairs.

Should you invest in real estate at a distance through a turnkey company? That's a decision only you can make after careful investigation into a particular company. There are both benefits and disadvantages, so you should weigh those against the possibility of investing in your own market. If you live in an expensive area and want to invest in lower-priced properties, turnkey can be a great alternative to being a local landlord. Just be sure to do your research and know what, and who, you are investing in.

WRAPPING IT UP

Do you live in an expensive area? Do you want to continue living there? Luckily, you don't need to choose between living where you want and investing in rental properties. But it's going to require some extra legwork, as I've outlined in this chapter.

Don't let "the prices are too high" be your excuse to continue sitting on your couch each night watching *Seinfeld* reruns. Get out there and find some sale prices, or identify an area where they exist.

Chapter Seven

TYPES OF RENTAL PROPERTIES

"It is hard to imagine a more stupid or more dangerous way of making decisions than by putting those decisions in the hands of people who pay no price for being wrong."

—THOMAS SOWELL

"Sir," I began, my voice trembling, "I would like to ask your daughter out."

The other end of the line went silent, just long enough to make my 18-year-old-self wish I had never called. My stomach sank. I simply wanted to be a gentleman and ask her father's permission before officially asking out the girl of my dreams. Yes, it's a bit old fashioned, but I knew (rightly so) from the depths of my soul that this would be the girl I would marry, so I might as well start the family relationship out on the right foot.

Finally, her father spoke up and asked a simple question, "Well, where do you want to go?"

I hadn't expected that response. I didn't want to "go" anywhere; I simply wanted her to be my girlfriend. But now I was getting 20 questions, and my already-nervous teenaged mind didn't know where to go next. "Ask her out" was the phrase all the young people used, wasn't it? I hadn't thought any deeper than that.

"Well, um, I don't, uh, I'm not, um ...well," I stammered on for what seemed like an eternity, sounding like a complete idiot every awkward second. Finally, in a stroke of genius, I managed to spit out, "A movie! Yeah, I'd like to take her to a movie."

"Oh yeah?" he replied, "Which movie?"

Uh oh. More questions! This wasn't supposed to be so hard. I didn't have plans to go anywhere, but looking back, I see how my initial statement of "I'd like to ask your daughter out" could be confusing. I wracked my brain for the name of a movie, any movie, hoping the answer would suffice.

Finally, my future father-in-law let me off the hook and laughed, thanking me for the call and telling me, "Good luck."

You see, when I was 100 percent ready and committed to pursuing the girl of my dreams, the woman I would someday marry, I quickly realized I didn't have a plan. I didn't have specifics in mind. I knew the end result I wanted, but the details were fuzzy.

Real estate investing is a lot like this. You tell me, "Hey, Brandon, I want to invest in real estate," and my response is in the same spirit as my father-in-law during that awkward conversation more than a decade ago: "Okay, what do you want to invest in?"

It's not enough to simply *want* to invest in real estate. You need to have a plan for what you will invest in. Given that you are reading this book on rental properties, I think I can assume you want to invest in rental properties, but that's not enough. What *kind* of rental properties? Are you even sure?

In this chapter, I want to give you an overview of the different types of buy-and-hold investment properties that exist, as well as the subsets within each type. The better you understand the different kinds of investments available, the better decisions you'll be able to make about what to buy.

Let's start by talking about the most common: the single-family house.

Single-Family Homes

Description: A single-family residence, commonly abbreviated as SFR, is your typical "house." One kitchen, one bathroom, a few bedrooms, and usually on its own plot of land. Ownership of a single-family home is often seen as "the American dream," and as such, is the most common type of real estate in existence. Prices for SFRs are based on what other similar homes have recently sold for, which means the price fluctuates wildly based on local market trends.

Pros

- **Plentiful.** There are a lot of SFRs out there. Nearly every street in America has a single-family home on it, and new SFRs are being built every day.
- **Strong Exit Strategy.** SFRs are generally fairly easy and fast to sell, compared with many other property types. This is because of the large number of people in the world always looking to buy a home.
- **Involve Fewer Bills.** With an SFR, the tenant will typically pay for their own utilities, including water, sewer, garbage, and electricity. (The owner is still usually responsible for insurance and property taxes, as well as repairs and mortgage.)
- **Easy to Finance.** SFRs are fairly easy to finance because, again, they are so commonplace. There are thousands and thousands of banks willing to lend on a single-family home, if your credit and income look okay.
- **Easier to Manage.** When a family rents an SFR, the property can be much more "hands off" than a multifamily property. For example, your SFR tenant will typically not call and complain to you about the neighbor being noisy—they'll call the cops. In a multifamily property, however, they *will* call the landlord about noise.
- **More Stable Tenants.** Tenants who rent SFRs tend to stay for many years and be higher-quality renters than multifamily. An SFR is less "transitional" than an apartment and caters to people who are already "settled" in life (with a stable job, income, etc.).
- **Better Appreciation.** SFR prices are based on "the market," which is largely based on emotion and the U.S. economy. While this can be both a good and bad thing, the fact is that if you can time the market correctly you can often buy low and sell high, making a significant profit through that appreciation. (The same principle applies, of course, to a market that is dropping. However, in a declining market, you can simply hold on to the property and wait for prices to go back up.)
- **Less Expensive to Buy.** Although the *cost per unit* is significantly higher than for multifamily properties, overall it is generally cheaper to buy an

SFR than it is to buy a multifamily, commercial, or most other kinds of properties. This is because of both the simple cost (one house is probably cheaper than a ten-unit apartment) and the fact that single-family homes often require smaller down payments than larger multifamily properties do.

Now that we've looked at a number of the benefits to investing in single-family homes, let's look at some of the negatives to doing so.

Cons

- **High Cost Per Unit.** When buying an SFR, the price per unit can be exceptionally high compared with a multifamily property. For example, in my neighborhood, I can buy a nice SFR for approximately $100,000, which makes the price per unit $100,000. I can buy a duplex for approximately $120,000, which makes the cost per unit roughly $60,000. Or I can buy a ten-plex for approximately $300,000, which makes the cost per unit around $30,000. As you can see, the cost per unit, at least in my area, is definitely much higher with an SFR.
- **Slower to Scale.** Building wealth one house at a time can take a while, because each transaction requires you to engage in the entire buying transaction for just one property—one loan, one insurance policy, one manager (if desired). When buying multifamily properties, however, you might be able to acquire two, four, ten, fifty, or even 1,000 units with one transaction. If your goal is to get 100 units, doing so with SFRs can be tough.
- **Limited Loans.** When trying to buy SFRs, you are often limited by the number of properties you can have financed on your personal credit report. Currently, the limit is usually four or ten depending on your bank, and if they are packaging and selling their loans to Fannie Mae or Freddie Mac. However, you may have trouble reaching even those limits because of how quickly an SFR can raise your debt-to-income level above the bank's limit.
- **Expensive Rehabs.** After a tenant vacates one of my apartment units, tenant turnover is generally fairly easy and relatively inexpensive. Mostly, this is because of the property's smaller square footage and the shorter residence of the tenant. On the other hand, when one of my house tenants vacates, the rehab costs can often reach into the thousands, as the tenants have "dug in" more than they would in an apartment.

- **More Competition.** When you are shopping for an SFR, you are fighting to find a good deal in a sea of wannabe homeowners who don't care about a good deal. They don't care about cash flow or ROI or future appreciation. They care about getting a pretty house in a pretty location with a pretty front porch. As such, the competition for SFRs can simply drive you away from most of the properties on the market. Trying to find that one deal that will provide you with the cash flow you need can feel like finding a needle in a haystack.

Now, let's compare that with multifamily residential real estate.

Multifamily Real Estate

Multifamily properties, on the other hand, are buildings with more than one unit. A multifamily could be as small as two units in a duplex or as big as thousands of units in a large apartment complex. Few people ever buy a multifamily to live in (though I do love the strategy of "house hacking," where an individual lives in one unit and rents the other units out), but instead, most multifamily properties are owned by real estate investors who rent the properties out to those who can't, or won't, buy a single-family home of their own.

Multifamily classification is generally split into two categories: small and large. Small multifamily properties are those that contain two, three, or four units. Large multifamily properties, therefore, are those with five or more units. This is an important distinction because of the way these properties are valued and financed. Smaller multifamily properties are considered "residential" to most lenders, and are thus seen as no different from an SFR. Large multifamily, however, is considered commercial real estate, and the rules change drastically.

While the value of a residential property (single family or small multifamily) is determined by what the similar house down the street sold for, value on commercial property is determined by comparing the ROI one would achieve with that of other commercial properties down the street. More technically, it is based on the ROI an investor would achieve if they did not use a loan. This is known as a "cap rate," and every location has a different normal cap rate to compare different properties against.

Let's talk about the pros and cons of investing in multifamily properties.

Pros

- **More Cash Flow Possibilities.** If purchased right, multifamily properties have a likelihood of producing positive cash flow from day one. In addition, rents can be increased a small amount for each unit or expenses decreased, and the ripple effect of those changes can cause huge increases in cash flow.

- **One Loan, Multiple Units.** Trying to get a loan is a long, arduous process that no one enjoys. But it is a necessary evil for most real estate investors. This is a huge benefit of investing in multifamily properties: There are fewer loans to obtain! If you were to go out and buy twenty SFRs in the next few years, that's twenty loan applications you'd need to fill out, twenty financial statements you'd need to prepare, twenty "yeses" you'd need to hear from the underwriting department. Exhausting, isn't it? Instead, you can buy a twenty-unit apartment building and get just one loan—one application, one set of financials, only one yes.

- **One Insurance Policy.** I hate insurance. I understand the importance of it, but the insurance world is just so cumbersome and frustrating. A good amount of my wife's administrative time is spent just dealing with insurance. We have boxes and boxes of paperwork with nothing but insurance documents. When you invest in a multifamily property, you have *one* insurance policy on it. It's so much easier to keep track of and manage.

- **Math Over Emotion.** When investing in multifamily units, I am able to separate emotion from the transaction much more easily than with a single-family home. Multifamily is all about the math, the numbers.

- **Business, Not Hobby.** Furthermore, it's much easier to treat multifamily investments as a business rather than a hobby because of the nature of the beast. Multifamily properties are designed for investors to own and management companies to run; thus, the cost of hiring such a management company is often figured into the cost of owning the property, leading to less hands-on management by you.

- **Income Valuation.** As I mentioned earlier, multifamily units with five or more units are not valued the same way as SFRs. If I were to sell you my single-family home, the appraiser would look at a few other single-family homes that were similar and base their appraisal on the selling price of those other homes. Commercial properties, on the other hand, are valued based on the ROI they give their owners. After all, it's not easy to compare a twenty-four-unit apartment building with another twenty-four-unit apartment building with the exact same returns, because you'll never find that exact same property. Commercial investments are just too different from one another. Instead, we rely on the cap rate to base value on. If three properties that recently sold gave the owner a 10 percent ROI, then this one should also. Why is this income valuation so important? Because the value can be changed internally, rather than relying on others, by simply lowering expenses or raising the income. Small changes to the income can make drastic swings to the value of the property, and a savvy investor can use this to their advantage to supercharge the wealth-building process.

- **Less Competition from Homeowners.** When shopping for a single-family home, an investor is competing against tens of thousands of others looking for a home. Most of this competition is in the form of non-investors who buy property for *way* too much money because the front porch is "so cute" or the backyard is "perfect for Fido!" This can make competition much more difficult, because you are playing the game with a different objective. Instead, when you buy multifamily properties, you are competing with other investors, which means there is *far* less competition.

Okay, multifamily properties sound pretty terrific. What's the downside? Let's find out.

Cons

- **More Expensive.** First, multifamily properties typically cost much more to buy than a single-family house. This can be a barrier to entry for many people trying to get started, so multifamily is often not considered until much later in one's investment career. That said, smaller multifamily properties have some lower down payment financing options, and larger multifamily properties often include raising money from other people.
- **More Management Intensive.** I'll be the first to admit it, multifamily tenants cause more headaches than single-family tenants. They are generally more "transitional," and thus have much more drama in their lives. Tenants stay for shorter periods of time, which can add significant expense to your bottom line. They call and complain for pettier reasons, have more difficulty paying the rent on time, and tend to be

harder on units because they don't always feel like the place is their real "home." That said, as I mentioned earlier, multifamily properties are often managed by third parties, so the owner doesn't need to be very involved in the management drama.

- **More Savvy Competition.** Although there is less competition from homeowners when investing in multifamily properties, the folks you are competing against are far more sophisticated than the average homeowner. They can spot a deal just like you can and generally have a lot more capital with which to buy those deals.
- **More Complicated.** Most people can easily wrap their head around a single-family investment property, but the more units there are in a property, the more complicated (and expensive) it all becomes. Suddenly, you are dealing with 20 moving parts rather than just two or three.
- **Fewer to Choose from.** Depending on where you live, there may be a lack of available multifamily properties from which to choose. While single-family homes are plentiful across the world, multifamily properties may be sparser in your location.
- **Government Regulations.** Finally, when you invest in multifamily properties *and* raise money from others to fund it, you enter a whole new world of government regulations that dictate what you can and cannot do while raising that money. If you do it wrong, you might end up wearing an orange jumpsuit and earning $1.38 an hour serving soup to other white-collar inmates.

Which should you choose? Single family or multifamily?

I wish it were that simple. I'm not going to be the guy who says, "*This* is the right path" or "*This* is the only way to invest!" There is never one right path, but there may be a right path for you. My goal is to help you see the pros and cons of each choice, and allow you to weigh the options to make the best decision for you and your family. Furthermore, although I believe that focusing on one niche is helpful, it is possible to try to invest in either single family *or* multifamily, and just see which comes up first. As long as you are willing to do the work and learn to run the numbers on either one, you can pursue both and buy whatever crosses your radar first.

While we are on the subject of property types, let's discuss some of the more common ones you may consider investing in. Each of the following could fall in either the single-family or the multifamily category.

Condos

Condos (short for condominiums) are a property ownership structure in which there are many individually owned units within one complex. A collection of condos often looks like an apartment complex (though it definitely doesn't have to), but rather than having one owner who leases out all the units, each unit is individually owned by a person who either lives in the unit or rents it out. The individual owners legally own each unit, but the exterior walls, roofs, foundation, and other common areas are owned jointly by the entire community and managed by the homeowner's association (HOA). The HOA collects a monthly fee and pays for repairs and upkeep to the common areas. Condos can be decent investment properties because of the minimal expenses (for example, you won't need to directly pay to fix a roof leak, paint the outside, or other such maintenance), but there are a few concerns you should be aware of:

1. Some condo associations forbid using a unit for rental purposes, especially for the first year or two. Before investing, be sure to investigate the rules outlined in the condominium map (often called a condominium plan), and the covenants, conditions, restrictions, and easements (CC&Rs).

2. The HOA fee can be hefty and cause your cash flow to dwindle. Obviously, you should know this before buying the property by doing your homework and including this fee in your analysis.

3. As Joshua Dorkin, founder of BiggerPockets, often shares about his experience owning a condo, the HOA operations board can get "crazy" when normal people get into a position of power and can make life miserable for others just because they can.

4. Condos can charge "special assessments," which are extra monthly fees tacked on to your HOA fee to pay for certain upgrades or repairs to the property that the HOA can't cover with its normal budget. These special assessments can quickly turn a positive cash flow property into a negative cash flow property, and there isn't much you can do about it.

5. Condo prices, especially in large cities, tend to swing wildly with the economy.

Many investors find success with condos, but risks do exist, so if condo rentals are the path you want to take, be sure to do your homework, plan for the worst, and hope for the best.

Townhomes

Townhomes are very similar to condos in that they often involve multiple units, individually owned, within one complex. Townhouses, however, have much less of an "apartment feel" and are typically multiple stories in height, giving the townhouse the feel of a single-family, detached home. Townhouses usually share a wall with another unit, because multiple townhouses are lined up side by side.

Townhouses share most of the advantages and disadvantages of a condo, in that an HOA generally governs the property and can make changes that affect your investment.

REOs/Foreclosures

An REO (short for real estate owned) is a property that has been fore-closed upon by a bank and is now owned *by* the bank. The terms "REO property" and "foreclosed property" are often used interchangeably, but both refer to the same concept: a bank-owned property. Although in the past it was possible to buy an REO directly from a bank through its REO department, today REOs are usually listed on the MLS with other conventional homes. The homes are listed through local real estate agents and sold to the highest or best buyer.

In my experience, 90 percent of the deals I've purchased have been REOs, because they have been the best deals on the market over the past few years. REOs can be exceptionally good for investors for two reasons:

1. There is usually something distressed about the property. Most REO properties have been vacant for months or even years, so problems such as bad smells, mold, and vandalism are common. For this reason, many people simply avoid these properties, because they don't want to deal with the problems. This gives investors—who can hopefully see past superficial surface problems—less competition and a better chance of snagging a great deal. I'll talk more about buying fixer-uppers in a moment.

2. Unlike typical home sellers, banks are not emotional creatures. They are not likely to get offended by a low offer and will look at your offer analytically, not emotionally. For this reason, banks are often willing to drop their price fast to get the property sold and off their books.

Fixer-Uppers

Remember that high school movie where the homely girl was transformed into the beautiful prom queen when she removed her glasses and put on some makeup? (Yeah, me neither. I was watching *Die Hard*.) The point is this: Human nature loves to see transformations. We love to see the before and after, and marvel at what it must have taken to get from A to B. Just tune in to any episode on HGTV to see what I'm talking about.

For this reason, people love to buy fixer-uppers. But is this always a good idea when investing in real estate? Should you invest in a fixer-upper when getting into rental properties?

What Is a Fixer-Upper?

First, let's all get on the same page as to what I'm even talking about when I use the term "fixer-upper." A fixer-upper is a home that needs either minor or significant rehabilitation before it can be used for its intended purpose. Being that this is a book on rental property investing, that intended purpose would be to rent out to tenants. The repairs a fixer-upper can need range from light cosmetic work, such as fresh paint or new carpet, to more intensive renovations, such as a new roof, foundation, plumbing, or electrical.

I actually love investing in fixer-uppers. In fact, I've never purchased a property that didn't require some level of rehab to get it to a rentable condition. For me, it has just made sense. On the forty-fourth episode of the *BiggerPockets Podcast*, Michael Woodward tells a story about taking his kids to look at potential houses to buy. Michael mentions that when they walk into a house with an absolutely terrible odor, he turns and asks his kids, "Boys, what does that smell like?" In unison, they shout, "Money!" What this cute story represents is often the truth with fixer-uppers. There can be money in the mending, riches in the restoration, freedom in the fixing! At the same time, fixer-uppers do carry a large degree of risk and can turn your investment into a money pit. Let's examine both the pros and cons of buying a fixer-upper.

Pros
- **Less Competition.** Finding good, nice homes can be tough in a crowded market, because everyone is looking for a nice house. This is especially true in the single-family space when you are competing with owner-occupants for properties. People don't want to buy a project; they

want to buy a home that is move-in ready. The same is often true for multifamily properties. Investors don't usually want to buy a problem; they'd rather buy something that is easy to simply purchase and rent out. Therefore, when you invest in a fixer-upper, you clear out the vast majority of the competition because most people simply do not want to do the work needed to bring a home up to par. Instead of competing with 100 percent of the population, you are competing with perhaps 10 percent of those who are willing to look at fixer-uppers. This can make finding a deal much easier, even in a hot market.

- **Forced Appreciation.** I also love fixer-uppers because you can build some immediate equity in the property through a concept known as "forced appreciation." Earlier in this book, I talked about the four wealth generators of real estate (appreciation, cash flow, tax savings, and loan paydown). Appreciation is the concept that properties tend to gain value over time. But what if I wanted to shorten that time? What if I didn't want to wait twenty years for inflation to push my property value up? While it's very difficult to raise the value of a nice home, it *is* possible to raise the value of a fixer-upper and take advantage of this amazing wealth generator called appreciation.

     For example, three years ago I purchased my own primary residence for $62,000, and it was a fixer-upper. It needed paint, flooring, some foundation work, new windows, new counters, and a whole lot more. I ended up putting about $20,000 worth of work into the property, so I currently have approximately $82,000 in the home. However, the home is not worth $82,000. As soon as I finished the rehab, it became worth what other fixed-up homes of its size and condition are worth in my neighborhood—about $132,000. I was able to raise the value of the home from $62,000 to $132,000 through just the power of the rehab. Now I will be able to take further advantage of that great wealth generator we call appreciation (which is guided by inflation and the real estate market) from a starting point of $132,000 rather than $62,000. In other words, if the market appreciates 2 percent per year, it's going up 2 percent from $132,000 (to $134,640 next year, $137,333 the following year, $140,079 the following year, and so on). My wealth creation was supercharged through the power of buying a fixer-upper.

- **Potentially More Cash Flow.** Because fixer-uppers allow you to buy a property for far less than other properties in the area, a fixer-upper can also help you achieve greater cash flow. To illustrate what I mean, let's return to the story I just shared about my own primary residence. Had I purchased this home for the full value of what it was worth, my ability to earn any cash flow from the property would have been severely diminished, because my mortgage payment would have been much higher. Instead, my mortgage is cheap enough that if I rented the home out today, I would be renting it for what a $132,000 house would rent for, *but* I'd only be paying a mortgage on an $82,000 house (because I refinanced to a $82,000 loan, getting all my rehab money back). Therefore, my cash flow is also being supercharged because I bought a fixer-upper.

- **Unique Financing Options.** Finally, one of the reasons I like fixer-uppers so much is the unique financing ideas it can offer. I'll also discuss financing in the cons section for fixer-uppers, but let's first talk about how fixer-uppers can lend themselves to greater financing options.

Although most lenders do not lend on properties that need a lot of work, I've found a unique way to invest in fixer-uppers that allows me to ultimately get the rental property for very little of my own cash. To accomplish this, I find a great deal, get a private lender or hard money lender to finance the purchase (and hopefully the rehab), and then, after a "seasoning" period of six to twelve months, I refinance the home into a long-term mortgage. I call this the BRRRR strategy (for buy, rehab, rent, refinance, repeat), which I outlined in Chapter 3.

I recently accomplished this with the purchase of a fiveplex in my town. The property was listed at $120,000 (and had been reduced from a starting price of $150,000). I offered the sellers (a local bank) $90,000 for the property, and they accepted. The property needed about $10,000 of work (mostly interior and exterior paint, some carpet, and some cleaning). To fund the purchase of this property, I called a friend I'd met on BiggerPockets who I knew lent money to individuals for short-term rehabs. He agreed to fund the entire $90,000 purchase price if I funded the rehab costs. A little over one year later, I went to a local bank and refinanced (obtained a new loan) for $90,000 to pay off my friend. In the end, I have about $10,000 invested in this deal, with cash flow of $800 per month, and have about $60,000 of equity built into the property. All this was made possible because it was a fixer-upper.

Now before you go out and buy a fixer-upper because of what I've just said, let's talk about some of the dangers, risks, and disadvantages, because there are many.

Cons

- **Hidden Expenses.** Any time you open up a wall, rip up a floor cover-ing, remove part of the roof, or undertake another rehab project on a fixer-upper, you increase the risk of finding more that needs to be fixed. For example, you might decide that you need new cabinets, but suddenly you realize that you also need new electrical work in the wall behind those cabinets. Maybe you'll discover some lead-based paint. Maybe you'll find rotten wood. The point is this: It's very difficult, espe-cially as a new investor, to accurately estimate the total cost of rehab on a project.

- **Stress.** Rehabbing a home is usually not a peaceful experience. From the first swing of the hammer to the final change of the locks, deal-ing with the drama associated with rehabbing can be stressful. If you plan to do the work yourself, plan on coming home each day with cuts, bruises, and a lot of frustration. If you plan on hiring it out, expect to deal with contractors who say one thing and do another, show up late, and miss deadlines. As you get more proficient at rehabbing a home, it can become an easier task, but learning how to efficiently rehab a house takes time.

- **Potentially More Out-of-Pocket Costs.** Because of the two items I just mentioned, maintaining your budget while rehabbing a home is difficult. The same applies for maintaining your timeline. Therefore, when investing in fixer-uppers, it's easy to spend more money than you planned and for the project to take longer, thus throwing your analysis out the window. This can affect your ROI and turn a great deal into no deal at all.

Five Questions to Ask Before Investing in a Fixer-Upper

Should you invest in a fixer-upper? Despite the cons I outlined, I would say *yes*, you should definitely consider it because of the overwhelming pros. However, before you jump into your next project, ask yourself these five questions about the deal.

1. **How Bad Is It?** There are many levels of severity when dealing with fixer-uppers. Some properties need just a few thousand dollars of paint, while others need a complete overhaul. As common sense would suggest, the less work a property needs, the less risk you'll have that

something will go wrong during the rehab. At the same time, however, the less work a property needs, the more competition you'll face. This is why I generally look for properties that *appear* to need a lot of work to the general public but that actually just need minor fixes. For example, homes that have a bad smell because of pets or cigarettes are a prime candidate for me, because smells are easy to rectify. An ugly exterior paint job or a bad roof are also fairly easy (if costly) to remedy, but they scare away more potential homeowners. Before you buy a fixer-upper, I encourage you really look at the property and have an accurate estimate of what it's going to take to fix it up. Don't go into a fixer-upper blind.

2. **Is It Worth It?** Let me ask you a question: Is it better to buy a house for $120,000 that needs $30,000 worth of repairs, or a house that is $150,000 that is 100 percent finished? With all other factors being equal, the finished house clearly has the advantage. However, many investors fail to comprehend this logic and instead think "fixer-upper" automatically means "great deal." It doesn't! Often, the cost of rehabbing a project will negate any discount you might get. On the other hand, if you could get that same property for $90,000 and put $30,000 into it to make it worth $150,000, now we're talking.

3. **Do I Have the Time?** Whether you plan to do the work yourself or not, fixer-uppers take time. You have to be present at the property often to make sure the work is being finished correctly, or maybe you'll end up having to do the work yourself. I have a friend who bought a fixer-upper triplex with plans to live in one unit and rent the other two out, but it took him three years to fix up the two other units and get them rented. While this friend may still have a great investment on his hands, he lost close to $40,000 in potential rent over those three years because he didn't have time to handle a fixer-upper.

4. **Do I Have the Skills?** Most people who are looking to get started with fixer-upper rental properties plan to do the work themselves. I actually encourage this, as long as the work is on a small scale. Being able to do your own rehab can save you a ton of money *and* can help you get a good feel for how long projects take so you can better manage the hiring out of those projects in the future. However, if this is your plan, do you really have the skills to take on the project? If not, see the next question in this list.

5. **Do I Have the Drive?** Or more importantly, do you have the mental

skills and motivation needed to *learn* how to accomplish those projects? My first home was a fixer-upper, and I had never swung a hammer in my life. However, I picked up a book on home improvement and began learning on the job. I also called in a lot of favors from other people I knew and had them teach me how to do things. By the end of the project, I could install carpet, tile a bathroom, lay laminate wood flooring, solder copper pipes, and fix a leaky roof—not because I had the *skill*, but because I had the desire and motivation to learn.

By answering these five questions for every project you are about to take on, you can better decide whether it is the right path for you. Fixer-uppers can be a great way to supercharge your wealth creation, but they also present increased risk. Just be sure to do your due diligence on any fixer-upper you plan to buy and accurately account for the hurdles you might face. Then take action, and get a little dirty!

Commercial Real Estate

Commercial real estate consists of property leased to businesses for work purposes rather than to individuals for living space. Doctors offices, grocery stores, strip malls, restaurants, the building that houses the local Starbucks, the office building down the street, and hundreds of other buildings that house businesses fall within the commercial real estate realm. Commercial real estate can be advantageous because it requires less hands-on interaction from the owner. After all, a commercial tenant is not likely to call to complain about the neighbor being noisy or the toilet being clogged, or to give excuses about why the rent is late (though, depending on the commercial tenant, all these *could* be possible). As a result of their more stable nature, commercial real estate tends to offer lower returns, but this may be ideal for an investor later in their real estate career.

Commercial properties also usually require a higher down payment, 30 percent or more, and may encounter much longer periods of vacancy. When you own a single-family house, there are generally thousands of potential families waiting to move in. When you own a specialized commercial property, the property's shape and size may mean only one kind of tenant could ever move in there, which, in turn, means it might sit vacant for months or even years before the right tenant comes along.

One of the most popular types of commercial investments is known as "triple-net" or NNN. In an NNN lease, the commercial tenant pays for nearly every single expense, including maintenance, improvements, remodeling, capital expenditures, insurance, and taxes. This can be one of the most passive real estate methods on earth, but as such, the return will likely also be significantly lower than you might see in other more active niches.

Although there are certain principles within this book that relate to commercial real estate investing, most of my experience lies in residential, so that is where I will keep my focus.

WRAPPING IT UP

The goal of this chapter was to give you an in-depth look at the most common types of rental properties a person can invest in. Next time someone asks you, "What kind of real estate do you want to invest in?" you won't need to stumble around for an answer like an 18-year-old kid trying to impress his girlfriend's dad!

There is no one "right" path for you to take. Rather, the type of real estate you choose to invest in will depend on the kind of real estate that works well in your area, with your budget, within your time frame, and with your skill set. In truth, any of these types of rental properties could help you achieve financial freedom and independence. Which will you choose?

In addition, you are not limited to just one of these types. My first deal was a single-family house, but my second deal was a duplex. Within a few years, I had purchased a 24-unit apartment complex, and now I'm looking at more commercial properties. A diverse real estate portfolio is definitely possible, but each type of rental property requires a whole new set of rules, so I recommend starting with one type and expanding as you gain experience.

Hopefully, you now have a solid grasp of the different types of investment properties you could buy. However, one thing matters even more than the type of investment, and that's location. Even a great investment, if purchased in a poor area, could turn into a horrific experience. But how do you find the best location? Let's find out in the next chapter.

Chapter Eight
LOCATION, LOCATION, LOCATION!

"Even in a bad market, location, location, location is a way to still buy and sell property."

—VANILLA ICE

My wife and I once had a fantastic opportunity to take a road trip around the entire United States, leaving Seattle and driving to New York City, down the East Coast, and across the South. For almost five weeks, we rode (and often slept!) in our little Prius, traversing through mountains, deserts, forests, and more cornfields than I knew existed. This trip was definitely one of the highlights of my life, and not just because of the scenery. Along the way, we met with hundreds of real estate investors from the BiggerPockets community, hearing their stories of real estate success and struggles.

I talked with Josh and Summer, a young couple from Montana who were beginning to build wealth through a small duplex they created by moving a mobile home onto the same land as a single-family house. I met with Jered in Ohio, whose knowledge of the construction industry allowed him to buy more than twenty rental units before his twenty-fifth birthday. C.C. in New York is buying brownstone townhouses near New York City to craft his financial independence in a market that most people consider "too expensive."

Real estate investing is possible in any market and in any location. However, understanding the location you are investing in is key to being successful with that investment. Each of the stories I just mentioned demonstrate a different style of real estate investing, crafted out of the location each investor found themselves in. Your investing journey will likewise be specific to you and your location. You need to gain an in-depth understanding of the location you plan to invest in so you can find a strategy that will work best for you there. That is the goal of this chapter: to help you master the concept of location.

In this chapter, I will explain several key indicators that define an area's strength. Keep in mind that money can be made in any real estate market and in pretty much any location. The purpose of this section is not to give you a checklist of where you should and should not buy, but to help you know what to look out for and to consider when analyzing a location, as well as provide you with some links to resources where you can investigate these indicators more thoroughly.

Neighborhood Classes

As you begin investing in real estate, you'll likely hear people talk about a property being in an A, B, C, or D location. Just like your high school class grades, a neighborhood can receive a grade, though the classification is a bit more subjective than a simple high school test. There is no government organization, board, or company that classifies locations. It's honestly more of an unwritten rule accepted by most investors, and the lines are not incredibly clear. *You* might think a location is an A location (the best), while *I* might think it's a B location (second best), but for the most part, investors will agree on the class distinctions.

Some investors grade locations on an A through C scale, whereas others grade on an A through F scale. In other words, you might say a location is a C location, meaning that you think it's the worst, because you grade on an A through C scale; at the same time, someone who grades on an A through F scale might think it's pretty middle of the road. For the sake of our discussion in this chapter, we'll use an A through D scale, which is probably the most common grading scale.

In addition to the location receiving a grade, the property itself can be classified as an A, B, C, or D property. You might hear someone say, "I have an A property in a B area." To add more specificity to the classification system, some will add a plus (+) or minus (-) to those grades, so you might hear "The property is a B- house in a B+ area." I'll leave out the + and - designations in this chapter, but you can always use them if you want to get more specific.

Let's take a minute and talk about the different classes of locations and property types.

Class A

A Class A location is an area that has the newest buildings, hottest restaurants, best schools, wealthiest people, and most expensive real estate. This is truly the best location you can find, and the highest-quality tenants are looking to rent here.

A Class A building follows the same concept. It is generally newer, probably less than ten years old, and therefore has fewer maintenance issues. The building has modern amenities, such as granite countertops, hardwood floors, and other in-demand features. Class A properties generally command the highest rent but may provide a lower amount of cash flow, because of the high demand for an "easy investment." More demand and a higher purchase cost equal lower cash flow.

Class B

A Class B location might be slightly older than a Class A one, but perhaps still has decent restaurants, schools, and people. These might be your "middle-class" areas, but these will attract more blue-collar workers who live paycheck to paycheck.

A Class B building follows the same concept. It is probably 15-30 years old, mostly upgraded but perhaps lacking the shine of a Class A property. Rental income is probably lower than what you might find with a Class A property, and the maintenance costs will likely be higher because of the age of the home.

Class C

A Class C location is likely a lower-income area with homes that are old—30 years or more. This area tends to attract people who are either on government subsidies or working low-wage jobs. You'll likely find a lot of check-cashing businesses, pawnshops, and other such businesses in this area.

A Class C building follows the same concept. The property is likely older than 30 years and looks the part. Numerous repairs are likely needed, and ongoing maintenance should be expected. Systems in the property, such as plumbing and electrical, may be outdated and require ongoing attention. Properties will typically rent for a low amount in this area, but the properties will also be much more affordable than Classes A or B.

Class D

A Class D location is somewhere you likely would not want to travel alone. Not every city has a Class D area, but you'll recognize one when you see one. Often, even the police are nervous about entering these areas and crime and drug use/sales run rampant. There are probably numerous buildings with boarded-up windows and other indications of being vacant.

A Class D building is likely old, similar to a Class C one, but with far more neglect. Chances are, the property is currently uninhabitable, needing significant repairs before it could be lived in. Class D properties are generally exceptionally cheap, but getting good tenants can be difficult and dangerous. Unless you *really* know what you are doing, I don't recommend getting involved with a Class D building or location.

As I mentioned earlier, the class distinctions are not very rigid or defined, but the classifications I just outlined here should give you a general indication of how investors view properties and neighborhoods. There is no right or wrong answer to the question "What classification should I invest in?" You'll likely find investors who only buy A, others who only buy B, others who only buy C, and still others who only buy D (God help them!). Each has pros and cons. Typically, the nicer properties will cost the most but may produce the least amount of headache—though this is not always true.

Because I am largely a "value-add" investor (someone looking to rehab a property to bring its value up), I tend to look for Class C properties in Class B areas, but you'll likely find a strategy that works well for you.

Now that I've introduced you to the concept of location classification, let's move on to talk in depth about some of the different location characteristics that help define an area.

Crime

An area with a lot of crime can make finding and keeping good tenants difficult for a rental property owner. Therefore, it's important to understand the criminal activity of the location you want to invest in. There are several great tools you can use to help you investigate the criminal activity in a particular area. I recommend the following resources:

- www.cityprotect.com (Free)
- www.neighborhoodscout.com (Paid)
- www.city-data.com (Free)
- www.usa.com/rank (Free)

Each of these sites allows you to access in-depth information on the volume and types of crime in an area. I recommend beginning with www.cityprotect.com and typing in the zip code of the area where you want to invest. You'll see a crime map of that area that shows robberies, thefts, assaults, murders, sex offenders, and other offenses.

Keep in mind, crime maps, while helpful, don't show the kind of "invisible borders" that exist in a community. For example, let's say that there is a four-block area in the middle of your town where crime is high. On the crime map, you can see that most of the crime takes place within this zone, but what about immediately outside that zone? There may not be a lot of crime there, but the proximity to the high-crime area may make finding good tenants just as hard as in the high-crime area. Or perhaps the general public's perception of this area is that the "bad" area *is* confined to this smaller footprint. You see, a crime map can't give you the public's perception; only talking with locals can help you know that.

Drugs

High-drug-abuse locations are a bit more difficult to determine, but generally speaking, drug abuse is highly related to the criminal activities in an area. High-crime areas tend to have the most trouble with illegal drugs. To get more specific, honestly, the best way to know is by simply talking to people in the area. Head to a local grocery store and ask people about the surrounding neighborhoods. Drug abuse affects many families, so most people will have an idea of where the high-drug-use areas are. You can also call your local police station and ask to speak with an officer who can shed some light on the areas of your town with the most drug-abuse problems.

Schools

In doing research for this book, I posed a question on the BiggerPockets Forums about what indicators people considered when deciding on a location. Although I received dozens of responses, the number one response that was mentioned over and over and over again was great schools.

At the time, I didn't realize how important this aspect is to people, but it makes absolute sense. People (myself included) will typically do anything for their children, so getting them into a good public school is incredibly important for many parents. Since the school a student is assigned to is based on location, a property located near a good school district should rent for a higher amount and maintain a lower vacancy than one near a bad school district.

To research school districts, head to www.greatschools.org and simply type in an address or zip code for your potential rental property. GreatSchools gives each school a rating "based on test scores and other available data, including student academic growth and college readiness."[4] According to the GreatSchools website, "The GreatSchools Rating is on a 1-10 scale, where 10 is the highest and 1 is the lowest. Ratings are broken down into three categories: ratings 1–3 signal that the school is 'below average,' 4–7 indicate 'average,' and 8–10 are 'above average.'"

Jobs versus Unemployment

In general, a high number of jobs make for a strong rental market, whereas high levels of unemployment can make it more difficult to find tenants who consistently pay their rent. While you may hear things like "The national unemployment level is at 5.9 percent," this really means very little for you and your rental properties. You need to get specific and look at the unemployment rate in your city. To do this, you could dig around the United States Department of Labor's website (which operates exactly how you'd imagine a government website would operate!), but I usually just head to www.city-data.com and look up the city to discover

---

4 http://www.greatschools.org/about/ratings.page

the local unemployment rate.

Again, keep in mind that higher unemployment does not necessarily mean you shouldn't invest there. In 2014, my area had a 9.9 percent unemployment rate, which is 50 percent higher than the Washington State average. While that seems terribly high, remember that this also means we have a 90.1 percent employment rate, so 90 percent of our population is employed. A higher unemployment rate just means I need to screen my tenants even better than I normally might to make sure they are in the 90 percent who are employed, and I need to make sure their job has a high likelihood of lasting (in other words, their job is not a temporary one).

Population Growth

A growing population should allow you to raise rents over time, and should also increase the value of your property through appreciation because of supply and demand. Yes, you know that I advocate primarily buying for cash flow when investing in rental properties, and that appreciation is just "icing on the cake." But why not buy cash-flowing properties in areas that have the highest chance for getting that icing?

Population growth is impossible to predict with 100 percent accuracy, but educated guesses can be made based on historical data and current trends. To research population historical data, I like to head to www.usa.com/rank, where you can enter your target market's zip code to see data such as population, population growth, and population density, and to learn where your city ranks among other cities in your state. You can also research the fastest-growing cities in your area to spot trends.

Housing Starts and Building Permits

Another key indicator of population growth (and of the potential for appreciation with your property) is the data for housing starts and building permits. This publicly available data shows you the number of new homes being constructed in a certain area, which can help you determine whether an area is being overbuilt, underbuilt, or right on track. An area that is declining or holding steady in population but rapidly expanding in housing starts or building permits could indicate higher vacancy in the future, because supply will outpace demand.

To research housing starts and/or building permit applications, check out the National Association of Home Builders site at www.nahb.org.

Transportation

If you want to rent to good people who have good jobs, you'll likely want to invest in areas where those people can get to work. Although it's entirely possible to invest in rental properties in rural areas, as I do, your choice of the best tenants will increase if you are in an area where good tenants can travel to work reasonably easily. Look for locations with close access to mass public transit. My good friend and fellow BiggerPockets member Darren Sager recommends buying properties within walking distance of the local light rail, because economic growth tends to follow the rail. But even if your area doesn't have a light rail, look for places within a moderate commute to major centers of employment.

Proximity to Local Businesses

When seeking a good economic market, why reinvent the wheel? Consider this: When Starbucks decides to open a new store, do you think they do their research? How about Walmart? Or Costco? Of course they do! Large businesses like these spend millions of dollars a year doing research on every aspect of a community before deciding to invest their money into a new store there. Therefore, it would make sense that if Starbucks or other national businesses begin to invest in an area, it might be a good area for you to consider.

This is also helpful because your tenants will want local businesses to shop at, and if they have to travel 30 minutes to get their tall extra-hot peppermint hot chocolate with whip but no mocha drizzle, it might be a bit tougher to find a tenant.

Price-to-Rent Ratio

One of the most popular numbers people like to consider when analyzing a location is the price-to-rent ratio. In other words, what is the average ratio of the median monthly rent divided by the median purchase price in the area? If that confused you, let me break it down a little further. The median sales price of an area is the point at which half the properties are more expensive and half the properties are less expensive. You can find this data in a number of places, but I've found the most accurate figures at www.zillow.com/research/data, where you can download a *massive* amount of data about nearly every zip code in America.

You'll be able to download a CSV (comma separated values) file, which you can open with Excel or Google Docs, and see the current and historical median sale price data for almost every zip code in the country. Find your local median sale price by searching for your zip code and write that number down somewhere.

Then, head back to www.zillow.com/research/data, and use Zillow Rent Index to download the data based on zip code. Simply find your zip code and look in the column representing the most current quarter (all the way to the right). There you will find the median rental price for your zip code.

To find the price-to-rent ratio, simply divide the first number by the second:

Price-to-Rent Ratio = Median Monthly Rental Price / Median Sales Price

In my area, according to the data from Zillow, I've found my median monthly rental price is $839 and my median sales price is $106,846.15; therefore, my price-to-rent ratio is .7 percent.

Now that I've shown you how to calculate this number, let me explain why you might not want to use it. As with any calculation, everything comes down to the data you input. Garbage in, garbage out. In the case of my area, I know that this data might be *technically* correct, but I also know it doesn't take into account numerous factors. For example, it doesn't separate out the properties in the lower-income areas of this zip code. It doesn't look at the condition of the properties. It doesn't distinguish between properties of different sizes or number of bedrooms. It doesn't look at a lot of things. When I purchase a single-family house in my area, I typically will pay approximately $50,000 for the home, which will rent for around $750 a month. This is a price-to-rent ratio of 1.5 percent, double what the data showed. Keep in mind that although this data does have some use, especially in comparing one area with another, you must take this information with a grain of salt and look at properties with specifics, not averages, or you might miss out on a great location simply because of bad data.

Vacancy Rates

You heard me mention the concept of vacancy rate a few times thus far in this book. This term denotes the percentage of a year that a property will sit empty. It is a very important calculation to include in your numbers when you buy a rental property, but it is also an "average" number that you should consider when determining the best location in which to purchase a rental property. Buying in an area with a high average vacancy rate means that *your* property will likely be vacant more often. Because vacancy is one of the most costly expenses for a landlord, it would make sense that you would want to buy in areas with below-average vacancy rates.

How do you find an area's average vacancy rate? There are three different approaches to finding this data:

1. **Census.** The U.S. Census Bureau tracks vacancy rates with data points in many areas of the country, including the largest 75 markets in the country. This data is fairly "raw" and will require you to download information to a spreadsheet to analyze it. This data also does not get down to the level of specific neighborhoods, which can dramatically affect the vacancy rate.

2. **Agents.** If your specific location uses real estate agents to fill vacant units, you can call in a favor and ask a real estate agent to conduct a comparative market analysis on local rental property stats. This can show you how long currently available properties on the MLS have been vacant. This will also show you how long properties sat before being rented, original listing prices versus rented prices, and other data points.

3. **Property Managers/Landlords.** The third—and, in my opinion, best—approach to finding an area's vacancy rate is by calling up a local property manager or large landlord (in number of units, not body fat) and asking them. They should know this number off the top of their head and can probably give you a more accurate picture than either of the other options listed here. Property managers can tell you specifics about which streets or neighborhoods have a higher or

lower vacancy, as well as other nuances about locations. In addition, this gives you the chance to interview some property managers on the phone in case you decide you want to hire one to watch over your investment.

What is a good vacancy rate? The truth is that there is no standard right or wrong number, but according to the U.S. Census Bureau,[5] in 2014, the nationwide average was 7.6 percent, compared with a record high of 10.6 percent in 2009 and record low of 5.0 percent in 1981. Your area will likely have a different number, and honestly, that's okay. No matter what the vacancy rate is for your area, the truth is this: Make sure you incorporate this vacancy rate into your analysis. Furthermore, know that vacancy rates are largely affected by the way you manage a property. I'll talk more about the specifics of lowering your vacancy rates later in this book, but consider this: The average vacancy rate in my area hovers around 6 percent to 8 percent, but in my company, we run under 2 percent all year round. Of course, when I analyze a deal, I am sure to include a 6 percent to 8 percent vacancy rate, knowing that I will not always be the one managing my properties so efficiently.

Property Tax and Insurance Rates

Finally, as with vacancy rates, every location has different taxes and insurance rates, and this is something you should both be aware of when purchasing and include in your estimates when analyzing a property. Some areas of the country have surprisingly low property tax rates (Denver, Colorado, for example), while other areas have exceptionally high rates (such as much of the northeastern areas of the country). The same is true for insurance rates, because some areas require higher insurance rates as a result of the weather or climate. (Florida, for example, tends to have higher insurance rates because of hurricanes.)

Also, be sure to consider whether or not the area you are considering is located in a one hundred-year floodplain. This is a designation given by the Federal Emergency Management Agency for areas that have a 1 percent probability or greater within a one hundred-year time frame of flooding. If you buy a property in such an area, any bank or traditional

---

[5] http://www.census.gov/housing/hvs/data/ann14ind.html

lender will require you to have flood insurance on the property, because traditional insurance policies do *not* cover damage caused by floods.

Flood insurance is required on several of my properties, and trust me, it can add a significant expense. Additionally, the future cost of flood insurance is a political issue because it is currently subsidized by the United States government, which keeps prices down for those who are required to have it.

What's my advice on buying in an area that requires flood insurance? I can't say not to do it, because some of my best properties are located in these kinds of areas. (The property's location in a flood zone is one of the reasons I was able to get such a good deal.) It is just imperative that you include the cost of flood insurance in your estimates and plan for that price to increase over time. Furthermore, look into the actual risk of the property. For example, I purchased a triplex last year in a flood zone, but the property's first floor was physically 15 feet off the ground—so I had little to worry about.

That said, I will also caution you with this: For years, everyone laughed at the idea of a flood in my area, and we joked about the whole "flood insurance thing" being unnecessary—until this past winter, when that once-in-one hundred-years flood hit my town. We received 7 inches of rain in twenty-four hours, overflowing the city's water control systems and flooding the town. I spent the morning walking through 3 feet of rainwater, checking out my properties and, in total, ended up with $5,000 worth of damage. My deductible on my flood insurance was $5,000 per property, so the insurance didn't even help, but I escaped relatively easy. All of this is to say that you must understand that floods, in a floodplain, are a very real possibility, so if you are considering investing in rental properties in this kind of location, plan for the worst and hope for the best.

WRAPPING IT UP

I don't know what your location is like, so I can't craft the perfect investment strategy for you. However, you now have all the tools needed to go out and research your prospective location to fully understand what you are getting into. Success through real estate investing can be found in any location, but only if you understand that location. Take the time needed to dig in, get the facts, understand the location, and then build your plan around that.

After you've studied your market, it's time to take some action and begin shopping for a great deal. Therefore, in the next chapter, I'll dive into the concept of finding great real estate deals within that market.

Chapter Nine

HOW TO FIND RENTAL PROPERTIES

"Things may come to those who wait, but only the things left by those who hustle."

—ABRAHAM LINCOLN

An ancient proverb tells the story of a young man who wanted to jump over a hill.

In preparation for this feat, he trained night and day for many months. He worked on his leg muscles, ate the right food, talked with others who had made the same jump, and visualized success.

On the day of the big jump, he stood facing the hill, determined to make the jump a success. He knew he would need a good running start, so he backed up. Then he backed up some more. Then he backed up some more, until he could barely see the hill. Then, with all his effort, he took off like a rocket, running at full speed. He ran so fast and so hard that by the time he made it to the hill, he was too tired to make the jump, so he stopped, gave up, and went home.

The first eight chapters of this book have been a warm-up. You've done your stretching, your preparation, your education. You've likely "flipped the switch" and have fully decided that rental properties will be the key to your success. You've nailed down a niche that you want to enter, and you've begun building your plan for buy-and-hold domination. You even know how to analyze a location and a deal to make sure the investment is solid. But up until this point, it's all been talk, preparation, and backing up. I firmly believe that everything you've done so far has been necessary, but like the young man in the story, this is often as far as many new investors make it in their journey. They prepare and prepare and prepare—and then give up.

But not you! For you, the time has come to stop preparing and start running toward the hill. It's time to jump.

In this chapter, I'll focus on how you can find a great rental property with which to start building your future wealth. I'll talk about eight different ways you can find investment properties, starting with the most common: the MLS.

1. The MLS

The MLS, or Multiple Listing Service, is the collection of all homes listed for sale by real estate agents in your area. In truth, the MLS is not one specific list but rather hundreds of lists from different, smaller MLSs across the country. In the years before modern technology, agents would pass around a physical copy of this list so that other agents in the area would know what was on the market. Today, however, the internet has simplified the process dramatically. Now, all the little MLSs have been combined into one master list we commonly refer to as simply "the MLS." Before you jump on your computer and try to download this list for yourself, understand that you can't—at least not completely. The MLS is a tool owned and used by licensed real estate agents, so unless you or your spouse have your license, you will have to start your search elsewhere.

Several websites allow you to search some of the MLS, such as www.zillow.com, www.trulia.com, www.realtor.com, and www.redfin.com. However, none of these offer the full picture of what's available in a given area. To get the most up-to-date, correct, and complete data, you must access the MLS directly through an agent. It's a slightly annoying process to always have to go through a third party, and this is the primary reason many investors get their real estate license.

However, if you don't have your license and don't plan to get it in the near future, you will need to deal with it.

Your agent will send over real estate deals, hopefully automatically and electronically, that fit what you might be seeking, as mentioned earlier when I discussed working with an agent. Your agent will likely send you a link to a website that has more information about a property, usually including photos, property specifics, and other data that will help you decide if the property is worth pursuing. At this point, the ball is in your court to decide whether the property is worth looking at in more depth. If you toured every single property you came across, you'd waste a lot of time, and your agent would probably stop working with you. Instead, you will do some quick math and make some quick decisions based on the numbers, location, and property type.

If the property seems to have potential, you may want to set up a showing to check it out as soon as possible, or if you have time, perhaps you drive to the property right then and there to investigate further. A few nights ago, my agent sent me a listing that he thought I would be interested in, and I was. After some quick number-crunching at home, I jumped in my car to go dig in a little more, since I was unfamiliar with the location. I discovered a lot just by looking at the outside of the home and peering in the windows (don't worry, it was a vacant HUD property). I made my decision that night to pursue the property, set up a time with my agent to see it, and make an offer.

I typically "look" at several dozen properties per week on the computer screen, but I only actually physically look at maybe one in one hundred. There are simply too many bad deals on the MLS. This doesn't mean you can't find good deals, though. In fact, the vast majority of the properties I have purchased have been on the MLS; you just need to be smart. Let me share with you my top ten list for getting a great deal on the MLS.

1. **Find a *Great* Agent.** A great agent who is fast and motivated is the key to success on the MLS. Because there is such high competition for properties on the MLS, you need someone who is responsive and will get the job done. If you can't find this person, consider becoming an agent yourself.

2. **Set Up Automatic Alerts.** With the help of your agent, be sure to set up automatic alerts about properties when they come on the market or drop in price. I have an automatic alert set so that any multifamily in my area will be emailed to me immediately, as well as any house

under $100,000 in my town. This way, I can check it out right away.

3. **Quickly Screen Out the Duds.** Most of the properties on those automatic alerts won't be good enough, so learn to quickly screen out the bad ones. This will save both you and your agent a lot of time, so you can focus on the small percentage of deals that will be worth pursuing.

4. **Be Faster Than the Rest.** Again, your success using the MLS is strictly tied to your ability to be fast. You may not have the highest or best offer on a property, but if you get it in before the other guys, you might just hear a "yes" before the competition has even looked at the property. Too late for them!

5. **Look for Hidden Value-Add Opportunities.** Look for properties that can be changed slightly to increase their value dramatically. For example, I'm sure I've mentioned this before in this book, but I'll say it again: I love finding two-bedroom houses and turning them into three-bedroom homes. This is not always possible, of course, but many two-bedroom homes have an extra "bonus room" or attic that can be converted this way, and huge equity can be added through the conversion. This is just one example of something that most people don't see, but if you can envision the possibilities, you can take a mediocre property that most people would pass on and turn it into an incredible deal.

6. **Make Lots of Offers and Fail Often.** Finding great deals on the MLS is largely a numbers game. You are playing with statistics when trying to find that one deal that will provide great cash flow. Perhaps only one in one hundred deals are worth buying, so you need to look at one hundred properties (on paper or screen) before you offer on one. And because most properties for which you submit an offer will not work out, you need to offer often and fail often. That's right: fail often. A wise investor once told me that if he gets more than one in ten offers accepted, he knows he is offering too much. Although the ratio may be different for you, the point of his statement is solid: Don't be afraid to submit a lot of offers.

7. **Look for Old Listings.** While speed is incredibly helpful when buying on the MLS, the opposite end of that spectrum can also be a gold mine for investors to find hidden deals: old listings. If you've ever tried to sell a home, you'll understand what I mean when I say, "It's stressful." There is always that worry that your property won't sell, and you'll be stuck holding it forever. Therefore, the longer a property sits on

the MLS without an offer, the better chance you'll have of getting a great deal. And the longer it sits on the MLS, the more searchers forget about it. It's no longer the "cute new kid in school." It's just another overpriced property that most people are ignoring, and as a result, it might just be your ticket to getting a deal put together that makes financial sense (and cents).

8. **Focus on Distressed.** When buying a property on the MLS, focus on the deals that need work. I have already talked about the pros and cons of buying a fixer-upper, so I don't need to belabor the point. Just remember that homes that have some kind of "problem" are the ones that 90 percent of the homebuyers out there are avoiding, so focus in on those for the best chance at a deal.

9. **Make Your Offer Clean.** A clean offer is one without a lot of contingencies. I'll discuss contingencies more in depth later, but a contingency in an offer is a legal reason to back out. The more contingencies you have in your offer, the less inclined the seller will be to accept it. Common contingencies include the "inspection contingency," which allows you to back out if you uncover something bad about the property's condition during the inspection, or the "financing contingency," which allows you to back out if you can't get financing. I'm not telling you to necessarily remove those contingencies, especially if you are new to this game, because they help you limit risk. However, understand that the more contingencies you have in your offer, the less inclined the seller will be to accept. Imagine that a seller receives two offers: one from you with numerous contingencies that would allow you to back out of the deal any time before closing for almost any reason, and another offer with no contingencies. The seller will likely choose the "cleaner" offer because they don't want to be jerked around—even if the cleaner offer was for less. Therefore, keep your offer as clean as possible to increase your chance of getting an acceptance.

10. **Work When No One Else Is Working.** Finally, when dealing with the MLS, make it your goal to submit offers when your competition is relaxing. Real estate investor Mark Ferguson often talks about the success he has had by offering on deals on Fridays, when most agents and investors have already begun wrapping up for the week and are planning their weekend fishing trip or barbecue. By the time Monday rolls around and other agents and investors start working, he's got the contract accepted and the property tied up, and he is already getting

his inspection scheduled. This same principle applies to holidays and especially to the end of the year. Most people see the time between Thanksgiving and New Year's Day as "holiday" time, so they work half as hard. Savvy investors, however, know that this is the best time all year to find deals, for two reasons. One, during this season, banks are in a hurry to unload their properties before the new year, and two, there is less competition for properties.

The MLS can be a great source of deals for a real estate investor, but because of the sheer quantity of deals and the number of competitors, you need to be both fast and smart. As real estate investing becomes more and more popular, the MLS will also become more and more difficult to find deals on. Even terrible deals will be snatched up quickly, because people generally have no idea what makes a good deal. Therefore, you may need to expand your horizons and look elsewhere for a deal, and that is what I'll focus on for the rest of this chapter.

2. Direct Mail Marketing for Deals

One of the most common methods used by house flippers and wholesalers to find deals, yet neglected by nearly all rental property investors, is direct mail marketing. Direct mail is the act of sending out a large number of targeted letters or postcards to people who *might* be interested in selling their property, knowing that a small percentage will call you to talk more about the possibility, and that a small percentage of *those* will end up actually selling you their properties.

While this may seem to be a lost cause, direct mail marketers know that the proof is in the percentages. If they can get, for example, 5 percent of those mailed to call about selling their property, and if they can buy, for example, 5 percent of the homes of the people who call, they can still make far more than those letters or postcards cost. Let's say that a wannabe landlord sent out 1,000 letters and got 5 percent of those people to call for more information about selling their property to that landlord, resulting in 50 phone calls. Now let's say that 5 percent of those 50 phone calls resulted in a property being purchased, or 2.5 homes—but since a person can't really buy half of a home, we'll round down to two homes. Could you spend the money needed to send 1,000 letters if you knew you were going to buy two properties? If those deals are as financially solid as they should be, I hope your answer is *yes*! (Keep in mind that these numbers are hypothetical. Every direct mail campaign will have different results, based on numerous factors.)

It's easy to see why flippers and wholesalers might do direct mail—because they get repaid right away when they sell the home. Buy-and-hold investors, on the other hand, do not quickly sell, so they don't see that money spent returning to them soon, which explains the lack of use of this tactic among rental property investors. However, if you consider the cost of direct mail just part of your investment (think of it as an additional closing cost), then it's hard to *not* want to try this method.

Who is actually saying yes to selling you their properties? Typically, these are motivated people who can't or won't sell with a real estate agent. It might be someone caught in a nasty divorce who is just trying to liquidate the property as fast as possible. It might be someone who is in danger of losing the home to foreclosure. It might be someone who inherited the house but doesn't want it. It might be someone who tried to be a landlord but failed miserably, and now has a deadbeat tenant who won't pay rent and won't leave. Do you see a pattern here? Direct mail marketing is about finding people with problems and helping solve their problems. You are not taking advantage of anyone or trying to trick someone into selling their house. You are simply canvassing a large number of people and trying to find those with whom you can find a win-win solution for all parties.

There are a number of different contact lists you can buy and mail to, but the most common is the "absentee" list. This means that the person on record for owning a property does not actually live in the property. You can find and purchase these lists from companies such as www.listsource.com or www.melissadata.com, and then send letters, postcards, or whatever you think will work best to secure you a deal. Typically, you'll spend approximately $0.60 for each postcard and approximately $1 for each letter, but this can depend on how much work you do yourself and how much you outsource.

One final note about direct mail marketing: Success is found in repetition. It is unlikely that the person you mail to this month will respond with an immediate "yes." Trust and brand recognition need to be built first. We've all heard it said that before someone buys a product from a company, they need eight interactions with that brand. The same is true for your direct mail, so I encourage you to mail regularly and to the same list. Some direct mail marketers send letters monthly to the same list, while others send quarterly. You will likely find a solution that works well for you, but again, the point is this: Repetition is key! If John Homeowner gets a letter from you every month for a year, and he suddenly realizes he needs to sell fast, who do you think he will call? Some stranger from an ugly yellow sign taped to a telephone pole by the laundromat, or you, the company that has been reaching out to him for twelve months?

For a much more in-depth look at direct mail marketing, check out "The Ultimate Guide to Using Direct Mail Advertising to Grow Your Real Estate Business" at www.biggerpockets.com/directmailadvertising.

3. Driving for Dollars

Have you ever been driving in your car and noticed a house that made you think, "Boy, that house needs some work!"

If so, then you are already proficient at "driving for dollars."

Driving for dollars is the practice of getting in your car, and driving up and down the streets of neighborhoods where you want to invest, looking for potential deals. Then you simply try to buy those properties.

But what does a "deal" look like?

Typically, when you're driving for dollars, you want to focus on properties that look like they're distressed, vacant, or transitioning negatively. For example, a property with 18-inch-high grass indicates that someone probably doesn't care about the property much. A mailbox stuffed with old, wet pieces of mail shows that someone might not live there. A tarp on the roof that seems to have been there a while shows that the house might have some problems that the owner can't fix.

While driving in the neighborhoods where you want to buy, you'll likely encounter dozens of potential properties. Write down the address of each one, including notes about its condition, and snap a photo as well. When you get home, do some digging into the public records to see who owns the property. Many times you can even do a reverse phone number search to get the owner's number. Or perhaps you just want to write a letter offering to buy the property and mail it to the owner's address listed in the tax records.

Driving for dollars is one of the lowest-cost methods of finding potential properties, because it involves nothing but a tank of gas and your time, which makes it great for those who are looking to get started investing in real estate but have limited funds. It can also help you get to know your prospective neighborhoods really well, which will help you make smarter decisions about your real estate.

4. Eviction Records

I'll never forget my first eviction.

Cockroaches. Filth. Anger. A crazy lady. And a hefty bill at the end.

As any landlord reading this can testify, evictions are not fun. They are messy, stressful, time intensive, and expensive. During this period of time, many landlords begin to question why they are even in this game to begin with. And this is why targeting landlords who are in the midst of an eviction can be so powerful. They have a problem, and there is a great chance they will be motivated to get rid of the property as fast as possible. Had someone talked to me while I was going through my first eviction, I would have seriously considered unloading the property right then and there.

How can you target landlords who are going through an eviction?

Public records.

That's right, evictions are part of the public record in most counties of America. In other words, you can take a trip to your local county administration office and ask to see a list of the current evictions. Different counties and states do evictions a little differently, so I can't tell you exactly how to track down the list of evictions in your area, but if you ask around enough, it shouldn't be hard to find.

Then make some phone calls or send some letters!

5. BiggerPockets Marketplace

What if there was a single source online where real estate investors came together to buy and sell their properties?

What a coincidence! There happens to be such a place, and we call it the BiggerPockets Marketplace. Every day, dozens of listings are posted, and real transactions happen as a result. You can post an ad for either something you want or something you have.

- Looking for a certain kind of property in a certain area? Make a post!
- Looking to sell one of your properties? Make a post!
- Looking to partner with someone? Make a post!

The beauty of the marketplace is in its connection to the keyword alerts on BiggerPockets that I described in Chapter 2.

You never know who is looking to sell you a deal in your area.

6. Craigslist

In the "good ol' days," people used the newspaper to place classified ads. Today, it's all about Craigslist.

Craigslist.org is an online classified section where it is free to post and free to browse, so it makes a great resource for finding real estate deals.

There are three strategies I want to share for using Craigslist:

1. **Search for Sellers.** Perhaps the easiest and most passive way to use Craigslist is to simply search the site for real estate postings in your area. You can do this fairly easily and can even automate the process so new posts that contain certain words that you choose are sent directly to your email inbox (you can do this through www.ifttt.com). The problem with this strategy is that there are a lot of folks doing this. If you want to get really creative, you need to go on the offensive, which brings me to the next tip in this list.

2. **Post an Ad.** Why wait for the deals to come to you? Instead, post an ad that says you are looking for a house to buy. Make it big, and make it flashy. Get people's attention!

3. **Search for Landlords.** Perhaps my favorite use of Craigslist is actually in contacting landlords who are posting on Craigslist. Landlording is not easy, and as I often say, 90 percent of landlords out there suck. Many landlords lose money year after year and are only hanging on to their property because they know it would be hard to sell without first fixing it up. Therefore, you can use Craigslist to search for rental listings that appear to have been placed by "mom-and-pop" landlords (not professional property management companies). Most likely, the landlord put their phone number directly in the post, so call them. Explain that you are looking to invest in real estate in their area and saw their post, and although you aren't interested in renting it, you may be interested in buying a property. Even if they don't want to sell that particular property, there is a chance they will have something else they do want to sell *or* they know someone else who does. Worst-case scenario, you build a relationship with a local investor. Maybe you'll even gain a mentor out of the deal.

Craigslist truly is a no-brainer when you are on the hunt for a good deal. Not only is it free, but it's also where people go to buy and sell things. Why not take five minutes today and find a great deal on Craigslist?

7. Wholesalers

How great would it be if you could sit at home while someone else was out there, pounding the pavement, looking to bring you a killer deal?

That's exactly what could happen if you get your deals from a wholesaler.

Wholesaling is the business of finding incredible real estate deals (usually through the methods I've already mentioned), putting those deals under contract, and selling (or assigning) that contract to another investor for a slightly higher amount.

For example, a wholesaler might find a deal and put it under contract for $110,000, and then sell that deal to you for $115,000, netting a $5,000 profit for himself/herself and helping you get a great deal.

The key to working with wholesalers is this: Find a good one! This is actually trickier than it sounds, because there are a *lot* of wannabe wholesalers out there who claim to know what they are doing but who really don't. Wholesaling is one of the most difficult real estate "jobs," because you have to be great at almost every aspect of the transaction (marketing, analyzing, communication, sales, negotiation, etc.). Nevertheless, the approach is consistently taught by real estate gurus as a get-rich-quick way to build wealth with real estate. However, if you are able to connect with a great wholesaler, you truly can get hot deals delivered straight to your inbox.

To find wholesalers, I recommend the following:

- Call the numbers you see on those ugly "bandit signs" on the side of the road.
- Go to every real estate club in your area.
- Create a Marketplace posting on BiggerPockets.
- Train your own wholesaler on how to find you deals.

8. Passion

Finally, the last method to find great deals is what I call "passion," and this is hard to describe exactly, but here's the gist: People want to help you achieve your goals. Once you let the world know what you want, other people will help you get it.

Let me tell you a quick story. When I was 24 years old, I had just finished reading Ken McElroy's book, *The ABCs of Real Estate Investing: The Secrets of Finding Hidden Profits Most Investors Miss*. I quickly fell in love with the concept of investing in apartment complexes. At church the next morning, I mentioned my newfound love of apartment investing to a nice older couple who told me that they actually had an apartment complex they were looking to sell.

Now, was that luck, or was that something I did? I think both. As the saying goes, "The harder I work, the luckier I get!" I didn't tell just this one couple about my goals, I told everyone I knew, because I was so passionate about it. This is the concept of finding deals through passion. Let your goals and passions be heard, and amazing things can happen.

WRAPPING IT UP

As real estate grows in popularity, you have two choices:

1. Sit out and wait until the next crash.
2. Do what needs to be done to find a deal.

I know which option I'll be taking. Do you?

Now that you have some good ideas for finding properties, let's talk about the process of determining whether a deal is worth buying.

Chapter Ten
WHICH PROPERTIES MAKE THE BEST RENTALS?

Jim Halpert: "Question: What kind of bear is best?"

Dwight Schrute: "That's a ridiculous question."

Jim Halpert: "False. Black bear."

—NBC'S *THE OFFICE*

In 2006, NASA admitted it had accidentally taped over the original recording of the first lunar landing.

In 1962, Decca Records had a choice to sign one of two bands. They chose Brian Poole and the Tremeloes. Which band did they reject? The Beatles.

In 1788, the Austrian army accidentally attacked itself and lost 10,000 men.

Clearly, mistakes happen. The same will be true for your real estate business, though hopefully to a lesser extent than the examples above. But one mistake that *can* be fatal to your real estate business is choosing the *wrong* property. Picking the wrong property is a lot like picking the wrong spouse. It can be incredibly stressful, expensive to get out of, and detrimental to your well-being. But how do you know what the right property is? After all, there are a lot of properties out there. What should you buy? What should you avoid? Are four bedrooms better or worse than two bedrooms? What about garages? Neighbors? These are important questions you should be asking if you want to buy the right deal and have the most success as a landlord, so let's examine several things I look for when shopping for a rental property.

Keep in mind, as with all things in this book, all of this depends heavily on the trends in your location. Furthermore, the following list is not a bunch of rules you must follow, but rather pieces of wisdom that I've picked up and that have served me well.

Bedrooms

It's hard to get long-term tenants in a one- or two-bedroom house. Tenants who are single tend to choose a one-bedroom but quickly hook up with that cute guy/girl from work, and then need a larger place. They move into a two-bedroom and soon start having kids, and again find they need more space. Therefore, in my experience, three- or four-bedroom houses tend to make the best rentals because they attract long-term tenants, which cuts down your vacancy expenses. Furthermore, three-bedroom houses are generally the best kind of property to sell, which can be great when that time comes.

If you are looking for a multifamily property, two-bedroom apartments are usually acceptable, and incredibly common. Single-bedroom and studio apartments are also common, but they tend to attract a more transient tenant, so expect more turnover in that style.

Also, understand that having more bedrooms is not always better. Once you get into five-bedroom homes or higher, you'll find the only tenants willing to rent them are families with a lot of kids. Now, I like kids as much as the next person, and I would never discriminate against them (that's illegal, anyway!), but the truth is that having a lot of kids is hard on a property—broken windows, stained carpet, etc. Keeping a house to three bedrooms (maybe four) is the best way to keep the kid count down legally.

Age

The older the property you buy is, the more expensive it's going to be to fix. I invest in a lot of older homes because they offer the best price in my market, but I definitely pay dearly for my choices. Projects that seem to be fairly simple have a tendency to get out of hand quickly, as existing but previously unknown problems are discovered. You have to deal with the work that others who were far less skilled have done over the years, and live with the consequences of past shoddy work.

Older homes are also generally less energy efficient than newer homes, which can cause the utility bills to be much higher. You might not think that matters much if the tenant will pay for their own heating or cooling, but trust me, tenants know. If your property costs an extra $100 to heat or cool, your tenants will do the math, and you may have a more difficult time keeping a property rented long-term.

Again, I'm not telling you that you should not invest in older homes. Just understand that the newer a property is, generally the fewer issues you will need to deal with.

Garage

When you are investing in single-family houses, you may have difficulty finding a stable, long-term tenant for a house without a garage. Tenants tend to accumulate a lot of stuff, and they need a place to store it. Plus, in areas that get a fair amount of snow or rain, tenants like the luxury of being able to park in a garage. I've generally found that the homes I own that have garages stay rented far longer than those that do not.

Utilities

Some properties, especially older ones, have all the utilities paid by the owner, which is *not* ideal. Buy these kinds of properties only if the numbers truly make sense, because having so little control over this major expense will give you a major headache. When tenants don't need to pay for their own heat, they tend to leave windows open in the winter or the air conditioner running 24/7 in the summer. If they don't need to pay for water, they'll never let you know about the constant drip in the bathroom, thereby costing you hundreds of dollars a year.

When looking for single-family homes, look for ones for which all utilities (including water, sewer, garbage, electricity, and heat) can be paid directly by the tenant. When shopping for multifamily, at least look for ones where heat and electricity can be paid by the tenant, and if you can find properties that can be converted to a master metered system to allow tenants to pay for their own water, you've potentially struck gold.

Lawn

Properties with large lawns, gardens, and other outside features will never be taken care of by tenants the way that you or I would take care of them. Although there are exceptions to every rule, I look for properties that have smaller yards to keep the yard work for the tenant at a minimum. That said, recreational space is very important in attracting a stable, long-term tenant, so make sure there is somewhere the tenant (and/or their kids) can run around and have fun.

Parking

Stable tenants need a place to park their vehicles. Off-street parking (a driveway, carport, or garage) is something nearly all great tenants prefer, so look for properties with this feature. And generally, two parking spots are better than one, three are better than two, and so on.

Location

I talked about location a lot already in the previous chapter, so I don't need to belabor the point. However, when shopping for a property, keep an eye out for what's nearby. A tenant is just like you: They want to eat out occasionally, take a jog in a park, pick up milk from the grocery store. Buy in locations where tenants want to live, and you'll find a more stable rental.

These are just a few of the property characteristics I look for when buying a property. You don't need to get each and every one perfect to get a great rental property, but these factors are important to consider when shopping.

Now, this might surprise you, but I actually don't like to buy "perfect" properties. The fact is that perfect properties come at a premium.

A savvy investor is always looking to snag a great deal, which is why I tend to avoid *perfect* properties and instead look for *problem* properties. I'll explain.

Eight Problems I Look for When Shopping for Rental Properties

Yes, you read that correctly.

When looking for a rental property, I actually *proactively look* for problems. Sure, it's entirely possible to buy a rental property that is 100 percent finished and great, and perhaps for you and your business model, that is what you should do. But for me, I want to find problems that I can fix that will help me get a better deal.

How do problems get me a better deal?

It's simple: When most people encounter the following eight problems, they turn around and walk out the door, repulsed and saying, "No way!" I walk into that same property, take a look around, and start to get excited. In fact, it's hard for me to be excited about a property that *doesn't* have problems. It's the fear of dealing with problems that drives most people away, and with less competition, I know I can find better deals.

Before I get to the list, I will caution you: with problems comes risk. It's imperative that you understand the full nature of the problem at hand, and that you include an accurate budget to fix that problem when doing your numbers. Whether you are using a spreadsheet you created or the BiggerPockets Rental Property Calculator, be sure to include an accurate amount to cover each problem.

With that, let's get to the eight problems.

1. The Bigfoot Smell

When you walk into a house, and it smells like Bigfoot died in the kitchen, is your first thought, "I gotta get outta here?" The truth is, most people respond with disgust, but seasoned investors see opportunity. Bad smells are one of the easiest problems to fix in a property but one of the things that drives away 99 percent of the competition. Bad smells are generally caused by one or more of a few things, none of which are difficult to solve:

- Rotten food in the cupboards or rubbed into the carpet
- Cat or dog urine soaked into the floor
- Smoke residue on the walls, ceiling, and floor

- Mildew on the windows, walls, or other surfaces
- Bigfoot dead in the kitchen

As long as you are not dealing with some kind of environmental issue or a major sewer leak under the house, you'll likely find smells are fairly easy to eliminate with some cleaning. To get rid of the smell, go through the following list in order and stop when the smell is gone:

1. **Carpet.** In my experience, getting rid of the carpet and the pad underneath will get rid of 90 percent of the problem immediately, so plan on hiring a couple people for a few hours to remove the smelly carpet. For less than $100, most of your problem will be solved. Open all the windows and let the property air out for a few hours.

2. **Mop.** Mop the floor with a mixture of bleach and water. Let it dry, and open the windows to air the place out. (It can take a day or two for the smell of bleach to disappear and let you know if the smell is truly gone.)

3. **Clean.** Make sure every crumb in the kitchen is picked up and all windows have been washed. Obviously, you will need to do this anyway, so find a professional cleaner who can come in and clean every square inch.

4. **Prime the Floors.** If the smell persists, buy some cans of Kilz Oil-Based Primer and a long-handled paint roller from the local hardware store. Pour the primer out onto the floor (this is a lot of fun, actually!) and spread it over every square inch. I will warn you: Oil-based primer is *strong smelling*, so be sure to use a respirator (they run about $30) so you don't pass out. I'm not kidding—you will pass out otherwise. I've been there, done that. The chemicals are just too potent.

5. **Wash the Walls.** This approach is most commonly used when dealing with a stale smoke smell. Get a good sponge and a bucket of soapy water, and scrub the walls. Often, you will be able to physically watch the smoke residue wipe away from the walls, which is an oddly satisfying experience.

6. **Prime/Paint the Walls/Ceiling.** Lastly, and for situations where the other approaches have not solved the problem, hire someone to spray the entire inside of the house with that Kilz Oil-Based Primer (about $200 in primer will do a whole house, plus two days of labor).

Following these steps, I've never had a problem smell I could not eliminate. Whether you do the task yourself or hire a local handyman to do it for you, the entire process is unlikely to cost more than $1,000 (not including the cost of the new carpet, which you are likely planning to replace anyway), and you'll have a fresh, clean, and newly painted property, ready for a new tenant. The great news is that a bad smell can drive the cost of a home down considerably, maybe even tens of thousands of dollars. Now you understand why investors often say, "Mmmmm, it smells like money!"

One final caveat on the smell issue: Make sure the smell is not coming from a busted sewer line under the property or in the basement or something tragic like that. That fix could be much more expensive. If you are unsure what is causing the bad smell in a property, bring along someone with more experience and/or be sure to get a professional inspection on the property.

2. The Hidden Third Bedroom

I mentioned earlier that I don't like two-bedroom homes for a rental property. However, there is one case where I get very excited about buying a two-bedroom home: when there is a hidden third bedroom.

No, I'm not talking about some mysterious bedroom hidden behind a wall (though admittedly, that would be pretty cool!). I'm talking about taking a room that is not considered a bedroom and turning it into one.

For example, the other day, I checked out a house that had two bedrooms, one bathroom, a laundry room, and then a large "storage room" next to the laundry. This storage room was 10 feet by 12 feet—the perfect size for a bedroom. The walls were finished, the floor just needed carpet, and a door needed to be added. In other words, to turn this two-bedroom home into a three-bedroom home, I was looking at maybe $3,000 of labor and materials. As a two-bedroom, the property was worth about $90,000. However, as a three-bedroom home, that same house was worth closer to $115,000. Why the agent didn't list it as a three-bedroom, I'll never know. But I see this kind of thing all the time.

In many cases, the difference in house value between a two-bedroom and a three-bedroom can be significantly higher than the cost of converting a "hidden bedroom" into a functional, legal bedroom. This helps build some immediate equity in the property, since you're paying for a two-bedroom but will own a three-bedroom. In case you are wondering, the jump from three bedrooms to four bedrooms is likely not the same as from two to three, so I usually stick to the latter.

Of course, not all two-bedroom homes have this hidden bedroom; most don't. But I've found that around 20 percent of two-bedroom properties do have some potential for a third bedroom. Keep an eye out for this kind of property, and look for keywords like "bonus room," "attic," and "huge bedroom" (which can often be split in two).

3. Ugly Countertops and Cabinets

You've likely heard the phrase "kitchens and baths sell houses," and it's not an exaggeration. People spend a large amount of time in the kitchen, and nothing says "1979" like bright orange countertops or ugly cabinets. Most people simply avoid houses with these problems. Those people don't realize how easy it can be to transform an ugly kitchen into a modern, beautiful one with just some new counters and a fresh coat of paint on the cabinets.

Yes, that's right, many times you can paint old cabinets to make them look brand new. Rust-Oleum sells a really nice cabinet refinishing kit for less than $100 at Home Depot that will turn nasty cabinets into modern works of art.

Furthermore, replacing countertops is a fairly straightforward process. You can pick up prefabricated laminate countertops from Home Depot or Lowe's for a few hundred bucks and have it installed in a couple of hours, or you can spring for nicer granite or quartz if the neighborhood style demands it. All in all, don't be scared off by 1979. It's entirely possible to turn a dated, ugly kitchen into a gorgeous one for less than $1,000, so look for easy wins like that to snag a great deal.

4. The Bad Roof

This one might come as a bit of a shock to people, because a leaking roof seems like it would be a pretty major problem. However, I like finding properties that are in desperate need of a new roof, because it scares off a lot of the competition, and getting a new roof is not a difficult process. Yes, it can be fairly expensive, but I can usually get the current roof removed and a new one put on for less than $6,000, and it's completed in just one or two days. Now I don't need to worry about the roof leaking on my rental property for many, many years, and I can factor that into my budget.

Keep in mind that roofing costs can vary wildly depending on the contractor you consult. In my area, the two largest contractors will typically charge between $15,000 and $20,000 to replace a roof, and because they are the largest roofing contractors in my area, most people call both and get bids from both, only to find that the bids are within a few hundred dollars of each other. Little do they know that the companies are actually owned by the same person, so of course the bids come in the same. If they took the time to call a few more contractors, they'd discover that the cost of a roof is usually less than $6,000 from nearly everyone else in town—same materials, same quality, but drastically different prices. Keep that in mind when shopping for your next roof. Don't get taken advantage of. Shop around, ask for referrals, and then check up on those referrals. Don't let a bad roof overwhelm you, but instead, look at the opportunity.

5. M... M... Mold?!

Uh oh, did I just say the "M" word? Yep! And yes, mold is one of the *best* problems I look for when buying a property. You see, mold is a scary thing to the average consumer, maybe even to you, but it shouldn't be. You see, mold is a fungus that grows naturally *everywhere*. It's in your house right now. It's in your car. It's probably in your beard and in your hair. It's in the air you breathe all the time if you live in a wet climate. (Still scared?) Mold is everywhere that there is moisture.

However, when mold spores begin to settle and accumulate in large quantities, suddenly the human eye can detect the mold and will start to see spots of black or green on certain surfaces. Now, if there is enough mold in an area, it can be dangerous to people with certain immune system problems, but in small quantities, it's not like anthrax, as much of the U.S. population seems to think. Let them keep thinking that mold is just slightly worse than eating a spoonful of ricin. While they are out there complaining about a few spots of mold in a property, I'm out there investigating *why* there is mold and snatching up amazing deals.

Mold is not a random occurrence; it happens for a reason. That reason is moisture. Eliminate the moisture, and you eliminate the visible mold! If you walk into a potential rental property and there is mold all over the bathroom walls, and then you notice that there are no windows or a vent in the bathroom, guess what? That's right, the mold is growing because the moisture from showers can't leave the bathroom. Install a vent, and the problem is probably solved. Mold all over the ceiling? I would wager that there is either a roof leak or no ceiling insulation directly above the moldy spot (so condensation in the room is forming on the cold spot where the insulation is missing, causing mold growth).

The only mold I would really worry about is mold in basement walls, because it indicates water seeping in through the foundation—and that begins to scare me. Fixing a bad, leaking foundation can be incredibly complicated and expensive, so unless you are more experienced, I would steer clear of those issues.

6. Compartmentalized Configuration

I think this might be the longest word in this entire book, but the concept is not hard to understand. Compartmentalization is the characteristic found in many homes, especially older properties, where the rooms were designed to be separate from each other. Today, there is a movement toward open-concept living, in which the living room, dining room, and kitchen have no clear borders and all kind of blend together. People want to cook in the kitchen while still engaging with the rest of their family in the living room or dining room. Properties that are severely compartmentalized do not allow for this and are therefore not as desirable to the average homeowner. As with the rest of the items in this list, anything that drives away the general population makes me take interest.

Compartmentalization is a problem that intrigues me for two different reasons. First, in a rental property, compartmentalization is not always a problem, so you can pick up a house for less than other similar homes, but it might not rent for any less. Second, compartmentalized properties can be "opened up" fairly easily to modernize them. Usually for less than $2,000, a contractor can go in and tear out a wall to open the property up, increasing the desirability, and thus, its value.

7. Jungle Landscaping

You've likely heard the term "curb appeal" before and probably know the importance of having a property look pristine from the street. After all, the landscaping is the very first thing potential buyers see when they visit the property. This is why I love to find properties where the yard looks less like a yard and more like Tarzan's jungle. Long grass, dead grass, overgrown bushes, pink flamingos—it's all good! Landscaping is not a terribly difficult or expensive thing to clean up, but the bad condition can drive away the bulk of the competition and help you snag a great deal. It's amazing what a simple cleaning, mowing, and edging can do to a property, and typically for less than $1,000, a problematic landscape situation can become a nice yard.

8. Junk, Junk, and More Junk

Have you ever watched the television show *Hoarders*? This show takes you inside the homes of individuals who have the compulsive habit of saving or collecting an absurd amount of junk.

Sometimes the house is filled so high with junk that it's impossible to get into certain rooms. While this makes for highly entertaining television, this is not some mythological thing: Hoarding is a real and very common problem for people around the world. When these hoarders need to move or they pass away, the junk they leave behind can be a major roadblock for casual buyers. However, when I see junk, I don't see a problem—I see opportunity. I might be able to get an incredible deal on the property because no one else wants to handle the problem. I can simply hire someone to come clean it out 100 percent, bringing it to a point where I can put in new carpet, perhaps paint it, and get it rented out for incredible cash flow.

We just looked at eight problems that I *like* to find in a potential rental property. Now I'll share three problems I *don't* want to see when I'm shopping for a deal.

Three Problems I Avoid When Shopping for a Rental Property

The following are three problems I try to avoid when I look for a rental property. This isn't to say I will never touch a property that has one of these issues, but there better be a really good reason for it, and I would have to factor it into my numbers.

1. Neighborhood

You cannot easily fix a neighborhood. Sure, you could join the local city council and start a neighborhood watch, but the neighborhood is not likely going to change because you want it to. Therefore, I don't want to buy a property where the neighborhood will always be an unsolvable problem. The property will continually be difficult to rent, the tenants will trash the house, I'll have to deal with evictions and late rent, and in the end, the property's value may never increase (and might actually decrease). I'm not saying I will only buy in a Class A neighborhood, but I'm definitely not going to buy in a Class D area.

2. Foundation Issues

Foundation issues scare me because they can be money pits to fix, and the cost of a solution can sometimes eclipse six figures. This is especially true with foundation issues on a house with a basement or slab. I would also put any property that has water leaking in the foundation in this problem category and steer clear. Yes, there are investors who specialize in properties that have bad foundations, but for me, the risk is too great.

3. Shared Driveways

I once bought a nice house in a nice area that shared a driveway with a neighbor's house. Literally, the two houses were 20 feet apart with the driveway in between, split evenly down the middle into "their side" and "my side." When I bought the house, I didn't see any issues with this situation, but within a few months I learned a terrible truth: The neighbor was a driveway hoarder.

He started to pile up garbage, boats, engines, tires, and everything else you could imagine in the driveway. Although he was polite enough to keep his junk on his side of the shared driveway, it made my property look incredibly bad, and we had a terrible time trying to rent or sell it. The junk in the neighbor's driveway reduced the value of my property by 20 percent, and there was nothing I could do about it. Now I don't buy properties where the neighbor could so easily affect my bottom line.

In addition to these three, there are other location-specific problems, such as being directly below a flight path or next door to loud/angry dogs. Likely, you'll have your own list of "won't touch" property features, and that's okay. Success is found more often in what you say "no" to than what you say "yes" to. You don't need to try to fix every deal you find. As the saying goes, "One man's junk is another man's treasure."

WRAPPING IT UP

There is no set rule as to what makes a perfect rental property. Instead, the perfect rental property is one that helps you achieve your goals. Period. Buying the wrong deal will take you further from those goals.

This chapter wasn't designed to give you a list of exactly what you should and should not buy, but I hope that the principles I covered will help you narrow your buying criteria down so you can focus on hunting for only the best properties and avoid potential mistakes.

As you begin to search for deals, a funny thing will happen: You'll likely find potential deals! This can be a little scary for a new investor, because it then becomes time to start interacting with—gasp!—other people. In the next chapter, I will cover the process of making an offer and negotiating your way into your dream rental property.

Chapter Eleven
SUBMITTING YOUR OFFER

*"I wanna make you smile whenever you're sad.
Carry you around when your arthritis is bad. All I
wanna do is grow old with you."*

—"GROW OLD WITH YOU,"
ADAM SANDLER IN *THE WEDDING SINGER*

My palms were sweaty, and I could barely hold the guitar pick in my right hand.

I had traveled 2,000 miles for this moment, by plane, three buses, and two hitched rides. The noise of the waves crashing on the sand and the crackling fire near my feet helped calm my nerves on this foggy October afternoon. All I could do now was wait for *her* to come to me.

I finally spotted her half a mile down the beach, walking with her friends toward me, completely unaware of my presence on the beach and in this part of the country. Her beauty was breathtaking, even from this distance. It had been several months since we had last seen each other, and it took everything in me not to run down the beach toward her and throw my arms around her small frame. When she finally approached, it took her a moment to realize who I was.

The surprise was worth every second of the journey.

Her friends, who had been in on the ruse, left us there alone to watch the fire and the waves. We talked of my internship on a U.S. Senate race that I had quit to come see her. We talked of my morning, stranded in downtown Tacoma, Washington, when the bus I was hoping to take didn't materialize. We talked about how much we missed each other.

And then Adam Sandler helped me win my bride.

I reached over and picked up an old acoustic guitar, struggling through a version of Adam Sandler's classic song from the 1998 movie *The Wedding Singer* titled "Grow Old with You." As I closed out the song, my sweaty fingers "accidentally" dropped the guitar pick into the hole on the front of the acoustic guitar. I tipped the guitar upside down but instead of the pick falling out, a small gold engagement ring came out and landed on the sand.

I picked it up, set down the guitar, and dropped to one knee.

She said yes.

Making an offer of marriage is scary stuff!

You never know, with 100 percent confidence, what the other person will say. But if you don't stick your neck out there and make the offer, you'll never experience the incredible joy of hearing that "yes" and spending a lifetime together.

Imagine if I had never worked up the courage to ask Heather to marry me. Imagine if I had stayed at that internship, where life was "safe." The thought is too tragic for me to even consider.

In a similar (yet much smaller) way, making an offer on a piece of real estate is also scary. As with marriage, you never know exactly what you are getting yourself into. There is risk. There is danger. But without the offer, you'll never experience the life that comes after. You'll never hear a "yes" without the request.

My goal in this chapter is to help you overcome the fear and complexity surrounding making an offer on your future rental property. I will give you the tools, tips, and process you need to not only present your offer, but also to get that same positive response I heard on that beach that day.

Yes!

How to Make an Offer

Everything in this book, up to this chapter, has walked you through the dating phase of your relationship with real estate. You've explored.

Learned. Grown. But now it's time to take action and move your relationship to a new level. It's time to quit thinking, planning, and talking. It's time to start *doing*.

As with a marriage proposal, making an offer to buy a piece of property can be overwhelming, but most of that is mental.

In reality, making an offer is a pretty easy task *if* you've done the rest of your homework up to that point. You've committed to doing this, made a plan, and done your math homework, so now you are ready to offer. Now is not the time to be timid. All the planning, all the analyzing, all the mindset changes you go through—they don't mean anything if you don't actually get out there and make an offer. Now is the time for boldness, confidence, and paperwork.

How you offer will depend a lot on *who* will receive the offer. For example, buying on the MLS is going to be very different from offering on a home from a motivated seller. I'll talk about both briefly.

Offering on a Property on the MLS

When you want to offer on a property currently listed on the MLS, you need to go through a real estate agent. Typically, one agent will represent the seller and another will represent the buyer, but the seller will pay the commission for both agents. In other words, a real estate agent is typically free for the buyer (you!). Therefore, your first step in offering on a deal on the MLS will be to find a real estate agent to work with.

Yes, you can use the same agent who is selling the property. In fact, some investors like to work this way, because the agent is incentivized to encourage their client to take your offer, because they would make double the commission. The downside to this, however, is the inherent conflict of interest present when the listing agent, who is morally bound to get the seller the highest price possible, is also working for you. Some states, in fact, make this practice illegal as a result. I recommend using the same agent (known as "dual agency") *only* if you are an experienced investor and don't need any advice from the agent.

Once you have your agent, offering on a property can be a quick process. The agent will walk you through each step using the forms supplied by the local MLS. You'll need to check the boxes, sign on the right lines, and send the offer off with your agent to deliver (electronically, most likely) to the seller. Most agents can do the entire offer process online, but I recommend sitting down with your agent if you are just getting started with real estate and having them walk you through each step of the process.

Once the offer has been sent off, you just need to wait for the seller to respond.

Offering on a Property Not Listed on the MLS

If you are buying a property that is *not* listed on the MLS, you will probably not be using a real estate agent. While this can seem intimidating, this happens all the time, and although an agent won't be there to hold your hand, you'll get through it just fine.

Making an offer to a private seller usually begins with a verbal offer during a casual conversation. It's usually far less official at first, and it's usually just brought up when touring the property. When I am trying to buy a home from a private seller, I like to start by asking the seller how much they would like to get. Then, after some negotiation (which I'll cover later in this chapter), you'll come to an agreement on price. At that point, you can pull out your official purchase and sale document, and sign in all the necessary places to make it official.

Another casual way to make an offer without being too official is by using a letter of intent. A letter of intent is a simple document that lists the conditions of the purchase and sale, usually on one page, and doesn't use all the legalese. It's not a legal document, just a way for both parties to see the summary of what's being offered. Often, the official purchase and sale document can be dozens of pages long just to explain a few important facts. A letter of intent simply places those facts on one page, so both parties can decide whether an official purchase and sale agreement is worth drafting.

If you don't have a purchase and sale (P&S) agreement lying around, don't worry. There are several places you can go to get one:

- **Local Title Company.** Title companies will often give away legal P&S agreements because they know that by providing this free form, you will likely end up using them for the sale closing.
- **Online.** There are several online websites that offer state-specific legal forms for purchase. You can also check the BiggerPockets File-Place at www.biggerpockets.com/files for other useful forms and documents.
- **Office Supply Store.** Many office supply stores, especially the big-box stores, carry P&S agreements, along with many other legal forms.

- **Other Investors.** Ask around at your local real estate club to see if anyone has the form you need. Most investors would have no problem sharing theirs.

Finally, no matter how you obtain your P&S form, I recommend that you have a local attorney take a glance at it. You want to be sure you are covering all the necessary bases, and a lawyer can help you do that. You can also simply get a P&S agreement from an attorney, though this might be the most expensive option.

The Earnest Money Deposit

The earnest money deposit, also known as a good faith deposit or, simply, earnest money, is money provided by the buyer when an offer is submitted as a way of showing the seriousness of the offer. This deposit is essentially the buyer saying, "Look, I really want to buy this property, and I'm putting my money where my mouth is."

The earnest money is pledged, and should the buyer not fulfill his end of the contract, the seller can keep the money. Yes, you can lose your earnest money. However, there are certain conditions that allow you to back out without losing it, which I'll talk about later in this chapter.

How Much Is the Earnest Money Deposit?

The amount of earnest money supplied depends greatly on the price of the property and the person from whom you are buying the property. For example, the earnest money on a $40,000 house will probably be far less than the earnest money on a $1,000,000 apartment complex. Although there is no hard-and-fast rule that governs the amount required, most earnest money deposits tend to be 1 percent to 2 percent of the purchase price.

Because the seller gets to keep the earnest money if the buyer backs out without a legitimate reason, the higher the earnest money deposit, the better the chance that your offer will be accepted. (I'll talk more about this in a moment.) That said, when dealing with motivated sellers, the earnest money becomes much less "normal," because the seller generally doesn't know or care much about the amount. Some investors simply make the earnest money $1, and most private sellers don't seem to notice or mind.

Who Holds On to the Earnest Money Deposit?

The earnest money should not be given directly to the seller. Instead, this money is usually held by a third party, most likely the title company or attorney who is handling the closing. This ensures that the rules that govern what happens to the earnest money are followed. This is most commonly done when the contract has been accepted and signed by both parties, not before. If you are working with a real estate agent, your agent will mostly likely tell you when and where to drop off the earnest money check.

What Happens to the Earnest Money?

What exactly is the earnest money used for? What ultimately happens to it? There are three possible scenarios that could play out, depending on how the deal is done (or *not* done).

1. If the sale goes through, the earnest money becomes part of the cash the buyer would be required to bring to closing. For example, if your down payment plus closing costs came to $50,000, but you gave a $2,000 earnest money deposit, you would only be required to bring $48,000 to the closing table, as directed by the title company or attorney who closes the sale.
2. If the sale does not go through, and the buyer does *not* have a legal reason to back out, then the deposit is forfeited to the seller, and the seller receives the deposit.
3. If the sale does not go through, and the buyer *does* have a legal reason to back out, the deposit is returned to the buyer.

What are these "legal reasons" I have mentioned?

Most contracts, real estate or otherwise, contain certain provisions that outline conditions in which the contract could be terminated. These provisions are known as "contingencies." In other words, the property sale is *contingent* on some specifically listed things. These are legal loopholes that allow you to not follow through on your contract, should one of those contingencies happen to occur.

Technically, you could have contingencies for anything you can think of. Yes, that means you *could* write up a contingency in the contract that says, "This contract is contingent on the grass being colored purple" or "This contract is contingent on my hair falling out before closing." If you were to include those, and the grass was not colored purple or your hair did not fall out, you could cancel the contract and back out with no repercussions. Of course, these are absurd examples meant only to illustrate what a contingency is.

What kind of contingencies *should* you put in your offer?

First, understand that the more contingencies you put in your offer, the more leery a seller will be to accept it. Think about it: If someone offered to buy your home, but only if fifty little contingencies happened, would you feel comfortable accepting? Probably not! However, at the same time, contingencies are often necessary to protect yourself from things you couldn't anticipate. Like knowing how much to offer, knowing which contingencies to include in the contract depends on the deal itself and the person you are submitting the offer to. If I was competing with numerous other people for a property, I might include far fewer contingencies than I would if I was offering on a deal with no competition. But let me share the two most common contingencies you'll likely encounter:

1. **Inspection.** You can only learn so much about a property by walking through it on a quick tour. As I'll talk about more later in this book, it's pretty important to do a deep inspection of a property before buying it, using a professional inspector to find every imperfection they can about the property. An inspection contingency, therefore, gives you the ability to inspect everything about the property within a certain time frame, and back out if you find something that you didn't expect. On residential homes, a ten-day inspection contingency is most common. This means that after ten days, the contingency is no longer applicable.

   Inspection contingencies are very common in real estate contracts, but some experienced investors do choose to waive this contingency, opting instead to take the risk that nothing unforeseen will come up in the inspection. If it does and they have to back out because of it, they could lose their earnest money. Other investors, including me, often designate much shorter inspection periods (often as brief as three days), knowing that this will still allow time to get in and get the property looked at in detail, but it will look better than those who need ten days. (Of course, you need to know that you can get it inspected in this time frame. Often, professional inspectors are booked out several days in advance and take a couple of days to get the report to you.)

2. **Financing.** What would happen if you tried to buy a property, but at the last minute, you found out that your financing had fallen through?

As disappointing as that might be, you could also lose your earnest money if you don't have the financing contingency in place. The financing contingency allows a buyer to back out and to keep their earnest money should the buyer not be able to obtain a loan.

Of course, if you are paying cash for a house, you will have no need for a financing contingency, and your offer will likely look much stronger to the seller. Some investors choose to avoid using the financing contingency, even if they are using a loan. This can help make their offer stand out, because the seller knows that either the deal will close or they'll get the earnest money, no matter what happens. Of course, if you choose to waive the financing contingency but still plan to use a loan, this can increase your risk of losing that earnest money should something go wrong with your financing.

What Should the Offer Include?

Every real estate offer can basically be boiled down to the who, what, where, when, why, and how of the deal.

- WHO is making the offer and to WHOM?
- WHAT is being bought and for WHAT amount?
- WHERE am I getting the funds? (the financing)
- WHEN am I planning to buy it? (the closing date)
- WHY would I back out of this offer? (the contingencies)
- HOW is this all going to happen? (the fine print)

In essence, everything from a transaction can be summed up in this. When offering on a deal on the MLS, your agent will likely walk you through every step of the document, but if you are offering on a property directly to a seller without an agent, you are on your own. Therefore, let's go through these elements in a bit more detail.

The who and whom are fairly obvious when you're making an offer. The what and when should be clear as well. So let's focus on the where, why, and how.

Where Are You Getting the Funds?
Yes, the chapter on funding your purchase comes later in this book, but let's touch on the subject now. When you submit an offer, you'll likely

include what kind of financing you'll be using for the purchase. Will you be using all cash? Will you be obtaining conventional financing through a local bank? Will you be using private or hard money? Most sellers want to know this information before they allow you to tie up their property for the next month or two, only to back out at the last moment because you can't actually buy it. If you are using financing, it can help to provide a letter from the lender showing that you have already been approved for a loan (known as a pre-approval letter).

Why Would You Back Out of the Offer?
In other words, as we discussed earlier in this chapter, what are the contract contingencies? Can the buyer back out if they can't obtain financing? What if they find some surprise problems during the inspection, like asbestos in the attic or plumbing that hasn't worked in a generation? What if the house appraises for far less than what was offered? Make sure your P&S document spells all this out.

How Will This All Happen?
In other words, the contract should spell out the exact process by which the sale will proceed. This includes all the small print that helps the title company or attorney know exactly how to move forward with the sale.

How Much Should You Offer?
Now for the difficult question: How much should you offer?

Hopefully, you did your preliminary numbers on the deal and have a decent idea of what you can pay for the property. But should you offer that exact amount? Should you lowball the seller (offer an extremely low price, hoping they take it)?

The truth is this: There is no one right way.

Some investors choose to submit a lot of lowball offers, hoping something, somewhere pans out. Others choose to give their highest and best offer up front. Still others find room in the middle. Each of these techniques have a time and place, but each individual deal will dictate the kind of offer you should submit.

For example, if the home has been sitting on the market for a long time, and you have a good indication that the seller is eager to sell, there is no real danger in submitting a lowball offer to see what happens. However, if you are in a competitive market and a new listing hits the MLS at a great price, and you know that it's going to sell quickly, you may want to cut out the chase and simply offer your highest amount, right then and there. Sometimes, you may even need to offer more than the asking price.

The transaction for a triplex I recently purchased went exactly that way. The big, ugly purple triplex REO hit the market at $70,000, and I knew just by the photos that this thing would go quickly. It needed some work, but the property was in overall great shape and would bring in almost $2,000 per month in income. Within hours of the home hitting the MLS, I submitted a bid of $72,000 for the property, wanting to be the first and assuming that any other offers would be full-priced but that few would go over. I was right, and today this property is one of my highest-cash-flow deals. Had I tried to lowball the seller with a $50,000 offer, they would have laughed at me and moved on to another interested party. But for me, even at $72,000, the numbers worked great. And that's key! The numbers worked at $72,000. I would never pay more than asking price just to win a bid if the numbers didn't pencil out, and you shouldn't either, unless you have some dramatic future reason for doing so.

As I mentioned earlier in this book, I walked through another home on the MLS, and the seller was home, so we struck up a conversation. She was trying to move to California, and the house, which she could not take care of, was the only thing keeping her from doing so. She was eager to go be with the rest of her family and just wanted out. The seller was asking $30,000 for the piece-of-junk property, but because of the condition, I didn't expect any other investors to be pounding down her door. It was only a mediocre deal. I offered her $16,000 for the property and told her I could close in two weeks. She took it.

As you can see from these two examples, I submitted an offer on both these properties the day they were listed, yet my strategy was different for each. The motivation was different, as was the relative price. These are just a few nuances in the real estate game that you'll master quickly once you start making offers. Never assume that the offer process is always black and white, and keep your eyes open to cues that will help you make a solid offer with the best chance of being a win-win for all parties involved.

There is no silver bullet in knowing exactly how much you should offer. Each deal is different, and requires a different analysis and strategy. Yes, this means it takes work. However, the more offers you make, the more deals you'll close, and the faster you'll reach your financial destination. Just keep one eye on the financials and the other on the situation, and you'll do great.

Sixteen Tips for Getting Your Offer Accepted

Making offers—and getting them accepted—is often as much about art as math. This section will give you sixteen tips for getting your offer accepted. No one tip is applicable to every situation, but to paraphrase an analogy, "The more tools you have in your tool shed, the more projects you can build." Consider each of these a tool in your shed.

1. **Work Fast.** As they say, the early bird gets the worm. Sometimes, the secret to getting a "yes" is as simple as being the first to offer on a property. Be sure to have automatic alerts set up with your real estate agent, so you'll instantly be notified about new properties as they hit the market. Then, don't hesitate. Run the numbers and make the offer. Don't let fear slow you down.

2. **Offer Your Best Up Front.** Rather than playing a game with the seller, give your maximum offer right up front. If they counter and try to make you go higher, just say no. If the numbers work at $90,000, sometimes it's best to just offer $90,000 and not try to shoot for $85,000.

3. **Submit a Letter with Your Offer.** When offering on a piece of property, remember that there is always a person at the other end of the line making the decision, even if it's a bank REO. If you want to get your deal accepted, get that person to like you. I think the best way to do this is simple: Include a letter with your offer. This doesn't have to be anything formal, just a quick message letting the seller know who you are and what you plan to do with the house. I use this strategy almost every time I submit an offer, and I can promise you, it works!

   I also believe it's important to include a photo with the letter. This lets the seller know that you are not just "some investor." You are a real person. Here's the letter I use for an example. Feel free to modify this and submit it with your next offer:

Hello!

My name is Brandon; my wife and I are active real estate investors here in Grays Harbor County...and have a special love for ugly properties, which attaracted us to yours! :) We love this community and love to make old properties new again, revitalizing this area and improving the neighborhoods where we live and work!

As you know, ___*address*___ has a few maintenance concerns, but that's my specialty. I'd love to put new electircal, windows, fencing, and foundation in, plus the ususal paint/etc.

As ___*my real estate agent's name*___ can testify to, I am a very active buyer here in town and always do what I say I'm going to do. I don't put properites under contract unless I'm sure I can deliver.

Hopefully this attached offer sounds reasonable to you! I know I'm offering less than you were asking, but due to the repairs needed, these are the numbers that make it work for me.

Either way—I wish you the best of luck!

I look forward to working with you.

Sincerely,

Brandon and Heather Turner

4. **Discover the Seller's True Motivation.** Always try to determine what the seller's true motivation is. Are they looking for the absolute highest price? Are they in need of a fast closing? Just yesterday, I walked through a house with someone who called me after finding my "I buy houses" website. While touring the house, I learned that the home is owned by his grandmother, who can no longer afford the tax or insurance payments on the home. They want to use the money to buy her a new car, and soon. This person's main motivation was not getting the highest price but solving a problem quickly.

5. **Feel Uncomfortable.** A real estate agent friend of mine once told me, "If I submit an offer and it doesn't make me blush, I offered too much!" In other words, when you're trying to get a good deal, submitting offers should make you a bit uncomfortable. Get out there, make some offers, blush a bit, and get a few killer good deals.

6. **All Cash Helps.** If you can afford to offer all cash on a property, this can help you get an offer accepted, even if other potential buyers have offered more. Sellers love cash buyers, because they know the money is there, and the risk that the buyer will not be able to follow through drops significantly.

7. **Remove the Financing Contingency.** Even if you can't afford to offer all cash, you can always remove the financing contingency from the offer. Of course, if you remove the financing contingency and then can't get a loan for the property, you could lose your earnest money deposit. This is a risk, of course, but if you are confident taking this risk, it can help grease the offer and help you get to "yes."

8. **Waive the Inspection Contingency.** Most sellers know that their property needs a lot of work. Therefore, sellers get nervous when people want to do an inspection of the property. They fear that they will accept an offer, and then a week later, the buyer will back out because they discovered how bad the property really is. Therefore, if you want to dramatically increase your chance of getting an offer accepted, don't include an inspection contingency. Again, this will increase your risk, because if you learn something about the condition that you did not expect, you can't back out without losing your earnest money deposit. However, removing the inspection contingency can be a powerful way to make your offer stand out.

9. **Close Faster.** Once a seller decides to sell their property, they can't wait to get that burden off their shoulders. Make your offer stand out by offering a shorter (sooner) closing date. Of course, if you are using a normal bank loan, you might not have much of a choice (banks typically take thirty to forty-five days to get through all the paperwork to buy a property). But if you are using cash, private, or hard money, set a quick close date.

10. **Give Two Offers.** When you submit an offer on a property, the seller will compare what you offered with what they are asking. If you offer $150,000 on a $190,000 house, they will instinctively do the math and say to themselves, "Wow, they are offering me $40,000 less than what

I'm asking." Instead, consider submitting two offers on a property, so the seller compares the two offers, rather than the asking price and your offer. Perhaps one offer could be for $150,000 cash, and the other for $165,000 with financing that will take 60 days to close. The seller is now trying to decide which offer is better—and ignoring their asking price. This "price anchoring" strategy is used in many different industries but only rarely in real estate (which is too bad, because it works really well).

11. **More Earnest Money.** Show the seller you are serious by offering a larger earnest money deposit. Although 1 percent to 2 percent is customary, consider offering significantly more to show the seller how dedicated you are. Just be sure you have those contingencies in place, should you later want to back out. I've even known some investors who offer all cash, with no contingencies, and they make their earnest money the exact same amount as the purchase price. In other words, they guarantee a sale in the offer. Now that is a powerful offer.

12. **Provide Your Pre-Approval Letter with the Offer.** If you'll be using bank financing for the purchase, be proactive and include a copy of your pre-approval letter with your offer. It's one thing to tell the seller that you can qualify, but it's another for them to physically hold the pre-approval letter in their hands so they *know* that the sale will go through.

13. **Include an Escalation Clause.** An escalation clause is used when a property might have multiple bidders. It essentially says, "If someone else bids higher than me, this offer will automatically increase to $X above theirs, up to a certain point." You might offer $100,000 on a property but include an escalation clause that says you will pay $500 higher than any other offer that comes in, up to $110,000. This way, if someone comes and offers $106,000, your bid will automatically increase up to $106,500. The danger of an escalation clause, of course, is that it tells the seller exactly how high you will go. Therefore, only use an escalation clause if you know there will be multiple offers, and never make your maximum price higher than what you should pay.

14. **Offer to Clean Out the Property.** Houses can accumulate a lot of stuff over time, and removing this stuff can be incredibly overwhelming for the seller. Therefore, if you are offering on a property that has a lot of junk in it, make your offer stand out by offering to clean out the property for the seller. Or, to tie in one of the tips I mentioned earlier,

give the seller two offers: one that includes junk removal and one that doesn't.

15. **Pay the Seller's Closing Costs.** Selling a home can be expensive, so if the math works for you, consider offering to pay part or all of the seller's closing costs.

16. **Offer Again.** Finally, remember this: Just because your offer was turned down, that doesn't mean you can't offer again soon. I once offered $60,000 on a property that was listed at $80,000 and was rejected. I let it go. After the property sat on the market for three more months, the seller dropped their price down to $59,000. I offered $40,000 at that point, and my offer was accepted—$20,000 less than I had originally offered to pay.

WRAPPING IT UP

Making an offer is scary, it's overwhelming, it's a big deal.

However, it's also necessary if you want to get off the sidelines and take your future by the tail so it submits to your desires. As with a marriage proposal, if you want to hear "yes," you need to first present the offer. There are no two ways about it. The dating phase is over; it's time to get serious.

Of course, certain discussions need to take place before the transaction can happen. Who's going to pay for what? When is it going to happen? How do we know this is really the right thing? In real estate, this is known as the negotiation period, and your success at this stage will determine the success of your financial future.

Chapter Twelve
REAL ESTATE NEGOTIATION

"In business as in life, you don't get what you deserve, you get what you negotiate."

—CHESTER L. KARRASS

It started with a flock of Canadian geese in the wrong place at the wrong time.

On an average, cold January afternoon in 2009, Captain Chesley "Sully" Sullenberger lifted the Airbus A320 carrying 150 passengers and four other crew members out of LaGuardia airport in New York City. At 3:27 p.m., two minutes after takeoff, the plane struck the flock of birds, which disabled both engines and caused a fire in at least one. The plane was dead in the air. Without sufficient altitude and with no power to climb much higher, Captain Sully promptly determined that returning to the airport was not an option, and only one alternative existed: a water landing on the Hudson River.

As Captain Sully lined the plane up with the water, he focused on keeping it level. Too far left or right, and the wings could hit the water first, causing the plane to tear apart. If the plane tilted down too much, it could cartwheel head over heels, killing everyone on board. If it tilted back too much, the plane's tail would catch the water, causing the Airbus to slam down on the surface with the force of a bomb. Minor adjustments were made, both by the onboard electronics and by the captain himself—a little bump left, a little bump right. At 3:29 p.m., Captain Sully radioed the three most terrifying words any airline passenger could hear: "Brace for impact."

The plane collided with the water of the Hudson River at 3:31 p.m., in full view of the lawyers, stockbrokers, and other professionals in the skyscrapers along the Manhattan skyline. Because of the precise leveling of the plane and Captain Sully's experience, the plane did not tear apart, nor did it flip. It landed perfectly on the water, and Captain Sully, along with the four other members of the crew, assisted all 150 passengers to safety. Captain Sully was an American hero.

In an interview with news anchor Katie Couric after the event, Sullenberger said, "One way of looking at this might be that, for forty-two years, I've been making small, regular deposits in this bank of experience, education, and training. And on January 15, the balance was sufficient so that I could make a very large withdrawal."

As I prepared to write this chapter on negotiation, my thoughts immediately went to the concept of an emergency water landing and the "Miracle on the Hudson." Negotiation is the art of staying steady in a turbulent situation. It's about making minor adjustments to the left, to the right, backward, and forward. It's about keeping calm when hope seems lost. It's about successfully handling the unforeseen circumstances that hit you right in the face.

Although you may never safely crash-land an airliner onto the Hudson River, I believe that you have—that every person has—the skills to become a great negotiator. All you need are "small, regular deposits into the bank of experience, education, and training."

In this chapter, I will give you that.

The Negotiation Process

In the previous chapter, I talked about the process of offering on a piece of real estate. What happens next, however, is somewhat out of your control. You wait for a response. A seller could respond to your offer in three different ways:

1. Accept it
2. Reject (or ignore) it
3. Make a counteroffer

If they accept it, great! If they reject it, that's okay; there is always another deal, or you could reoffer again when the seller wises up. However, when a seller submits a counteroffer, that's when the real fun begins.

A counteroffer (often just called a "counter") is a response to another earlier offer. In other words, if you offered $100,000 on a property, and the seller says, "No, I want $110,000," that response from the seller is the counteroffer.

In most of the deals I've offered on, the original offer has not been accepted; the same will likely be true for you. And that's not a bad thing. I argue that if your initial offer is accepted, you probably offered too much. Of course, if you are in a highly competitive market, this might not be the case, but generally, I consider a counteroffer a good thing. It means the seller wants to sell to me and is willing to find common ground where both parties can get what they want. The negotiation process is where the two sides try to make that happen. Remember, both parties want the exact same thing: a sale.

Many people see the word "negotiation," and envision one party winning and the other losing. However, in a good negotiation, both parties walk away feeling like they achieved pretty much, if not exactly, what they wanted. When there is no negotiation, that's when one of the parties tends to feel they got shafted. Remember, a little back-and-forth is a good thing. In this chapter, I will explain how to do that successfully.

Keep in mind, I'm not referring to negotiating just on the price. In fact, there are multiple parts of the contract that can be negotiated. For example, you could negotiate for any or all of the following:

- **Price.** How much are you actually going to pay for the property?
- **Closing date.** When will you close? Next week? Next month?
- **Closing location.** Where is the closing going to take place? Your title company? Theirs? An attorney's office?
- **Contingencies.** What contingencies could be removed from the P&S agreement?
- **Financing.** Will the seller agree to carry a second mortgage on the property?
- **Closing costs.** Who will pay for what during the closing process?
- **Home warranty.** A home warranty is sometimes included in the sale of a home and covers certain repair items after the sale happens. This can help smooth any concerns on the part of the buyer. Will your deal include one? If so, who will pay for it?

- **Repairs.** What do you need the seller to fix before you purchase the property? Will you hold them to it? Will you buy the property "as is"?
- **Credits.** What about getting credits at closing toward certain repairs that are needed? If a new roof is needed, and the seller doesn't want to put one on before closing, could you negotiate the cost of a new roof given to you at closing?
- **Possession date.** When will you actually take control of the property? While it's most common to transfer possession immediately after the title has been transferred, this is negotiable. Maybe the seller needs a few more weeks. Maybe you want to get in early. It's all negotiable.
- **Items left in the property.** What is the seller required to leave at the property? Appliances? Tools? Furniture? This is all negotiable.

Again, these are all elements you can negotiate, either offering or asking for a concession. (A concession is when the other party gives up something in the negotiation.) Perhaps the seller is firm on the price, but you can get more repairs done on the property before closing. Or perhaps they don't want to do anything with the condition or the price, but the seller is willing to carry a contract on the property (seller financing) for a short period while you fix it up. The possibilities are nearly endless as to what your negotiation can produce, so look at negotiation as a huge opportunity for you to creatively achieve your goals.

When you're offering on a property through the MLS, the negotiation will take place through the agents. You'll likely never sit down across from the seller to engage in some television-worthy negotiation. Instead, the negotiation will take place through a back-and-forth exchange of documents signed by you, given to your agent, sent to their agent, and finally given to the seller. The seller will then either accept, reject, or reply with a counteroffer. Your job, at that point, will be to either accept the counter, reject it, or reply with yet another counteroffer.

When offering on a property outside the MLS, through a private seller, your negotiations will likely be much more direct. In fact, you might negotiate every point on the hood of your car or sitting at the seller's kitchen table. Yesterday, I negotiated a deal while sitting inside the seller's truck, just outside the house I was buying. The back-and-forth will likely be much less formal, though I still recommend putting as much of the negotiation on paper as possible, even if that just means pulling out a sheet of blank paper and writing down the terms.

When to Negotiate

There are three primary times when you might consider negotiating the terms of the offer.

1. At the Beginning

The most intense negotiations you'll likely encounter when buying a property will happen at the beginning, immediately after you submit an offer. This is when the big items on the agenda are hashed out and your "ideal offer" is presented to the seller. You submit an offer, they counter-offer, you might counteroffer that, and so on, until either an agreement is reached or you go your separate ways.

2. After the Inspection

If the inspection reveals some defect in the property you were not expecting, you can negotiate again at this point. If you included an "inspection contingency" in your offer and you are within your inspection time frame, you can back out of the deal and will get your earnest money back. Some investors choose to negotiate very lightly at the beginning and instead push their weight around after the inspection. Personally, I don't recommend this tactic unless you absolutely have to. This is not a great time to negotiate, because at this point, you have likely spent a good deal of money on the inspection, possible appraisals, and other aspects of the deal. However, if you find something you didn't expect during the inspection, don't be afraid to renegotiate the deal. Just don't be a jerk about it.

3. Anytime!

In reality, negotiations can (and will) happen at every step of the process. Until the property's title is officially transferred from seller to buyer at closing, the real estate deal always feels as though it's balancing on the edge of a cliff, and the slightest breeze could push it over. Negotiation is about both parties keeping the deal from falling, so slight negotiation is needed throughout the process to make sure it closes.

Thirteen Tips for Successful Negotiation

Although the following tips may not work in *every* case, the more negotiation strategies you know, the better you'll be able to negotiate any deal. You'll likely find that you already use a number of these strategies in your daily life, whether negotiating with your kids, your spouse, or coworkers.

1. Be Prepared to Walk Away

Perhaps the most important negotiation strategy of all is being 100 percent prepared to walk away from a deal if you don't get what you want. When you don't need something as much as the other person, your position is strengthened. This is much more difficult than it might seem, though, especially for new investors. You work so hard to find a deal and finally locate something that might work, so you are now likely emotionally attached to the deal. You *really* want the deal to go through. I get it! But if you are desperate, you've already lost.

Also, make sure the other party knows that you are prepared to walk from the deal if you don't get what you need.

2. Know Your Role

Before going into a negotiation, and throughout the negotiation process, know your role and where you stand. What is the prize? If you walk into a negotiation like John Wayne and start demanding a ton of concessions, but the seller has five backup offers on their property because it's a seller's market, you'll just make a fool of yourself as they slam the door on your offer and turn to one of the other buyers. Have an accurate perspective on where you stand in the negotiation.

3. Always Get Last Concession

The negotiation process contains a lot of back-and-forth, asking for (and offering) concessions. For example, the seller might ask you to pay $100,000, and you can accept, but only if they pay for your closing costs. Maybe they'll come back and say, "I can't pay all of them, but I can pay some," so you can reply with, "Sure, as long as you throw in a home warranty." As J Scott, co-author of *The Book on Negotiating Real Estate,* wrote, "If the other party realizes that every time he asks for something that he will also need to give something, he will naturally shy away from asking for more than what he needs in fear that he will be asked to give up something important in return for additional (non-essential) demand on his part."

4. Find True Motivation

What does the other party really need from the negotiation? Often, the true motivation is not what you think it is. Maybe they need to close quickly, so price is less important. Maybe they don't want to lose their recurring income from their rental property, so they might be open to seller financing. Use the negotiation time to discover what their true motivation is, and try to give them what they need while you get everything else you want.

5. Use a Red Herring

This negotiation strategy is named after a technique used to train dogs for fox-hunting competitions by distracting the animal with the strong scent of a dead fish. The red herring tactic is meant to drive the negotiation to focus on something inconsequential, distracting the seller from what you really want. For example, you might really want the best price, but when you offer that low price, you also offer, and focus on, something you *know* the seller won't give up, like agreeing to leave their fine-dining china in the home. They may insist that the china is nonnegotiable, perhaps even be a little offended you asked, but it will make the low-priced offer appear even better. "This guy is crazy," they'll say. "There is no way we're giving you Grandma's fine china! We'll take the price, but we're keeping the china."

And you'll smile and accept.

6. Institute a Penalty When They Ask for Concessions

The negotiation process can be awkward and uncomfortable for all parties, but everyone wants the same thing. You can help your negotiation by making it a little more uncomfortable by instituting a penalty whenever the other party asks for a concession. A penalty could be as simple as not responding for several days or requiring your lawyer to look over the issue. This will train the other party to stop asking for concessions, because they'll quickly realize it hurts them every time they do.

7. Stick to Your Numbers

Real estate is largely a game of mathematics and numbers, so while negotiating, stick to your numbers, and don't let emotion take over. Appealing to the math is a great strategy when negotiating, because it's hard to argue with. "Mr. Seller," you'll say, "at $100,000, my expenses with taxes, insurance, vacancy, maintenance, and management will be almost $900 per month, and I can only rent the property out for $1,000 per month, which would only give me a 5 percent return on investment. This doesn't work for me. But at $90,000, it would push my return up to 9 percent, which does work for me." It's hard to argue with that.

8. Don't Get Offended

Keep the negotiation light, and don't get offended. Remember, it's all a game of back-and-forth. I've seen friends carry on negotiations that look a lot like this:

> My friend: "I can pay $100,000."
> The seller: "No, $100,000 is way too low. I need at least $120,000."
> My friend: "Screw you! You're crazy!"
> *End of negotiation.*

Don't be like my friend. Keep it light, so neither side gets offended. Your goal is to keep working the negotiation until both sides get what they want, so unbunch your panties and sit down at the negotiation table until you get what you came for.

9. Negotiate with Data

When possible, use data to negotiate your point. One of the best ways to do this when buying a piece of property is by having the comparable sales (comps) with you when negotiating. The seller may want $150,000 for their property, but if you can show them that other similar properties have sold recently for only between $120,000 and $130,000, you'll take them out of their fantasyland and ground them in cold, hard facts. It's tough to argue with data.

10. Don't Be Insulting

Don't insult the other party or their property. Don't tell them they are crazy, that their property is a pile of junk, or that they are terrible negotiators. You need to keep the other party liking you while negotiating.

11. Let the Other Party Feel Good

At the end of a good negotiation, both parties should feel as though they won and the terms are fair. You never want to leave a negotiation with the other party feeling ripped off. Therefore, be sure to give something as well when negotiating, and don't dominate every point. Let the seller believe that they are a good negotiator and got some great concessions out of you. Let them see you bleed a little bit. For example, if your maximum allowable offer on a deal is $67,000, make $62,000 your known "max offer," and let them push you a bit higher if needed. They'll feel good that they pushed you higher than you wanted, but you'll still get exactly what you wanted—they just don't know that.

12. Demonstrate Why You Are a Great Buyer

During the negotiation for a property, feel free to remind the other party often why you are a great buyer. If you are paying cash, drop that fact numerous times in the conversation. Let them know how consistent you are in your purchases, how strong your credit is, how pretty you can make houses look when fixed up. You want the other party to want to sell to you, so remind them often that you are the best. When talking with motivated sellers, I like to tell brief stories about other properties I've purchased and rehabbed, sharing how I closed so quickly and was able to help the seller out. I find ways to slip into the conversation the benefits of selling to me, without making it obvious that I'm "selling myself." This helps encourage the seller to keep negotiating and ultimately sell the property to me.

13. Ask for Their Lowest Price, Then Go Lower

When negotiating in person with a motivated seller, one tactic that works almost every time is simple: Ask the seller what their lowest price is. They'll usually tell you a number, but this is never their real lowest price—this is their starting price.

Then, ask them a follow-up question like: "Okay, but what if I could pay all cash and close next week?" They will almost always go a little lower. If you wanted to push it one more time, you could say something like, "So, if I were to offer you [amount even lower than their new lowest price] and get you the cash you need in the next ten days, that would be unreasonable?" No one likes to appear unreasonable, and there is a good chance they'll respond with, "Yeah, I could do that."

In less than one minute, you were able to talk them down twice from their "lowest price," potentially saving you thousands (or even tens of thousands) of dollars. Calculate that out to a per-hour cost, and it'll be the best, easiest money you've ever made.

WRAPPING IT UP

Like crash-landing a plane on an icy river, your goal with your negotiation is to keep it level and safely accomplish your task. Negotiation is about the give and take, the minor adjustments to the left and to the right that will help you bring your next deal to a happy landing.

However, unlike plane crashes, negotiation is not a rare occurrence. It takes place in every real estate transaction in every part of the world. It can be uncomfortable, awkward, and scary. It requires practice, patience, and guts. However, if you don't negotiate, finding a great deal and reaching your real estate goals will be incredibly hard. Overcome those fears, learn to master the art of negotiation, stick to your numbers, and go build yourself an incredible future.

Chapter Thirteen
FINANCING YOUR RENTAL PROPERTY

"Creativity is just connecting things. When you ask creative people how they did something, they feel a little guilty because they didn't really do it, they just saw something. It seemed obvious to them after a while. That's because they were able to connect experiences they've had and synthesize new things."

—STEVE JOBS

When I purchased my first home, my real estate agent gave me a $100 gift card to the local hardware store. I knew nothing about rehabbing properties, but I was ecstatic. For the first time in my life, I was going to buy *tools*. My *own* tools.

My first purchase consisted of the basics: hammer, screwdrivers, a drill, and a few miscellaneous objects I thought I might need to successfully tackle the rehab of my home. I went back to my newly purchased property and got to work. But I quickly ran into problems when my hammer and drill proved ineffective for most of what needed to be done. I found myself back at the hardware store, buying more tools so I could accomplish more tasks around the house. Over the past decade, I've acquired an entire garage of tools that allow me to handle anything from flooring to plumbing to roofing to foundations.

Understanding financing is a lot like collecting tools in a toolbox. The more tools you have, the more (and bigger) projects you'll be able to tackle, and the more successful you'll be. Since I began investing in real estate nearly a decade ago, I've purchased real estate in almost every way possible. If you are new to real estate, you might be asking yourself, "How many ways are there, really?" The answer is *a lot*.

My goal in this chapter is to educate you on all the most popular ways of financing rental properties, whether you have hundreds of thousands of dollars in the bank or just a few bucks. I'll cover traditional methods as well as more creative options, in hopes of giving you all the tools you need to tackle whatever projects are put in front of you. Let's get started with perhaps the oldest form of financing: cash.

All Cash

Many investors choose to pay all cash for an investment property. In 2012, BiggerPockets and Memphis Invest conducted a nationwide survey of American citizens and discovered a number of interesting facts, including that 24 percent of U.S. real estate investors were using 100 percent cash to finance their investments.

To be clear, even when investors use terms like "all cash," the truth is, no "cash" is actually traded. In most cases, the buyer brings a check (usually certified funds, such as a bank cashier's check) to the title company, and the title company writes a check to the seller. Other times, the money is sent via a wire transfer from the bank.

This is the easiest form of financing, because there are typically no complications, but for most investors (and probably the *vast* majority of new investors), all cash is not an option. However, let's talk about this for a moment longer.

There exists a debate in the investment world about using cash for a property versus getting a loan. In one camp, you have the "no-debt" people, who say a person should only invest in rental properties if they can pay all cash for the deal. The "leverage" camp responds with the math that shows that a person using leverage can obtain a much better ROI by using a loan. The no-debt camp fires back, "But 100 percent of foreclosures happen to people with debt." And the debate rages. Who is right? If you had $100,000, would it be better to buy one house for $100,000 or five houses with a $20,000 down payment on each?

Once again, I don't believe there is a right answer, but rather a right answer for you. In other words, what works for me might not work for you. Your decision to use debt will depend heavily on your personal finances, your goals, your age, and other key factors.

Using all cash is safer in some regards, of course. If you owned a piece of property worth $100,000 without a mortgage, you could easily sell the property if you needed to. If the property was tough to rent out, you could afford making the tax and insurance payment to keep the property floating until a renter began to pay. For simplicity, let's say that the house rented for $1,200 per month, taxes and insurance were $200 per month, and all other expenses, over time, averaged $400 per month (repairs, vacancy, CapEx, maintenance, etc.). This means your total expenses on the property, not including the mortgage, would be $600 per month, and your cash flow would be $600 per month, or $7,200 per year. While this isn't a bad amount of cash flow, it represents just a 7.2 percent cash-on-cash ROI.

On the other hand, let's say you bought this same property using a 20 percent down payment loan, meaning you took out an $80,000 mortgage. Eighty thousand dollars at 4.5 percent interest for 30 years is about $400 per month. Add that $400 to the $600 in expenses we already assumed, and you are at $1,000 per month in total expenses with the mortgage in place, leaving you with $200 per month in cash flow, or just $2,400 per year—far less, of course, than the $7,200 per year we saw with the all-cash purchase. However, $2,400 in cash flow on a $20,000 investment represents a 12 percent cash-on-cash ROI—a pretty drastic difference.

Maybe the difference between 7.2 percent and 12 percent doesn't seem that drastic, but check out this chart on the next page that shows what a $100,000 investment, over 30 years, looks like at 7.2 percent and 12 percent.

Clearly, leverage can increase the ROI with the property. But is the increase worth the increased risk you are also taking? That's a question for you to decide, so let me mention a few more possible concerns with paying all cash for a property.

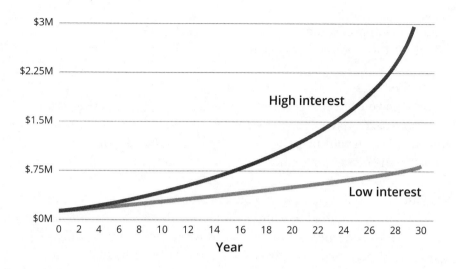

In Chapter 1, I talked about the four wealth generators of rental properties. Those were:

- appreciation
- cash flow
- tax savings
- loan paydown

We've already seen that paying all cash can help you get a higher cash flow dollar amount but potentially a lower cash-on-cash ROI. But let's look at how it affects the other three wealth generators.

Appreciation

The property will appreciate at the same amount whether you have a loan or not. But, again, what actually changes is the ROI. If you paid $100,000 for the property with all cash, and in one year, the property value climbs to $110,000, you have effectively increased your wealth by 10 percent and made $10,000 in equity. If you used that 20 percent down payment and only spent $20,000 on the property, and the value then climbed to $110,000, you'd have also made $10,000 in equity. But you've made $10,000 in equity and only invested $20,000, which means you've increased your wealth by 50 percent. Of course, the leverage game works both ways: If the property were to decrease in value, you could be looking at a catastrophic loss in value. However, if you are following the rest of the guidelines in this book and are buying great rental property deals, and if the appreciation is only the icing on the cake, you could continue holding until the value rose again.

Tax Savings

Although you will still get the depreciation benefit if you own a property free and clear, you will no longer be able to deduct the mortgage interest payment from your taxes, so you will likely end up paying the IRS each year on the money you make from your rental property. In the example of the $100,000 house, with the all-cash offer, the owner was clearing around $7,200 per year but can only deduct approximately $3,000 from depreciation, leaving them with a tax bill at the end of the year on their profit. However, when using leverage, the cash flow comes to only $2,400 per year after all expenses. At this point, the $3,000 deduction for depreciation would show a paper loss on the property, and no taxes would likely be due (depending on numerous factors, such as the percentage of the mortgage payment that was interest compared to principal). Again, keep in mind that this is a very simplistic discussion on depreciation, and you should consult with a CPA for more information.

Loan Paydown

Of course, if you have no loan on the property, you have no loan pay-down. You have essentially killed one of the four wealth generators. In the example of the $100,000 property, the tenant is paying off that $80,000 mortgage little by little, which increases your total return. Although you started with a mortgage of $80,000, after ten years, you might owe only $65,000 on the property, increasing your net worth by $15,000 because your tenant paid the mortgage each month. After 30 years (or whatever loan length you used), the property is 100 percent paid off, and you never (hopefully) had to make that payment yourself. (Of course, you are still physically making the payment, but it's your tenant's rent that is covering that payment.)

Liability with Cash Offers

Finally, let's talk about one more reason you may or may not want to use cash: liability.

When investing in real estate, there is a very good chance that some-day, someone will try to sue you. When you own a property free and clear, this is typically evident on the public record, because there is no bank lien on the property. Therefore, you are essentially holding up a sign that says, "I have lots of money that you can try to take!" If a disgruntled tenant approaches a lawyer to try to sue you, which scenario do you think will make the lawyer more excited to go after you: you have $100,000 of equity in a property or $20,000 of equity in a property? If the latter, the lawyer would understand that even if he did win the lawsuit, the most they could do is force the sale of the property, probably at a discount. After all the closing costs, there would be little or no meat left on the bone. Therefore, lawyers (especially those paid on the outcome of a lawsuit, as most lawyers of this type are) are reluctant to pursue rental owners who have a lot of leverage.

It may seem to you that I'm trying to influence you one way or another on using leverage, but honestly, that's not my goal. There are more important things in life than maximizing your ROI. Security, flexibility, and the "happy wife, happy life" (or happy husband) philosophy may matter to you more than maximizing your return. Maybe that 7.2 percent cash-on-cash return, for example, combined with the possible appreciation on the deal, would be more than enough for you. Great! My goal in this section was to simply share with you the benefits and risks of both options.

That said, here are a couple quick tips if you do plan to use all cash on your investment properties:

1. **Pretend You Aren't.** Using all cash makes people lazy. When buyers can simply write a check for a property, it's natural not to have the same motivation to find an incredible deal. Therefore, when buying a property for all cash, pretend you are *not* doing so. Run the numbers as though you had to obtain 100 percent financing for the property. Would it still cash flow? If not, you may want to think twice about buying it. Analyze your cash-on-cash return, and make sure you aren't using your all-cash purchase to justify a bad deal.

2. **Use Entities Wisely.** If you are going to own properties free and clear, at least try to hide the fact. Talk with your CPA and lawyer to discover the best way to hide your ownership from the public record.

3. **Consider Financing Later.** Using all cash when making an offer can help you get better deals because sellers love cash offers. However, just because you bought a property with all cash, that doesn't mean you have to keep it that way. You can place financing on the property after the purchase (usually six to twelve months later, depending on

the bank) and start taking advantage of the benefits of using leverage. It can be the best of both worlds. And if you are concerned about the risk, also understand that the financing doesn't need to be 80 percent. Maybe you want to obtain a 50 percent loan, or a 30 percent loan, or a 70 percent loan. The options are plentiful.

Using all cash is just one option for financing real estate, and for most people, the possibility doesn't even exit. Let's talk about some of the other strategies for financing real estate, beginning with a conventional loan.

Conventional Loans

Conventional loans are the standard loans you might obtain from a local bank, credit union, or mortgage lender. They are very similar to the kind of mortgage you would obtain when buying a home to live in. The bank or lender who lent the money on your own home (if you have obtained a mortgage in the past) can probably lend on your rental property, too. However, although loans on primary residences tend to have some fabulous low down payment options, with a conventional rental property loan, you will need to come up with a sizable down payment, typically 20 percent to 30 percent, depending on the lender. In addition, a conventional loan will require you to meet a certain debt-to-income requirement, income level, and other metrics (which I'll cover a lot more in the next chapter).

How Conventional Loans Work

When a lender creates a mortgage for you, it's actually fairly likely that they will sell the loan. In fact, that's the primary job of most lenders: issue a bunch of mortgages, package them together with a big bow, and sell the loan package so the lenders get their money back. The most likely buyer of these loan packages are the two government-sponsored enterprises Fannie Mae and Freddie Mac, the nicknames given to the Federal National Mortgage Association (FNMA, or Fannie Mae) and the Federal Home Loan Mortgage Corporation (FHLMC, or Freddie Mac). The purpose of these huge pseudo government institutions is to buy up mortgages from lenders so the lenders can get their money back and can re-loan again.

As such, Fannie Mae and Freddie Mac, like any other mortgage buyer, want to know exactly what they are getting, so they have strict requirements on what they will and will not buy. They'll define loan amount ranges, borrower credit score minimums, loan-to-value minimums, and other requirements. Again, I'll cover each of these much more specifically in the next chapter, but my point here is to let you know: If you plan to go conventional, you must be a round peg to fit their round hole. No square pegs allowed.

The Conventional Lending Process in Seven Steps

Getting a conventional loan is not a complicated process, but there are a lot of moving parts. Allow me to give you a quick summary of the entire process, so you'll best know what to expect when getting your loan.

Step One: Shop

When shopping for a conventional loan, I recommend beginning your loan search before you get your property under contract. After all, the bank needs to approve both you *and* the deal before lending, so you might as well get the first half of that equation out of the way to make sure you aren't wasting anyone's time. It would be best to know before shopping for a deal whether or not your credit score is high enough to secure that deal.

Start with the bank that you already have your primary checking account with. Schedule an appointment with the loan officer, and actually sit down with them. Ask them what kind of loan programs they have for rental property loans. Ask them the rental property loan amounts they typically lend on, the current interest rates, the term, and any other information. Have the same conversation with three or four other lenders in your area, and be sure to mix it up between banks, credit unions, and mortgage companies. Once you have the basics from each company, pick one and get pre-qualified.

Step Two: Pre-Approval

Getting pre-qualified means obtaining a conditional "yes" from the bank before you even find a deal by bringing in all your financial paperwork. In other words, the bank approves *you* before they even see whatever property you hope to buy. Now, of course, the deal will need to make sense to them, but getting yourself and your financials approved is the most difficult part. Of course, it's possible to skip the pre-approval and just bring a deal and your paperwork in, but when you're hunting for a killer real estate deal, this pre-approval can help a lot.

Step Three: Submit the Property Information
Once you find your deal, it's time to get the second half of your approval equation started: the approval of the property. The lender will require you to submit (or have your real estate agent submit) information about the property, most likely the P&S agreement. The lender may also want to see additional documents from you if it's been awhile since you got pre-approved (such as updated pay stubs and bank account information).

Step Four: Loan Goes to Underwriting
When all the information has been gathered, it is sent to the lender's underwriter, who will give the final "yes" or "no" on the loan. It's likely that, during this time, the underwriter will make you jump through numerous hoops before giving you the loan. In the next chapter, I will go into more detail on this process and how to ensure that you get a "yes."

Step Five: Lender Issues an Appraisal
The lender will likely hire a residential real estate appraiser to give them a valuation of the property. The lender's goal, of course, is to be secure in their investment, so they want to make sure they are not loaning more on the property than they should (and also that the property is in good enough condition for them to loan on). A typical single-family house appraisal will cost approximately $400, while a small multifamily appraisal might cost up to $1,000. If you are buying a commercial property, expect to be in for at least $4,000. This appraisal cost is not generally fronted by the lender, but you will be required to pay this before the appraiser will go out. This, of course, is to protect the lender from spending money on an appraiser and then having the loan not go through.

Step Six: Loan Goes Back to Underwriting
After the appraisal is complete, the underwriter once again reviews all the documents for the property, including the information just obtained in the appraisal, and decides whether or not they want to take the risk of lending to you. They may, once again, ask for you to jump through certain hoops. For example, I once had an appraiser require that the gutter downspouts on a property have "splash blocks" installed before they would issue a "yes" on the loan. They also, again, may want to see more pay stubs or other financials from you. Just get them what they need, and do it as quickly as possible. The biggest delay in the underwriting

process is usually the borrower needing to get paperwork to the lender, so don't be a clog in your own pipe. Ultimately, underwriting will either approve or deny the loan.

Step Seven: Loan Closes
If the loan is approved, the bank will let you or your real estate agent know. The title company or attorney will also be informed, and closing will take place soon after. At the closing table (typically at your title company or attorney's office), you will bring a check for the down payment, and your lender will wire over the funds for the purchase. The title company or attorney will take care of the paperwork, and you'll be the owner of a new property.

The Pros and Cons of Conventional Lending

Although conventional lending is perhaps the most common type of real estate loan, it may or may not be the best option for you. There are both advantages and disadvantages to be aware of before obtaining a loan, and the more aware you are, the better loan decisions you can make.

Pros
- **Low Interest Rates.** There's no denying it: Conventional loans likely have the best rates you'll find for long-term real estate financing. With investment loans usually .5 to 1 point higher than owner-occupied loans, you can borrow money at incredibly low rates. This will help keep your mortgage payment low and thereby maximize your cash flow.
- **Long Terms.** When you borrow from a conventional lender, your loan will likely be able to extend for a long term, maybe even up to thirty years if you're buying a residential property. This can help keep your payment low, though it will also extend the amount of time you'll have debt on the house.
- **Professional.** A conventional lender is in the business of lending, so the entire process is much more defined and professional than a relationship-based loan would be. This isn't the lender's first rodeo.

Cons
- **Max Number of Loans.** Conventional loans may have great terms and rates, but real estate investors are capped on the number of

conventional loans they can have. The current limit has been raised to ten loans, though many investors are not even able to get to that limit because of the rise in their debt-to-income (DTI) ratios. In other words, for every loan you obtain (debt), the percentage of your debt to your W-2 income rises, until you are pushed out of the "acceptable" range defined by the conventional lender. I'll talk more about this DTI issue in the next chapter.

- **Slow Process.** Conventional loans are not fast to obtain. Because of the legal scrutiny your loan must go through and the mounds of paperwork you must provide, the process of obtaining a loan can be arduous, usually taking thirty days or more.

- **Property Condition.** Conventional lenders only want to lend on properties that are in good shape. This can rule out a lot of the best properties for investors, because we tend to focus on properties that are in terrible condition so we can improve their quality and value. If the property is missing any of the basic necessities for home living (for example, it has bad flooring, a poor paint job, a leaky roof), the bank will likely not fund the deal until the issue is fixed.

- **Not Very Entity-Friendly.** Conventional lenders are also not very fond of loaning on properties owned by an entity, such as an LLC or corporation, especially for residential loans. In other words, if you want to keep your name off the public record and add some asset protection by purchasing the property with your LLC, a conventional lender will likely never do it. You could, as many investors do, buy the property in your personal name and then transfer it to your LLC, but you put yourself at risk of having the "due on sale" clause called by the bank. The due on sale clause is a part of nearly every mortgage's paperwork that says, "If you sell or transfer the property, we have the right to call your loan due now or foreclose on you." This has been happening more and more lately in the real estate space, so I can't suggest that this is a good idea. Be sure to talk to a lawyer and CPA who can help you sort these types of issues out. But the point is this: Conventional lenders don't like entities.

Should you use a conventional loan? Personally, I love getting conventional loans if I can get them. However, those days have long since passed for me, because I've hit the limit on the number of conventional loans I can obtain. If you are still able to do so, I would strongly encourage you to use a conventional loan for your next property. Very few financing strategies can live up to the low cost and stability of a conventional loan.

Let's now talk about another loan that operates very similarly to a conventional loan but that avoids some of the disadvantages conventional loans have.

Portfolio Lenders

In the previous section, I discussed how most financial lenders sell their loans in packages to Fannie Mae and Freddie Mac. As a result, those conventional lenders must abide by the strict rules handed down from those government-sponsored enterprises. However, not all banks operate the same way. Some banks choose to instead hold on to their loans and keep the money in the community. These are known as portfolio lenders, and they can be powerful allies for a growing real estate investor.

Because these portfolio lenders keep some of their loans "on their own books" (in their own portfolio of loans), they don't have to fit into the same government-prescribed box. Instead, because they are lending their own money, they can be a lot more creative. The maximum rule of four or ten properties? Not with a portfolio lender. The DTI (debt-to-income) problem? This is easily explained to a portfolio lender. Can you see how powerful these lenders can be?

Keep in mind, I'm not suggesting that a portfolio loan is easier to qualify for. Portfolio lenders still have minimum qualifications that must be met, and your loan will still need to be approved by the portfolio lender's board or underwriters. Don't think that a 520 credit score will work, and don't assume you'll be able to get a zero-percent-down loan. In these categories, the lender might even be stricter, but the rules are much more flexible, and you will likely be dealing with a person, not a faceless corporation.

How to Find a Portfolio Lender

Before the real estate crash of 2007 and 2008, there were many more portfolio lenders operating in the United States. Today, you will have to search a little harder. None of the "big banks" (the national ones with television commercials) will do portfolio lending. Instead, you'll want to focus your search on small, local community banks. Look for banks that have a maximum of twenty different branches. Credit unions might also be a good source of portfolio lending.

Of course, portfolio lenders will not be labeled as such. No brochure in their lobby will use the words "portfolio lender," and no category in the yellow pages will list them for you. Instead, you'll simply need to call them up and find out. In episode six of the *BiggerPockets Podcast*, investor Arthur Garcia talked about how he did just this. He picked up the phone book, called every lender listed, and simply asked, "Do you do any portfolio lending?" Eventually, he found a great portfolio lender in his area, ironically based out of a Walmart.

If you follow this strategy, just be sure to do the following:

1. Ask to speak with the loan officer, because the teller will likely have no idea how to help you.
2. Even the loan officer might not be familiar with the term "portfolio lender," so you may need to explain exactly what you mean and what you are seeking.

Portfolio lenders are often both conventional and portfolio lenders, and they can put you into whichever loan fits your needs best. Also, keep in mind that portfolio loans may be slightly higher in rate and shorter in term, or they may involve a balloon payment. (A balloon payment is a "due date" on a loan that is shorter than the amortized term. For example, you may have a thirty-year fixed-rate loan, but if it has a ten-year balloon, you must pay the entire balance of the loan off at year ten, most likely through a refinance.)

Portfolio lenders have been incredibly helpful in my own investing career, and if you can build a solid relationship with a portfolio lender, I think you'll have the same experience. Get out there this week, and start building that relationship.

Now, let's talk about a form of lending that doesn't involve a bank or credit union: private lenders.

Private Lenders

What is private lending?

Private lending is exactly what it sounds like: borrowing money from private individuals rather than from institutional lenders. Private lending is used all over the world by real estate investors and is, perhaps, the oldest of all forms of lending. Generally speaking, when investors use the words "private lending," they are referring to lending based heavily on relationships. Although the most common form of private lending is typically through family or friends, it doesn't have to be. You could borrow money from pretty much any person, anywhere, and as long as that entity is not a bank, mortgage company, or something similar, that transaction could be called private lending.

To illustrate how private lending works, let me tell you a story about a deal I'm putting together right now. The Cedar house is located about half a mile from my personal house in a great location. This 1960s-style house needs basic updating, including fresh paint and carpet, but it also needs new siding, new windows, and a new garage door. Now, if I wanted to, I could go to a local bank and drop 20 percent or 25 percent on a down payment for the property, and come up with the repair money out-of-pocket after closing. That is, of course, if the bank would lend on the house at all. After all, as I explained earlier, banks don't like to lend on properties that need work. Instead, I'm turning to private lending.

Through the reputation I built for myself on BiggerPockets, I received notices from several individuals who were interested in talking more about lending. These were not bankers, but just people looking for a good investment for their money. After several conversations with different lenders, I felt a strong connection with one in particular, and we're now in the process of closing on this deal. They'll lend the purchase price and maybe even the repair money, and I'll get into the house for little out-of-pocket money. Then, each month, rather than paying a bank the mortgage payment, I'll pay this individual the mortgage payment. In a year or so, after a period of "seasoning," I'll go to a bank and get a traditional thirty-year mortgage on the property; then, I'll pay off the private lender, drop my interest rate, and increase my cash flow.

Typically, a private money lender is looking for a fairly short-term loan, but this is not always the case. Some investors are in this lending game for the long haul. If you find these lenders, hang on tight and treat them right. They can be pure gold to you.

Now, let's address a fundamental question involving private lenders: Why would someone lend their money to you through a private loan, rather than placing it in the stock market or funding their own real estate deals?

- **Higher Return.** Private lenders lend money because they want a good ROI. Perhaps they believe they can get a higher return by investing with you than by putting the money in the stock market or somewhere else. Although private lending rates are not standard and are, essentially, whatever is negotiated, these rates are usually higher than a borrower would get from a bank or mortgage company. The most common private money rates I see fall between 6 percent and 12 percent, depending on the relationship.

- **Security.** Let's say a person places their cash in the stock market, investing in ABC Soda Company, and the very next week, the CEO of ABC Soda is photographed snorting drugs in a brothel, which drives the company's stock price down 80 percent. There is little the investor can do but pull their money out and take the loss. However, if you pull the same stunt and end up not paying your lender, the lender has far more security: the property. In other words, on a typical private lending deal, the lender will have a lien on the property, so if you don't live up to your end of the deal, they can take the house, sell it, and get their money back.
- **Passivity.** Private lending rates very high on the "scale of passivity." In other words, it requires very little physical or mental work over the long run to achieve a solid return. The lender is not crawling under houses. They are not yelling at contractors. They are not picking up rent checks and filing for evictions. They are walking out to their mailbox and picking up a check, and with direct deposit these days, they might not even be doing that much work. Of course, if the borrower does not pay, the level of passivity decreases dramatically, because the lender will need to take steps to get their money back, likely through foreclosure on the property. However, a lawyer typically handles that process.

Private versus Hard Money Lending

I feel it's probably a good idea to talk briefly here about the difference between hard money and private money. Both terms are tossed around interchangeably in the real estate industry, and there is a lot of confusion about the difference. Let me try to sort this out a bit.

Hard money is a form of private lending, and private lending is a form of hard money lending. There are a lot of similarities, and a lot of crossover, but most investors would agree to the following:

- *Hard money lending* is the process of borrowing money from a professional private lender, with the bulk of the lending decision based on the hard asset being bought. In other words, hard money lenders are professionals who lend out their own money, or other people's money, for a living. They have a set way of doing things, a predefined interest rate, a predefined set of fees (points), and a very short term (usually less than one year).

- *Private lending* is the process of borrowing money from nonprofessional lenders, so that the bulk of the lending decision is based on the relationship between the borrower and lender, but enhanced by the hard asset being bought. In other words, private lenders are lending their own money but don't typically do so for a living. They might be retired, or they might work a normal 9-to-5 job. The rates, fees, and terms are usually lower and much more negotiable.

Again, the difference between hard money lending and private lending is not always black and white, and some lenders fall somewhere in the gray middle. In the end, though, what they call themselves doesn't matter much. The questions are these: How much is it going to cost, and does the math still work for you?

Where to Find Private Lenders

Private lenders are everywhere.

A recent study by the U.S. Department of Labor and Training showed that 22 percent of American workers have at least $100,000 in their retirement fund. With 154 million workers in America, that means more than 30 million Americans have $100,000-plus in their retirement accounts, being shaken around by the stock market or collecting low fixed returns from CDs, annuities, savings accounts, or other conservative investments.

These individuals are in your grocery line, at your church, part of your local civic club, in your family. Anyone with a good chunk of money tied up in IRAs, savings accounts, or under a mattress could be a private lender. However, not just any rich person is ideal to work with. You'll want to find individuals who are easy to work with and understand that there is risk. You don't want to borrow Grandma's last dollar.

But how do you recognize these lenders? It's true, they don't wear a sign around their necks. Instead, you must let them come to you. Follow this simple three-step process:

1. Go to where private lenders might be.
2. Build your brand.
3. Ask.

Of course, this is easier said than done, so let me expound on it. First, you must go to where private lenders might be. This means getting out there and networking. Attend your local real estate club. Hang out in the BiggerPockets Forums. Attend civic events in your area. Next, talk about what you do. Don't brag, but simply let your passion for real estate shine through. And third, don't be afraid to ask people if they would consider private lending. This is the most crucial part of the entire process, so let's focus on "the ask."

In my previous book, I shared a strategy I like to use:

> "When talking with people about your business, it's a good idea to say something like, 'So, if you know anyone who's interested in lending on deals like this and working with me, definitely give them my number.' This opens up the conversation so they can say, 'You know, I might actually be interested in something like that' or 'I know a guy who very well might be interested.' Either way, the seed has been planted, and you didn't come across as begging for money—and you may just find some really valuable clients."

Of course, when you are just starting out and don't have a brand to build, this can be challenging. You may need to develop that brand first, through partnerships, doing small deals with hard money, or by just becoming the most knowledgeable guy or gal in the room.

How to Get Private Lenders to Say Yes

Anyone can ask someone to lend them money. I get asked all the time. I usually turn them down, though, and you will be turned down, too, unless you understand what the lender wants. The goal of a private lending relationship is to create a win-win solution for both parties, but to understand what "win-win" is, you need to have a firm grasp on what a private lender is seeking. To help illustrate this, I'll outline eight different things killing your private money chances, and I'll share how you can overcome these roadblocks so you hear a "yes" every time.

1. **Not Having a Deal.** First, if you are struggling to get financing, the simple answer might be that you don't have a good enough deal. The solution, of course, is to go out there and find an incredible deal. Run it by a few other experienced investors and see what they think. Is it *really* going to be a solid investment?

2. **Not Hanging with the Right People.** Who are you associating with? If you spend all your time hanging around your video game buddies,

it's unlikely you will meet the kind of people who will eventually fund your deal. Get out there and start networking with folks who are more successful than you.

3. **Not Building Your Personal Brand.** Here's the cold, hard truth: People don't lend money to people they don't trust. To build trust, you must build your personal brand, which is made up of your experience, knowledge, and the way you present yourself. Start building your personal brand today. Imagine a colleague of yours is telling one of their friends about you. What would they say? Is it, "That guy is hilarious on Friday nights!" or "That guy is wicked smart with real estate." That latter statement is the brand you need to build.

4. **Not Building Relationships.** In item two of this list, I talked about hanging out with the right people, but networking doesn't help if you don't start deepening those relationships. Get to know the people you are talking with on a deeper level. Take them out for coffee. Call them on the phone. Chat with them on BiggerPockets. Before you can expect someone to trust you with their money, you need to first build a solid relationship with them.

5. **Bad Math.** Math is incredibly important when buying rental property, and bad math can lead to bad deals and financial loss. To maximize your chance of getting private lending on a deal, be sure your math is solid. Prove to the lender that you'll make the profit you need. Of course, I recommend using the BiggerPockets Rental Property Calculator for doing this, but however you do the math, make sure you do it right.

6. **Asking Them to Take on Too Much Risk.** Private lenders need to be secure in their investments, so be sure that you are not asking them to take on an inordinate amount of risk. There are numerous ways to decrease their risk, such as lowering the loan amount, increasing the amount of money you are putting down, and requesting the repair money in draws after the repairs have been completed.

7. **Not Presenting the Deal Right.** Your deal might be great, but if you can't effectively communicate this to your lender, your chance of getting a "yes" is diminished. When presenting your deal, you need to abide by the five Cs of deal presentation, which are as follows:
   - **Confidence.** When you present the deal, are you confident in the numbers? If you aren't confident in the deal, why should they be confident in lending to you?

- **Clarity.** Is the information clear? Can the private lender clearly see the amount they need to lend, the ROI they'll receive, the income, the expenses, and any other pertinent information? If not, make this information clearer.
- **Conciseness.** Don't make the private lender sift through a document that is 200 pages long. Yes, they should have all the information they might need, but make the presentation concise so the information is easy to digest.
- **Convenience.** How easy is it for the lender to get the information they need? Don't make them sift through twenty different documents and webpages to learn what they need to know. Make it stupidly simple for them to access the data they must have to make a decision.
- **Creativity.** Finally, creativity. Although it's certainly possible to present a deal in a boring black-and-white spreadsheet, I really want to emphasize the use of great design in your presentation. How does your presentation look? Is it a bunch of chicken-scratch handwriting on the back of a cable bill? Or is it laid out nicely, with photos, charts, graphs, and easy-to-follow numbers? Design matters more than you think, so be sure your presentation is aesthetically pleasing.

8. **Not Asking.** Finally, this may be both the simplest and the most difficult part: ask! If you are having trouble getting private funding, it may simply be because you are too nervous to ask, so ask. Yes, you'll get rejected, but if you've followed the seven previous steps, you'll have a much greater chance of hearing "yes."

If you decide to use private lending to fund your next investment, you can usually have your attorney or title company prepare the note and deed of trust (or whatever recording method your state uses). The private lender will likely get a first-position lien on the property, and all the financing details will be handled through the closing process. You'll then make your payment to the private lender each month until the loan is paid off.

Private lending can be a terrific way to fund real estate deals, but it does take work. You'll need to build relationships, find great deals, and then execute the deal as flawlessly as possible. However, if you're willing to put in the work, you can find an inexhaustible source of funds for your real estate deals.

Let's talk about some other methods you might use to fund your rental property purchases.

Other Creative Methods

The methods I've outlined thus far are some of the most common for financing real estate, but they don't paint the whole picture of available financing methods. One of the things that makes real estate investing so exciting is the creativity one can implement to fund deals. In truth, your ability to fund is limited only by your imagination (and the law, of course), so the purpose of this section is to expand your mind and allow you to explore the more "creative" side of real estate.

Home Equity

If you own your own home, you may be able to use some of the equity in your home to purchase rental properties. As I've discussed before in this book, equity means the spread between what is owed on a property and what the property could sell for. In other words, if you owe $80,000 on your primary residence but it could sell for $200,000, you have $120,000 in equity. This equity can be borrowed against at very low interest rates through a home equity loan or home equity line of credit at your local bank or credit union. You may also see these loan products referred to as a "second mortgage," because the lender will place a lien on the property that is in second place to the primary loan on your house.

A home equity loan and a home equity line of credit are similar but have a few major differences. The loan is typically taken out all at one time and paid back in installments until it is paid off, much like a typical mortgage or car loan. The interest rate and payment are generally fixed for the life of the loan (but they don't have to be). A home equity line of credit, on the other hand, is a revolving account that works much like a credit card. You can borrow as much as you want, up to the limit, pay it back, and then borrow again. You pay interest only on the amount that is currently borrowed, so you could leave the balance at $0 until you need it. These lines of credit generally have lower interest rates than home equity loans, but since they are typically variable, they can rise or fall.

Partnerships

Partnerships have been one of my favorite creative methods of investing in real estate over the past decade, because even though I'm good at a lot of real estate things, I have a lot of shortcomings as well. Partnerships can be valuable tools when investing in rental properties, because two people can work together to cover for each other's shortcomings and do some amazing things. For example, if one person is great at getting a mortgage but has no time to find or manage deals, they could partner with someone who struggles with getting a loan but has more flexibility and knowledge to handle putting the deal together and managing it. Or perhaps both parties put in 50 percent of the income and split the responsibilities 50 percent also, making less work and less income for both partners.

If you plan to use a partner to invest in real estate, take incredible care in picking the right partner. Never pick a partner based on convenience; rather, choose a person because they are someone you would enjoy working with and because they have something you need, while you have something they need. Pick a partner the same way you would pick a spouse—after a lot of careful consideration. This is especially true when investing in long-term buy-and-hold real estate, because you'll be attached to this person for many years. You don't want to end up with a partner for the next twenty years with whom you don't get along. Be sure that your goals and work ethic are in near-perfect sync and that your roles are carefully defined (on paper) before buying a single piece of property. Have a lawyer write up a partnership agreement to protect you both, because as my friend Chris Clothier likes to say, "Every partnership will end. You decide at the beginning how it is going to end."

Seller Financing

When a seller owns a piece of real estate free and clear (meaning they have no mortgage on the property they own), they can sell the property using seller financing, which can be a really powerful method for investing in real estate without having to work with a bank. In seller financing, the owner sells the property to you, but they also act as the bank, so your mortgage is paid to them every month rather than to another lender. The title is transferred into your name, but the previous owner holds a lien on the property (a mortgage) so that if you don't pay, they can foreclose, just as a bank would. Once the loan is paid off (usually though a refinance or when the property is sold), the lien is released, and the two parties go their separate ways.

Seller financing can be a great win-win for both the buyer and the seller. The buyer can purchase a property without needing to go to a bank, fill out the paperwork, get approved, get an appraisal done, and provide a large down payment. The seller can go from "owner" to "lender" and start receiving monthly passive checks in the mail that are secured by real estate.

I purchased my twenty-four-unit apartment complex just after I turned 25 using seller financing. I put $15,000 down and the sellers financed the $550,000 purchase. A few years later, the property appraised for $900,000, and I was able to get a new loan for $650,000 through a local bank, keeping the $100,000 difference. This has helped me get into even more properties while still owning the twenty-four-unit one. And it was made possible through seller financing.

House Hacking

If you are just getting started on your real estate journey, one of the best ways to finance your real estate deal is through the process of house hacking.

House hacking refers to the unique strategy of combining your primary residence with an investment. There are two primary ways this can be accomplished:

1. **Live-In Flip.** Buy a single-family house with the intention of fixing it up and reselling it within a couple of years.
2. **Small Multifamily Property.** Buy a small multifamily property (two to four units), live in one unit, and rent the other units out.

My first two deals represented both sides of the house hacking coin. I was 22 years old and had purchased, fixed up, and sold my first property—my primary residence—clearing $20,000 in the process. I had successfully invested in my first property, but suddenly I found myself facing the very real possibility that I was going to be homeless. Sure, I could go find a place to rent, but I had been bitten by the real estate bug and knew that real estate investing was going to be my ticket to financial freedom.

I read a few books on the topic of buying a duplex, triplex, or four-plex so I knew that there was potential in a small multifamily property. I called my agent, found a small duplex that was a bank repo, and purchased it for $80,000. I spent a few weeks cleaning it up, painting it, and doing small maintenance work, and then I rented it out. My total mortgage payment was a little over $600 per month, and I rented the front house out for approximately that same amount—meaning I was living almost for free (just paying utilities). A year later, I moved and rented out the house I was living in, and ever since, I have been receiving significant cash flow each and every month, and I will continue to for the rest of my life, or for as long as I own the property.

I included the strategy of house hacking here in the financing portion of this book because of the relatively easy financing given to homeowners and the power this can have for investors who are willing to house hack. Financing through an FHA loan can get you into a property for just 3.5 percent down. In other words, if you buy a $200,000 triplex, you'll only need to come up with $7,000 plus closing costs to get into a thirty-year low-rate fixed mortgage. After one year, you can move out and keep the loan in place for as long as you need. This one loan can be a fantastic way to jump-start your investing career. However, keep in mind that the FHA currently only allows you to have one FHA loan in your name at any given time, so this is not a pattern that can be repeated over and over, unless you refinance out of the previous loan before undertaking the next.

House hacking can provide several other unique benefits, including the following:

- Great cash flow
- Rent paid to yourself, rather than some landlord
- The ability to gain multiple units in one transaction
- The ability to live free or cheap while the other tenant pays your bills
- A low-risk introduction to the world of landlording
- Relatively easy leasing of the unit(s)

Finally, know that simply buying a small multifamily to house hack is not the secret to success. If you buy a bad deal, you might as well keep renting. However, if you do your homework, shop smart, and snag a great deal, house hacking can be incredibly powerful in helping you build financial freedom.

BRRRR Investing

The final financing option I want to discuss here is not a type of loan but rather a strategy that combines several of the methods already mentioned into one. I call it BRRRR (short for Buy, Rehab, Rent, Refinance, Repeat) real estate investing, but it has also been called a "fix and rent" or "fix and hold" strategy. We looked at this strategy back in Chapter 3, but I want to touch on it here again for those who want to use this strategy to finance their deals. It combines the equity growth and quick financing of house flipping with the long-term stability and wealth creation of rental properties—a perfect hybrid of the two.

In BRRRR real estate investing, the property is treated like a flip, using short-term financing such as private money, hard money, a home equity loan, or cash to acquire and rehab. Then, after the property has been finished, it is rented out to a tenant. The owner then obtains a refinance on the property to pay off the short-term loan and turn the property into a stable, long-term, cash-flow-positive property.

Of course, as with all investments, the math has to work for the strategy to work. When a person goes to refinance such a property, a bank will typically only refinance up to 75 percent of the new value. Therefore, for you to get enough to refinance the entire short-term loan and to possibly get back your rehab money, the property needs to be worth significantly more than what you paid for it.

For example, let's say you bought a property for $100,000. The property needs a $25,000 rehab to be rent-ready, for a total cost of $125,000. You could use a short-term loan to buy the property (like hard money) and your own cash to rehab the place. Then, you'd refinance the property with a new loan from a lender. If the new lender's appraisal came in at $160,000, they might give you 75 percent of that amount in a new loan, which is $120,000. This would pay back your entire short-term loan, get you most of your rehab budget back, and give you a stable, long-term rental property with $40,000 of equity at the start.

Of course, this example only works if the ARV comes out at the $160,000 level. It wouldn't be as nice if the ARV were to come in at $100,000, and the bank would only give you a loan for $75,000—not even enough to pay back the short-term loan. This is what I mean when I say the math has to work for the strategy to work.

Before I conclude this section on BRRRR real estate investing, let me summarize some of the pros and cons of this strategy.

Pros
• **Potential No Money Down.** BRRRR investing is one of my favorite

strategies for investing without needing a lot of cash. If the numbers work out right, you could get into a deal for very little money out-of-pocket, or perhaps even none. Of course, the better the deal you can find, the less money you'll ultimately need to provide.

- **High ROI.** Because of the low amount of out-of-pocket cash you'll need for this strategy to work, your ROI should be astronomical. In other words, if you end up having only $10,000 in the deal, but you are cash flowing $2,500 per year, that's a 25 percent cash-on-cash return, and that doesn't account for all the equity you built during the rehab stage.
- **Equity.** BRRRR real estate investing allows you to build some serious equity right off the bat. Rather than owning a rental property that is worth what you paid for it, wouldn't owning one that you have $40,000 of equity in be better?
- **Renting a Rehabbed Property.** After the full rehab has been done, and the property is rented, you own and lease a property in Class A condition. This can help you attract the best tenants and reduce your maintenance budget on the property, making your landlording more hassle-free.

Cons
- **The Short-Term Loan.** The short-term loan you get at the beginning can be expensive, especially if you are using a hard money loan. Also, the short term on these loans can make the carrying costs expensive, possibly resulting in negative cash flow during the time you are paying on the loan. For this reason, many people use a home equity loan or cash to fund the first phase of the project, then refinance to get their cash back so they can rinse and repeat.
- **The Possibility It Doesn't Appraise.** Of course, if after the rehab the home doesn't appraise high enough, you could end up with a problem. This is why doing the correct math going into the deal is imperative.
- **Seasoning.** The refinancing bank will likely require you to wait six months or maybe even twelve months after the original purchase before they will refinance the property. This period of time is known as "seasoning," and most conventional and portfolio lenders require it. If your end lender requires you to wait twelve months, but your short-term loan is only good for nine months, you've got a problem. Therefore, when I use this hybrid real estate investing strategy, I try to make sure my short-term loan is for no less than eighteen months. This gives me

the time I need to refinance, and if something goes wrong after month twelve and the refinance won't work, I still have six months to sell the property or hunt for a new refinance.

- **Dealing with a Rehab.** Finally, when you use this strategy, you have to deal with the complications of a large rehab project. And trust me, rehabbing a property is not easy. Dealing with contractors, unknown problems, mold, asbestos, theft, and the rest of the headaches that come with a rehab are not fun.

In summary, BRRRR real estate investing can be a powerful way to build wealth through real estate and is one of my all-time-favorite strategies. Being able to capitalize on the forced appreciation the way a house flipper would while acquiring a great rental property that will provide years of cash flow is truly getting the best of both worlds. However, the strategy is not a simple undertaking; it requires exquisite math, planning, and the ability to find a great deal. But for those willing to take on the challenge, BRRRR real estate investing can supercharge your business and set you on a path to greatness.

WRAPPING IT UP

However you choose to finance your next rental property deal, my hope is that you now have the tools you need to get out there and make it happen. Whether you decide to go the conventional route, use a portfolio lender, get an equity line, or employ any other strategy I've discussed, get out there and learn more about that specific topic.

Sit down with a banker. Call up a mortgage broker. Apply for a home equity line of credit.

Do what you need to do to make financing the least of your concerns, and then get on with the rest of your investment strategy.

Chapter Fourteen
HOW TO GET A LOAN APPROVED, GUARANTEED

"I have always been afraid of banks."

—ANDREW JACKSON

One of the worst jobs I ever had was as the front-end personal banker at a national bank. Yep, I was the guy who sat at the desk, took loan applications, and tried to get you to refinance your house.

Man I hated that job; it was awful. So much sales pressure, so many hours of staring at the clock, so many loans—so many reminders that I should be out investing my money, rather than working for it. My job did, however, give me some insider information about how the loan process works. Want to know what I found out? Loans are like a gun safe. They can be opened with the right code—every time.

I included the word "guaranteed" in the title of this chapter not because I believe you will always be able to get a loan approved, but because I want to demonstrate that the lending process is not a mystery. It's a lock that can be opened with a code. If you enter the right code, you will get your loan approved. Can you enter that code today? Maybe, maybe not.

Unlike the code to a gun safe, though, this code is not one I can simply give you; the "digits" of the combination are something you must already have. But I do know that if you enter it correctly, if you have what it takes, you will get approved. Whether you are looking to buy your first home, purchase an investment property, refinance a current loan, or achieve something totally different, this chapter will give you the tools you need to crack that code and hear a resounding "yes" from the banker, every time.

Understanding How a Loan Works

Before getting into the details of just how to get your loan approved, let's talk about the basics. How does a loan even work?

Obviously, there are a lot of different kinds of loans and lenders. There are conventional banks, mortgage brokers, portfolio lenders, hard money lenders, private lenders, and still others. Each has their own system. However, let me make a few quick points about the loan process. Typically, the person you are talking with is just a salesperson (like I was). Here's the secret that makes the entire loan-procuring process ten times easier: **That person is not the one ultimately responsible for saying "yes" or "no" to your loan.**

When you go into a bank and sit down with a banker, most likely, they are simply there to collect your information and be your contact person. The real decision-maker is the underwriter. The underwriter is an individual trained to look at all the puzzle pieces that the salesperson gives them and to approve or deny a loan based on those facts. The underwriter knows all the rules, laws, and regulations, and can make an informed decision. Now, although the underwriter holds all the decision power, the underwriter is usually not very creative and definitely not emotionally involved (purposefully). Therefore, to get a loan approved, you must accomplish two things:

1. Convince the front-end sales guy that you and your loan are worthy.
2. Get the front-end guy to convince the back-end underwriter that you and your loan are worthy.

I find that the first part, convincing the front-end guy, is always easy. These people are very quick to say, "Yeah, no problem. We can do that." I ran across this about a dozen times when trying to refinance my recent fiveplex. Over and over, I heard it: "Yeah, Brandon, no problem. We can do that loan for you!" Then six weeks go by and I get that fateful call: "Hey Brandon, this is [insert sales banker's name here], and it actually looks like we can't do that loan. You see, our bank will only [insert excuse here]."

I don't blame the banker; I used to be one. I had one whole week of training, and I was sent out onto the sales floor to secure multi-million-dollar loans. In fact, I was paid commission on loan applications in addition to loan closings. In other words, as a front-end banker, it was in my best interest to get someone to apply for a loan, whether or not I thought they could actually get approved. Approval was the underwriter's job. I was just collecting leads and acting as the "middle man." Even though the banker is not the one ultimately responsible for approving your loan, they are the first person to focus your efforts on.

The Banker's Role in Your Loan Approval

Let me tell you a quick story about myself, not so I can pat myself on the back but to illustrate a point. When I worked at the bank, I was able to close twice as many deals as the other banker who worked there. We both had the same number of leads, the same number of applications, and the same underwriters, but I was able to do twice as much. Why?

It's the same reason I have been able to buy twice as much real estate as most, and for almost no money down: because I was creative. You see, most people don't punch the code in correctly the first time when trying to get a loan approved; there is something wrong with it. A boring banker or underwriter will simply say, "No, sorry" and give up, but I was different. Rather than saying, "I can't get this loan approved," I always asked myself, "How can I get this loan approved?" Remember the shift in thinking that I talked about in Chapter 1? This carries over into all parts of life.

Now, I didn't do anything unethical or illegal to get these loans pushed through. Sometimes it was as simple as paying off a small credit card first or changing the loan type. My point is this: When you start looking for a loan, look for a creative banker. You want someone who is not simply going to say "yes" or "no" like a computer, but someone who will fight to get your loan approved.

Perhaps the best way to find this, at least when looking to get a loan on a piece of property, is by asking some real estate agents who their preferred lender is. In my town, nine out of ten agents will say the same person. Find this person—that's your first step in getting your loan approved.

Even the best, most creative banker is not going to think of everything, however. This is why it's ultimately up to you to make sure your loan gets approved. No, you didn't misread that. Once you finish this chapter, you'll have no excuse for simply "applying and praying" for loans. You'll know, or at least have a very good indication, whether your loan will be approved or denied. No matter how good your banker is, they still can't turn a pig into a pancake. Your application must pencil out for the underwriter. To make sure it does, let's talk about how an underwriter thinks.

Understanding How an Underwriter Thinks

Let me tell you a little industry secret: Lenders need you more than you need them.

Think about that. Without borrowers, a lender makes no money. Why else do you think banks and mortgage companies spend hundreds of millions of dollars on advertising? They need us. So why does getting a loan seem so difficult?

To put it plainly, a lender follows the exact same advice I give new real estate investors: It's better to do no deal than a bad deal. In other words, they would rather deny a loan than lend on something that will go bad. This seems pretty obvious, but understanding it is the first step in getting your loan approved. A loan is a gamble for the lender, and the lender wants to bet only on sure things. This is why getting a loan seems so hard—because you have to prove you are a good bet.

What constitutes a "good bet"? I actually don't know, because I don't know your lender. However, there is a really easy way for you to find out ...ask them. Start building relationships with your local banks now, whether you plan to borrow this year or not. You never know when that relationship will come in handy. I'll now give you some specifics on exactly what your banker wants to see. It's time to unlock the code.

The Twelve-Digit Code You Need to Get Your Loan Approved

Remember, your lender needs to loan out money; you just need to get the safe open.

When an underwriter looks at your loan to decide whether to issue a "yes" or "no" verdict, they want to make sure you have the right code. This code is the minimum requirements the institution requires to lend. Some of these requirements are set by the bank policy, others are set by the government. Still others are set by the individual underwriter. Getting your loan approved is as easy as correctly entering the code. In this section, I will outline the twelve digits of that code. Some banks may require fewer digits, while others may require more, but these twelve should get you started.

1. Property Type
Some lenders loan only on certain types of property. The first thing you should ask yourself is whether the lender lends on the kind of property you want to buy. For example, if you are looking to purchase a commercial property, but the lender you are talking with only loans on residential properties, you'll see a door slam in your face. Trust me, I've been dealing with this.

2. Property Location
Typically, lenders have certain locations they will and will not lend in. Be sure that your lender is okay with the location of your property.

3. Property Condition
Many lenders will loan only on a property that is in great condition. Why? Because they want to ensure that the property can be sold if they later need to foreclose (and they want to ensure that it won't drop in value because of the condition). Therefore, be sure to check with your lender on what kind of condition they want. Keep in mind, there are strategies for buying properties that need work, so don't automatically rule out the fixer-upper.

4. Loan Amount
This is something I have run into often in my search for a loan over the past year. You see, the fiveplex I am refinancing is a commercial property, because it contains five units (anything over four is considered commercial). However, most commercial lenders have loan minimums, and since I only need $100,000 for the refinance, I've heard a lot of nos.

5. Debt-to-Income Ratio

When you're buying a property, lenders want to know that you can afford it. To determine this, they use a ratio known as debt-to-income or DTI. This is a percentage based on the relationship between your debt and your income. However, there are two different DTI numbers they care about, so let's look at both:

- **Front-End DTI Ratio.** Front-end DTI is the relationship between how much your total housing payment will be and how much debt you have each month. For example, if your primary residence house payment is $1,000 per month, and you earn $3,000 in gross monthly income from your job, your current front-end DTI would be 33.3 percent, because $1,000 / $3,000 = .333. For real estate investors trying to buy or refinance rental properties, this number is not as important as the back-end DTI.

- **Back-End DTI Ratio.** Back-end DTI is the relationship between how much total debt you have and how much income you make. In other words, your total monthly debt payment divided by your total monthly income is your back-end DTI. If your total debt payment each month is $2,000 per month, and you currently earn $4,000 per month from your job (gross), your back-end DTI would be 50 percent (because $2,000 / $4,000 = .50).

Every lender has a DTI number they care about, and one of the most important things you can do to ensure your loan gets approved is to ensure that you are below the threshold of what the bank likes to see. Typically, you probably want your front-end DTI to be less than 28 percent and your back-end DTI to be less than 36 percent. When checking with a lender on their DTI requirements, you will typically see these numbers in the following format: (28,36), in which the first number is the front-end DTI, and the second number is the back-end DTI.

6. Loan-to-Value Ratio

A lender's primary concern is to avoid risk. To do this, they want to ensure that no matter what happens in the future, they will be okay. If you continue to pay forever, they are happy with the interest. But if you stop paying, they want to know that they are not going to lose money. To ensure this, a lender wants to know that there is sufficient equity in the property to cover the costs, should they need to foreclose on you and sell the home. To gauge this, the lender relies on a percentage known as the loan-to-value ratio, or LTV. This is the ratio between the total loan amount(s) and the property's fair market value:

LTV = Total Loan Amount(s) / Fair Market Value

For example, if a property is worth $500,000, and you are looking to get a loan for $400,000, you are looking at an 80 percent LTV loan, because $400,000 / $500,000 = .80.

Lenders typically have different requirements for maximum LTV based on the property type. For example, for an owner-occupied property with an FHA loan, the lender will go up to 96.5 percent LTV. However, on a commercial property, a lender may not want to lend above 50 percent LTV.

If you are an investor, you are likely to find 70 percent to 80 percent LTV the norm for investment properties.

I have one additional note about LTV: The LTV is calculated using all the loans that have a lien on the property, including second and third mortgages. The lender will likely add all these loans together to determine the LTV.

7. Credit Score

This one is pretty self-explanatory, but banks want to know that you are trustworthy before they lend money to you, so they generally have a minimum credit score that they want to see. This number will depend on the lender and the loan type, but if you are below a 600, understand that obtaining any kind of loan could be difficult.

To check your credit score, I recommend visiting www.creditkarma. com, which allows you to see your score for free—actually *free*—no free trial and no credit card required. (They make their money by selling credit cards. Yes, kind of ironic.)

8. Repayment Source

Lenders want to ensure that your ability to repay the loan will stay consistent. To do this, they will dig in on your repayment source for the loan. For most borrowers, this means they will look into your job. They will want to know how long you have worked there and how much you have historically made.

If you just started a new job, getting approved can be more difficult than if you have had the same job for years. If you are a property investor, the lender will also look at your rental income and may be able to use that to offset your debt. However, most lenders will not give you any credit for this rental income unless you have been a landlord for more than two years (remember, they want stability).

In addition, no matter how long you've been a landlord, you likely will never get 100 percent of the rental income counted toward you. They will likely give you 70 percent to 80 percent just to be safe on their end.

9. Experience

Next, they may want to know your experience level. This is especially true on large, commercial, or multifamily loans. Why? Because the bank knows that you will not be able to cover the payment if something goes wrong. If the mortgage payment on your new apartment complex is $30,000 per month, the lender knows that there is no way you could pay that if all your tenants left. They'll want to look at your experience level to make sure you have the skills necessary to avoid such a catastrophic event.

10. Cash Reserves

The lender will want to ensure that you have the cash available to weather any storm. Be sure to have at least some cash in a savings account before applying for your next loan. The amount will depend on the lender and how many properties you own, but every lender will want to see something.

11. Recent Credit Changes

A lender wants to know that not only is the property going to be stable but that you will also be, especially with regard to your credit decisions. For this reason, it's important not to do anything crazy with your credit while you're trying to obtain a loan, such as opening up new credit accounts or adding on new debt.

12. Compensating Factors

Lastly, understand that, in the end, loan decisions are eventually brought to a real, live person, so there could be compensating factors if you fall short on a requirement or two. For example, if your credit score is a few points shy of what they like to see, but your LTV is exceptionally low, the lender may waive the minimum credit score requirement, because the equity in the LTV compensates for it. However, there is no way of knowing exactly what your lender will or won't do, so it's best to simply try to fit your peg within their round hole perfectly.

Now that you have a good idea of how a lender thinks, let's talk about how to fit your loan into a package that a banker will be excited about.

Make Your Lender's Job Easier to Get Your Loan Approved

Earlier in this chapter, I mentioned that getting a loan approved requires a certain code. If you can get the code right, you can get the "safe" to open.

However, a code does you no good if you can't find the keypad. In other words, you might know the twelve digits needed to open a safe, but if you don't know how to punch those numbers in, those digits will be worthless to you. Let's crack this safe together. As I said before, a lender wants to approve your loan. The banker wants to say yes. The underwriter wants to say yes. Why do we hear so many nos? Because people don't enter the digits correctly. What's the best way to make this process go more smoothly? How do you enter these digits correctly? It's simple: Do the heavy lifting for your banker.

Your banker has a lot of loans going on at the same time. They are doing a car loan for Bill Johnson, a house refinance for Sally Wiggins, and a broom loan for Harry Potter. Therefore, a banker will likely take the path of least resistance, and prioritize the loans that will be the quickest and easiest to enter. If you want your loan to get approved and get approved quickly, do the heavy lifting for them; make their job as easy as possible. You already know the twelve digits that the banker needs to enter, so write these out in great detail and make everything plain-as-the-nose-on-their-face simple for the banker, then provide documentation to back it up. When you speak with the front-end banker, ask them for a list of all the items you will need to have. Likely, that will be at least the following:

- Tax returns for previous two years
- W-2s for previous two years
- Pay stubs for previous two months
- Personal financial statement

- Bank statements
- Purchase and sale documents for the property
- Descriptions of all your properties

When the banker gives you this list, don't think of it as a wish list but as a must list. Your job is to compile this information in the most organized format possible. If there is one tip from this chapter you must remember, it is this: There is power in presentation. Go overboard. Have fun with it! When I applied for the loan that was ultimately approved for my recent fiveplex refinance, I organized the entire packet in a binder I bought from Staples, complete with a cover page, summary, photos, and divider tabs. There was nothing magical in this, but I simply gave him everything he wanted in the most organized way possible.

Furthermore, I ran this property through the BiggerPockets Rental Property Calculator, took the PDF report it generated, and included that on top of the organized packet. This enabled the lender, in one place, to see all the financials of the whole property. Upon receiving this application, besides being blown away by its organization, he commented how nice it was to see the summary document. And within a few days, I had a full loan approval.

WRAPPING IT UP

Whether you plan to use a traditional bank, a credit union, a hard money lender, a private lender, home equity, or another financing technique I discussed in the previous chapter, you will always hear "no" unless you can crack the combination. My goal in this chapter was to share the most common pieces of the code that bankers and other decision-makers need. I hope that you've finished this chapter with a solid understanding of how to get your loan approved so you can move forward with your rental property purchase.

Speaking of the rental property, at this point in the book, I've covered everything from the mindset to the planning to the shopping and now the financing. But there is one more step between getting your financing in order and becoming a landlord: the due diligence process.

Chapter Fifteen

THE DUE DILIGENCE PROCESS

"One of life's most painful moments comes when we must admit that we didn't do our homework, that we are not prepared."

—MERLIN OLSEN

Did you know that one of the most famous painters and sculptors in human history began his career as a fraud?

Michelangelo di Lodovico Buonarroti Simoni, more commonly known as simply Michelangelo, was a promising young artist working for the Medici family around the same time Columbus set out on his first navigation to the Americas. But before Michelangelo would go on to create some of the most renowned pieces of Renaissance art (such as *David* and the ceiling of the Sistine Chapel), he participated in a classic art forgery scheme. According to *The Life of Michelangelo*, a biography by Ascanio Condivi, Michelangelo's employer, Lorenzo de' Medici, looked at a sculpture the young man had made and asked him to "fix it so that it looked as if it had been buried." That way he could "send it to Rome and it would pass for an ancient work, and you would sell it much better." Of course, despite Michelangelo's best efforts, the deception was soon discovered by the buyer.

Art forgery is as much of a problem today as it was in Michelangelo's time. Millions of dollars are lost every year because of such deception, and many people have been made fools after spending inordinate amounts of money on something fake. The artwork an individual thinks they are buying is often very different from what they are actually buying. With art, discovering fakes can be incredibly difficult because of the impressive nature of the forger. However, with proper due diligence, a buyer can discover a fair amount of knowledge about the history of a piece of artwork.

The same problem art buyers face exists for real estate buyers, and investigating a property's hidden past is one of the most important aspects of the rental property investing process. After all, you don't want to buy a piece of real estate only to later discover that what you thought you were buying and what you actually bought were two separate things. In this chapter, I'll dive into the topic of doing your due diligence on a property to make sure you get what you pay for.

What Is Due Diligence?

Due diligence is the process you'll go through after getting an offer accepted but before you actually take ownership. This is your time to investigate the property as much as you can, trying to bring to light anything that is hidden (either purposefully or accidentally). After all, the information presented to the public when the home was "on the market" is rarely good enough.

Real estate agents and private sellers tend to diminish the negatives about a property while highlighting the positives. Sometimes there are problems that the seller never even knew existed. In some cases, the selling party flat out lies about the property, which can cause financial issues for you down the road. The due diligence process is there to help you uncover those things and assist you in getting an accurate picture of exactly what you are buying.

The due diligence process will differ, depending on what kind of property you plan to buy. If you are buying a 200-unit apartment complex, your due diligence list will be miles longer than what you'd have for a single-family house. Because this book is geared slightly toward the smaller end of the property scale, I'll focus on the due diligence you might want to do for a single-family or small multifamily property. This can be broken down into three major categories:

1. Title Inspection
2. Document Inspection
3. Physical Inspection

Title Inspection

How would you feel if I sold you a piece of property, and later you found out that I did not have the legal right to sell it? What if it was still owned by someone else, even after you bought it? Tragic, right? For this reason, every property you buy must go through the title inspection process.

Keep in mind, this may get a little complicated with legal terms, and you may start to want to look for the nearest exit while reading it. This information is important to understand, but don't let it overwhelm you. Your job in this process is actually fairly simple and straightforward. What I'm about to tell you is the legalese behind the title search. You will have very little interaction with what I'm about to say. That said, read it anyway to familiarize yourself with this step.

When a piece of real estate is sold, the title (a bundle of rights giving ownership to an individual) is transferred from one person to another through a legal document called a deed. In the United States, this deed is recorded at the county level to be made part of the public record and preserved forever. The deed simply shows that the title has been changed. When the property is later sold or transferred another time, the deed is once again recorded. This process begins when the property is first built or developed and continues forever. In other words, if you wanted to go to your local courthouse and see every single person or entity that has ever owned your house, you could do that. This is known as the chain of title, and is the process of going back in time, through research, to find each and every person who has ever owned the property to make sure the paperwork has been correct each time.

Furthermore, over the years, other documents can get recorded on the chain of title in addition to the deed that give people certain rights to the property. The most common examples would be easements, covenants, or liens. Easements (a legal right given by the property owner to another party to allow them to use or cross the property) and covenants (a legal document that explains how a property can be used) are fairly common and not a big deal, but a lien can make or break a sale.

A lien is a legal claim against a property made by a person or entity to secure the payment of a debt. The most common example would be a mortgage, where the bank places a mortgage or deed of trust on the property to make sure it gets paid back before the property is sold again. Another common example is when a contractor places a contractor lien or mechanics lien on a property, making sure they eventually get paid what they are owed.

When someone has a lien on a property, they can foreclose on the property under certain conditions. For example, if an owner/borrower stops paying the mortgage, the bank's lien allows the bank to foreclose and take the property. And because liens are attached directly to the property via the chain of title and the public record, no other bank will want to finance something that has an existing lien. It's too much risk.

Therefore, your goal when buying real estate is to only buy properties that have a clear title. This means a title that has been researched and found to be complete and free of liens or other issues. If this research sounds overwhelming, and you envision yourself pouring over hours of file cabinets at your local county courthouse, don't worry; it's much easier than that. This is when the attorney or title company comes into play.

Title Company or Attorney

Each state is different with respect to who researches the chain of title closing the sale of a property. In many East Coast states, an attorney handles the closing process as well as the title research. In the Midwest and on the West Coast, lenders, title companies, escrow companies, and attorneys generally handle the title research and closing. Talk to some local investors in your area (on the BiggerPockets Forums, perhaps?) to see how it's done in your area.

When you're working with a real estate agent, your agent will likely recommend an attorney or title company if you don't already have a favorite. They will send the necessary documents over, and the attorney or title company will get to work researching the chain of title. They will also order your title insurance.

Title insurance is simply a kind of insurance, just like car insurance, fire insurance, or any other type, except that it is designed to protect the owner and/or lender from problems with the title. In other words, if a title insurance policy is taken out on a piece of property, and later it was determined that a mistake had been made in the due diligence process and a mortgage was still in place on the property, the title insurance policy would cover any financial damage from that situation. Most title companies and attorneys are pretty good at researching the chain of title, so it's unlikely that you'll ever need to file a claim on title insurance, but nevertheless, most lenders will not fund a deal unless title insurance is in place to protect their loan. Title insurance can be purchased by either an attorney or a title company, and the cost is usually wrapped into the closing costs.

If you are buying the property without an agent, through a private sale, you will need to contact the title company yourself to get the title process rolling. If you are paying cash for the property, you may be able to skip the title search (or do your own), as well as the title insurance, but I do not recommend this. It usually doesn't cost more than $1,000, and you'll save yourself significant headache should a hidden lien be discovered years later.

As for the title inspection process, this pretty much covers it. Again, in most cases, you won't need to do much of anything for this process to happen—you just need to make sure the right people get it done. The other parts of the due diligence process, however, may require a lot more work on your part.

Document Inspection

After the purchase and sale agreement has been signed, it's time to start reviewing the documents. If you are buying a single-family home that has not recently been used as a rental, the documents you receive may be minimal. However, if you are buying a rental house, a multifamily property, or a commercial building, you'll likely have a lot to review.

As I mentioned at the beginning of this chapter, the purpose of the due diligence process is to make sure you are actually buying what you think you are buying. Inspecting the paperwork is a good way to do that. The seller may claim that the property's tax bill is $1,500 per year, but how would you know for sure if you don't investigate? They may say the property rents for $675 a month, but how would you know if you don't check to confirm this?

The following is a list of documents you may receive from the seller. Keep in mind, not all of these will be used in every situation, because it largely depends on the type of property you are buying. However, I'll list the most common possibilities here so you can know what to keep an eye out for.

- **Seller Disclosures.** Most states, if not all, require that the seller disclose any known defects in a property before selling it. Therefore, in most deals you purchase with the help of a real estate agent, the seller will give you a pile of forms in which the seller lists anything that might be wrong with the property. You'll want to read this document carefully, so you'll know immediately about any issues with the property that the owner knew about. Of course, the large loophole here is that the owner must know about the problems, so this should not take the place of you doing your own investigation on the property's condition.

- **Seller's Tax Returns.** One of the most powerful tools you can use to determine the truth about a property's financials is the seller's tax returns. A seller will not likely make a property look extra "cash flow plush" for the IRS, so tax returns will likely be the most accurate representation of how the property really performs. To get these, simply ask for them. Look for any discrepancies between tax returns filed and the financial information provided by the seller, but also recognize the difference between aggressive tax write-offs and deception. If you find inconsistencies between the numbers they provided and the numbers on the tax returns, you'll want to dig further into this.

- **Current Leases.** If the property is an existing rental property, be sure to dig through the lease(s) with a fine-tooth comb. After all, a lease goes with the property, so that lease between the seller and their tenant will become the lease between *you* and the tenant. Be sure to pay special attention to the rental rate, the length of the agreement, and any special, out-of-the-ordinary terms written into the lease. You don't want to discover after you buy the property that they had a twenty-year lease for $1 per month.

- **Current Rent Roll.** The rent roll is a list of all current tenants, their rental amount, and other information (such as move-in date and lease term length). In essence, it's a summary of what you'll hopefully find in their leases, but double-check that anyway. Make sure the numbers add up to what you think they should.

- **Tenant Estoppel Certificates.** If you are buying a property that is already rented, and especially if you are buying a property with multiple units, I highly recommend getting estoppel certificates from all the current tenants. An estoppel certificate is simply a form that the existing tenant fills out, letting you know what the terms of their current lease are. This can help you verify that the seller did not change the lease agreement without the tenant's knowledge or create a fake one, just to make the income seem higher (trust me, this happens).

- **Current Year's Tax Bill.** Be sure to verify that the tax amount you ran your numbers with is the actual tax bill. You can usually verify this online through your local assessor's office.
- **Recent Utility Bills.** Utilities are a major expense with real estate, so verify that the numbers you used for your math homework are accurate. Either ask for specific bills or call up the local utility companies and get the information directly from the source. Also verify who pays for which utility, especially if you are purchasing a multifamily property, and always check to make sure the utility bills have all been paid. When I first got started investing in real estate, I discovered several days after closing that there was a $400 garbage bill that the previous owner had not paid, and the debt was now mine. Now, I check to make sure all bills have been paid before closing.
- **Security Deposits.** If the property is already rented, make sure you verify the security deposit amounts to ensure you are given the correct cash at closing.
- **Recent or Current Maintenance on the Property.** Again, this is most helpful when a property is already rented. You'll want to get a good idea of what work has recently been completed on the property and what still needs to happen. This can also help you determine whether the owner has simply been deferring maintenance to make the expenses appear less than they really are.
- **HOA Documents.** If the property is governed by an HOA, you'll need to review the HOA's declaration of covenants, conditions, and restrictions, more commonly referred to as the CC&Rs. This document explains all the things you can and cannot do according to the HOA. For example, an investor I recently talked with told me that he bought a condo in Chicago, only to find out a few months later that the HOA would not allow the property to be used as a rental. Don't fall into that trap. Review the CC&Rs.

You may also review other documents, depending on the property and the rules or customs of the location in which you are buying. I simply could not list every possible document. The important thing to remember is this—verify everything. Let's now talk about the third inspection you'll need to do during the due diligence process: the physical inspection. Are you ready to get a little dirty?

Physical Inspection

Just as you can't judge a book by its cover, you also would be wise to avoid judging a property by its paint job. Below the surface of your property lies incredible amounts of risk that, if not discovered in advance, could cause immense financial loss later on. Therefore, the physical inspection of the rental property you are about to purchase is one of the most important steps in the entire due diligence process.

Should You Do Your Own Inspection?

The first thing I have to point out about inspections is that unless you are a licensed and experienced contractor, do not do your own inspection. Yes, you should walk through the property and make sure there are no major red flags before spending the money on an inspector, but your official inspection should be done by a real, licensed property inspector.

How to Find an Inspector

The easiest way to find a home inspector is by asking your real estate agent who they like to work with. They'll likely have the name of someone that they've worked with in the past. If you are not working with an agent, or if your agent doesn't have any recommendations, ask other local real estate investors, real estate agents, mortgage professionals, and/or property owners.

Speed is critical at this point, because you'll likely only have a week or so (depending on the details both parties signed in the P&S agreement). After the inspection, the inspector may take a couple of days to get their final report back into your hands, and you may need a day or two to think about what to do, so the moment you get the property under contract, the clock is ticking. I would try to get the inspector onto the property within four days of mutual acceptance.

The Day of the Inspection

If possible, make sure the power, water, and all other utilities for the property are turned on before the inspection. If there is no water, how can the inspector check for leaks? If there is no electricity, how can he or she tell which lights work and which don't?

After hiring the inspector, you or your agent will schedule a time for the inspector to look at the prospective property. Although you do not need to be present for the inspection, I highly recommend that you are. You are paying for the inspection anyway, so get your money's worth. Walk, crawl, climb, and touch every inch of the property as the inspector does, asking questions along the way. By doing this, you will be able to get a better idea of exactly what is wrong with the property so you can make the best decision on what you want to do with the problems you find. You may get a thirty-page (or longer!) report from the inspector, but it can be hard to tell from a written description how bad something really is. The report may say something scary like "illegal and dangerous wiring in bedroom two," but without being there to ask more questions, you might not realize the issue is simply two wires being mixed up in the light fixture—a thirty-second repair.

What Does the Inspector Look For?
Everything! The inspector will look at the property from the foundation to the roof and try to determine what they can about the condition of the property. If there is a crawlspace, they'll get down on their hands and knees to crawl through the entire thing, looking at the foundation posts, beams, and joists. They'll investigate for rot, incorrect past repairs, and evidence of rodents. Inside the house, they'll look at the condition of the doors, windows, walls, and flooring. They'll check the cabinets, the drawers, the plumbing, the electrical outlets. They'll look at the heat source and make sure it's working correctly. They'll crawl into the attic and look for issues there, and they'll hopefully walk up on the roof to check out the shingles and the chimney, if there is one. They'll also look at gutters, downspouts, and any landscaping issues that could affect the condition of the property.

After the Inspection
The report that the inspector provides you several days after the inspection will likely be scary. This is especially true with older homes. After all, the inspector's job is to discover every single possible problem they can about the property, and let's be honest, no property is perfect. In fact, I'd be nervous if the report didn't contain a laundry list of problems, because

I'd assume the inspector had been sleeping during the inspection. Your job, after the report comes in, is to decide which issues are important and which aren't. Again, being present for the inspection makes this process much easier.

Should You Use Your Contractor as Your Inspector?
Although there is nothing wrong with bringing your contractor through the property to take a look, I recommend hiring a third-party professional inspector to officially check out the property. Unlike the contractor, the inspector won't have any conflict of interest with the property, since they won't be doing the work. Moreover, contractors may be great at fixing things, but they are not generally trained to spot problems. A contractor might see a crack in the wall and begin talking about how to patch it, whereas an inspector will dive in to find out why it cracked. This distinction is very important.

How Much Does an Inspection Cost?
First, think of an inspection as an investment rather than an expense. The inspector will find things out about the property that you didn't know, and learning these things up front can either help you negotiate a better deal on the house or save you from problems later on. An inspection can also help you plan the entire rehab process on a property and allow you to create a checklist for addressing all the issues to make the property right.

The cost of an inspection depends largely on the size of the property, but for easy reference, a typical single-family home will cost between $350 and $500 for an inspection. A small multifamily property might cost up to $1,000. Larger multifamily properties (five or more units) get more expensive the larger they are. But again, don't think about the cost, think about the value and peace of mind you'll get.

Other Inspections You May Want to Get
I hope I've convinced you, at this point, that getting your property inspected by a professional inspector is important. However, even a great home inspector has their limits. There are several different types of inspections you may decide to have done on the property. Although these are fairly uncommon, they may end up saving you a lot of money in the long run. (Your home inspector may also suggest these separate

inspections after he completes his walk-through of the property.)

- **Plumbing.** A home inspector can look for leaks, and can test to make sure the water is running and draining well, but he can't see inside the drainpipes to confirm that there are no major problems. For this reason, you may decide to hire a plumber or plumbing inspector to stick a camera down the sewer lines and check for problems. After all, a cracked drain line can cost thousands of dollars to repair, especially if it's broken under a driveway or parking lot.

- **Asbestos.** Asbestos is a naturally occurring fibrous material used during the twentieth century in a lot of building materials, but it was later discovered to be dangerous, even deadly, to humans who might breathe in fibers that become airborne. Asbestos can be found in hundreds of different products but is most common in popcorn ceilings, exterior siding, and pipe insulation. If you or your inspector have concerns about asbestos being used on your property, get the house tested by a local environmental testing agency. Although asbestos can be removed, this must be done by a licensed professional trained to remove the lethal product.

- **Lead-Based Paint.** Before 1978, lead was often used in both interior and exterior paint. It was added to paint to speed the drying time, increase the longevity of the paint, and resist moisture, which can cause corrosion on the painted surface. It was later discovered that lead can cause damage to the human nervous system, especially in young children. In 1978, lead-based paint was outlawed in the United States for residential use. Therefore, anything built before 1978 may contain lead (the older the home, the greater the chance). Because of the danger this poses, there are some fairly strict laws in place concerning the disturbance or removal of lead-based paint from a property; this, of course, means that the issue can be very expensive to remediate. If you are buying a property that was built before 1978—and especially if you plan to do major work on it—you may want to test the surface of several painted areas of the property to determine whether lead exists. You can either hire a professional to do this, or you pick up a lead-test kit from any home improvement store and do it yourself.

- **Pests/Wood-Destroying Organisms.** Termites, flying beetles, carpenter ants, and other wood-eating bugs can cause tens of thousands of dollars in structural damage to a house, years before a homeowner or tenant even knows they are there. If your home inspector finds evidence of pests in the home, or if you simply live in an area of the country where this is common, hiring a professional pest inspector to perform a pest inspection would be wise. This is also known as an "inspection for wood-destroying organisms." These inspections are generally done by local pest control companies whose workers are specifically trained to spot signs of these "silent killers."

After the Inspections

After the property has been physically inspected and you've looked over the reports, you'll need to decide whether the property is still worth pursuing. If you included an inspection contingency in your offer, you could likely back out without losing any of your earnest money. However, if you did not include an inspection contingency and decide to back out, you will probably lose your earnest money deposit—though that might be better than losing tens of thousands of dollars on a money pit because you let your emotions keep you in a bad deal.

Also, remember this: It is an inspector's job to scare you with facts. If you are just getting started with your first deal, a scary inspection could raise unwarranted fear and make you back out of a deal that is actually totally manageable. I recommend consulting other local real estate investors about your concerns before backing out. A great place to do this is on the BiggerPockets Forums, where you can ask for advice any time, for free, from the community. Just go to www.biggerpockets.com/forums and let people know what the inspection report says.

Finally, keep in mind that the items you discover in your inspection can be used to negotiate a better price on the property. If you find things that you did not know about, you can ask the seller to either fix those issues, credit you the cost of those repairs at closing, or simply lower the price of the property. Of course, they may say "no," but if the issue is serious enough, there is a good chance they will make some concessions.

WRAPPING IT UP

The due diligence step is one of the most important aspects of the entire property-buying process. Without it, you may think you are buying a great deal when, in fact, you are buying a pig.

By having the title carefully inspected, you can ensure that the property will indeed be 100 percent yours. By verifying all the documents that come with the property, you can validate that the numbers advertised with the property align with the truth. And by having the property physically inspected, you help reduce the risk that hidden defects could cause untold damage later.

After the due diligence period, it's almost time to take ownership of the property. However, before the previous owner hands over the keys, you need to get a few more ducks in a row that will make the landlording process easier and the transition much smoother.

Chapter Sixteen
GETTING READY TO CLOSE

"Dig your well before you're thirsty."

—CHINESE PROVERB

After being accidentally abandoned on Mars with no hope of a quick rescue, NASA astronaut Mark Watney was forced to do what humans were designed to do best: survive.

This is the story told in the 2011 bestselling book by Andy Weir titled *The Martian*. Although the story is fiction, the incredible truths it contains about science, ingenuity, problem solving, and the human spirit have rocked millions of readers and tens of millions of viewers through the 2015 theatrical release of the film, starring Matt Damon. In the story, Watney must grow food in an unfruitful climate, maintain contact with Earth through a broken machine, and survive hundreds of days of unimaginable danger. Luckily for him, NASA was prepared.

In the tale, before Watney's spaceship left Earth for its 124-day journey to Mars, NASA sent fourteen advance unmanned missions to the red planet, depositing on Mars all the supplies the astronauts would need to live and explore there, including their home, vehicles, and tools. In other words, NASA knew that if it didn't prepare for everything before the mission, the mission could never succeed. After all, planning and building a new rocket to send forgotten supplies could take years, so if something were to break on Mars and the astronauts didn't already have the ability or tools to fix it, it would be too late. This preparation gave Mark Watney the resources he needed to extend his life on Mars.

Although again, the story is fiction, the underlying message is still true: Preparation is key to success. And like planning a space voyage, a rental property owner must properly prepare before purchasing. The way you set up your rental business before you close on a property will determine the success you'll have later. Therefore, in this chapter, I focus on the idea of preparation—the things you should do (or consider) before closing on your first, or next, rental property. This stuff might not be the most glamorous, but just as preparation saved Mark Watney, it just might save your life (or at least your financial life).

Let's start with the one thing every rental property owner must deal with: insurance.

Order Insurance

Fires, floods, and water leaks happen. Luckily, we live in a society that spreads this risk around to everyone to make sure such incidents don't bankrupt anyone. I'm talking about insurance. Therefore, before you close on your rental property, make sure that you have adequate insurance coverage. Although rental property insurance is slightly different from your normal homeowner's insurance policy, the process for getting it is nearly identical. Call up the same insurance agency that insures your house or car (or call up another, or several), and get a quote on the policy. Let them know this is for a rental property and that you are purchasing the property. If the quote looks good to you, you'll need to request that a "binder" be sent to the attorney or title/escrow company that is handling the closing of your property. Most likely, the cost of the insurance will be paid at closing directly to the insurance company, but that may not necessarily be the case for you. Your insurance agent will be able to fill you in on the details. Also keep in mind that if your lender is setting up an "escrow" account, which I'll talk about in a moment, you may be required to pay one full year in advance for the insurance. Be sure to plan for this possibility when you do your math.

What kind of insurance should you get on the property? To answer that question, I turned to my own insurance agent, Caleb Backholm of

Backholm Insurance, to write the next section of this chapter for me, and to help us all better understand the difference in policies.

Insurance for Landlords

Insuring an investment property is something every investor will want to do. In truth, it's probably an expense an investor would like to skip, but seeing your hard work and money go up in smoke is a nightmare that can ruin years of work. Here's how to avoid that, or at least insure against it.

How do you choose the right insurance? For homes that will need some fixing up, the choice may be partially made for you, because you may be limited to an actual cash value (ACV) policy. That means the insurance company will give you only enough insurance to cover what you paid for the property, minus the value of the land it sits on. This often occurs when the house is older, and the plumbing, electrical, and roof have not been fully updated.

The downside for those insured with an ACV policy is that if the structure sustains major damage, there likely won't be enough money paid out to rebuild. In a worst-case scenario, you may have only enough money to pay off the loan and be left with a vacant lot or a damaged building. But an ACV policy is still better than nothing and will often be sufficient for small losses, especially if you are prepared to pay a bit more than the deductible (because of depreciation) or do some of the work yourself.

An important note about ACV policies is this: about one-half of them don't cover water damage from frozen or broken pipes. In some cases, you just can't get it because of age or something else. But at least it's good to know that up front or get it endorsed to the policy if you can.

On the other hand, a replacement cost policy is the preferred option if you can get it. The coverage is better, and it will pay for the full cost of a covered loss (minus your deductible) or even to fully rebuild the house, if necessary. To qualify, the property must be in good condition, with the roof and paint in good shape. I can't tell you how many times over my years in insurance I've come across houses that couldn't get a good policy because of the condition of the roof or siding. Other problem issues include a lack of gutters, no handrail on the stairs, and debris left in the yard. Don't let your renters leave an old appliance or broken-down vehicle in the yard. An insurance inspector will usually cancel the policy if they see that.

When looking at a replacement cost policy, make sure the dwelling coverage (Coverage A) involves enough of a payout to rebuild, based on what contractors are charging in your area. In some cases, this number may not be even close to what you paid for the property. It could be much more or much less, and a lot of people are surprised by that. It does not matter what you paid; it matters what a contractor will charge you to rebuild that same home in the same construction style on the same lot.

With most policies, if you are more than 20 percent under market costs, you will be subject to a coinsurance penalty. This means that if the home would cost $200,000 to rebuild, and you are insured for less than $160,000 (80 percent of the value), any claim you have will be paid out at the same ratio. For easy math, if the value is $200,000, and you insure for $100,000, you are at 50 percent. If you have a toilet overflow that causes $8,000 in damage, the insurance company would pay only 50 percent of the cost—$4,000, minus the deductible. This is because you were only insured at 50 percent value on the home. Watch for this, and make sure your house is insured to full replacement value. (Note that with an ACV policy, you can usually get one that will pay 100 percent on partial losses, even though the home coverage is not at replacement value.)

Next, make sure your policy includes outbuildings (garage, shop, etc.), if you have any. Also look for "loss of rents coverage." If your renters have to move out after a fire or other covered damage to the home, this will pay you the rent you would have collected from them during that time.

Lastly, make sure you have liability coverage on the home. Common limits are $300,000, $500,000 and $1,000,000. It doesn't cost much to get the higher coverages here, so it's almost always worth it. If someone gets hurt and sues you, this coverage is a lifesaver. I recommend requiring your renters to carry their own renter's insurance as well. It's very inexpensive for them in most cases, and if they are found liable or negligent in an injury, it's good to have a policy for that claim to go against rather than having your insurance be the only option. And while we are talking about tenants, don't let them have dangerous dogs or other pets. If you're a serious investor, you don't want a dog bite claim on your record. Insurance companies hate those.

I hope that helps you out on your journey toward real estate success. And keep in mind, having a good agent who can look things over for you is always a plus, but being armed with at least basic knowledge is extremely valuable for every real estate investor.

Setting Up Your Bank Accounts

You must keep your rental property expenses separate from your personal income. I'll repeat this: Don't use your personal checking account to run your rental business. If you have the property owned by a legal entity, this could destroy any chance of protection that entity might otherwise offer. And even if you don't have such an entity, mixing your expenses will make your bookkeeping far more complicated.

Before purchasing your next rental property, head to your local bank and open a business checking and savings account for the property. Yes, you will need both a checking and a savings account. The checking account will handle the income and expenses, while the savings account will hold the security deposit given by the tenant. At most banks, basic business checking accounts are free, as are savings accounts. (You may need to pay for checks, though.) I also recommend setting up these accounts two to three weeks before closing on the property, to ensure you have time to get the checks and/or debit cards in the mail.

Speaking of checks, this is a good time to determine how you want to pay for expenses with your rental property. Although check writing seems to be a dying practice since the emergence of debit/credit cards, I still find that running much of my rental business using a good old-fashioned checkbook is much easier. You may find the opposite is true for you, but whatever you do, have a system for how you'll do it, and determine that system right now, at the beginning.

Preparing Forms

If you'll be managing your own rental properties, it's a good idea to pull together all the forms you'll need to do so. I recommend getting a small file cabinet and some file folders, and putting five copies of each form in the file cabinet. This way, when you suddenly need a lease, application, or other form, you won't have to go digging to find it.

If you are more comfortable with tech-related solutions, you could also place all the forms "in the cloud" using a service like Google Drive. You can create folders and upload forms there, which means you can access them anywhere. The benefit of this, of course, is the ability to retrieve a form even if you are not home.

If you are using computerized property management software, you may also have the ability to sign most forms directly on a smartphone or tablet, eliminating the need for paper forms altogether. But taking inventory of what you have and what you'll need would still be a good idea.

At minimum, I recommend gathering the following, along with any other forms required by your state, county, or city:

- Application
- Rental Minimum Qualifications Form
- Month-to-Month Lease
- Annual Lease
- Three-Day Notice to Pay or Quit (or Five-Day Notice, or whatever your state requires)
- A Deposit to Hold Agreement
- Property Rules and Regulations
- Adverse Action Notice (explaining why someone was turned down)
- Notice for Landlord or Maintenance to Enter a Unit
- The Lead-Based Paint Packet
- Ten-Day Notice to Comply (or whatever other notice your state allows for this purpose)
- Twenty- or Thirty-Day Notice to End Tenancy (as allowed by your state)
- Move-Out Packet (explaining the move-out process for tenants)
- Cleaning Expectations
- New Tenant Checklist
- Move-In and Move-Out Condition Report
- New Owner Announcement Form
- Pet Addendum
- Tenant Reference Questionnaire
- Disposition of Deposit
- Mold and Mildew Disclosure Form

Preparing Bookkeeping

Before closing on your property, you should also begin getting your bookkeeping in order. In other words, how will you track the income and expenses for the property? You may choose to use a computer-based accounting software, such as QuickBooks or Quicken Rental Properties, or an online property management tool such as www.appfolio.com, www.verticalrent.com, or www.buildium.com. Another option would be to simply use Excel or Google Sheets. Consider setting up a thirty-minute meeting with a CPA to go over the methods that they would prefer for keeping track of your income and expenses.

Do I Need an LLC?

This may be the most common question I receive from BiggerPockets members: "Should I set up an LLC for my real estate business?" It's a good question, because I'm sure you've heard horror stories of landlords getting sued by tenants and losing everything. You didn't spend years learning about real estate, growing your portfolio, and figuring out how to be an effective landlord just to lose it all to some deadbeat looking to game the legal system.

However, LLCs are also highly misunderstood in the real estate space, because they are just so darn complicated. What works for one person may not work for you, and what works for you might not work for me. I could easily give you the simple answer of "talk to an attorney," but I want to dive a little deeper. Of course, I am neither an attorney nor a CPA, so please take what I'm saying as my own personal opinion and get a qualified person to help you out with these legal discussions.

What Is an LLC?

First, let's start by talking about what an LLC is and what it isn't. An LLC is not equal to a get-out-of-jail-free card. You can be sued with an LLC, and you can still lose everything. An LLC is not designed to prevent you from ever being sued. An LLC is intended to help you manage and contain the fallout from such a lawsuit. According to the United States Small Business Administration[6] (SBA), a limited liability company is "a hybrid type of legal structure that provides the limited liability features of a corporation, and the tax efficiencies and operational flexibility of a partnership." Given this definition, an LLC's benefits are threefold:

1. **Limited Liability.** *If* you were to get sued, your liability (the damage to your wallet) could be contained to the assets within the LLC, not everything else you own. In other words, if the LLC is set up correctly, and you get sued and lose, the creditors probably would not be able to take your personal house or car, or garnish your W-2 job wages. Of course, there are ways a judge might "pierce" the protection of an LLC and go after these things if every "I" is not dotted and every "T" not crossed.

2. **Tax Efficiency.** The LLC is fairly easy to handle during tax time, especially if it is a "single-member LLC," which means an LLC owned by just you or by you and your spouse. LLCs are known as "pass-through

---

6 https://www.sba.gov/content/limited-liability-company-llc

entities," which means the income and expenses flow magically through the LLC and are reported (and paid) by each individual member on their personal income statement. There is no "corporate tax" like a corporation might pay. This can definitely make taxes easier and less expensive than for, let's say, a corporation. That said, although a single-member LLC does not require its own business tax return, a multimember LLC does. Don't make this mistake.

3. **Operational Flexibility.** Finally, an LLC is fairly flexible in terms of running it. You don't need thousands of documents or to issue stock. An LLC can be set up fairly easily and inexpensively, and requires just a few documents.

It's easy to see why an LLC might be advantageous to a real estate investor. Let's say a tenant slipped on the stairs and broke their hip. The tenant decides to sue the landlord for "neglect," and the court sides with the tenant. For whatever reason—let's say your insurance doesn't cover all the legal penalties—you, as the owner, are required to pay $500,000 out-of-pocket to the tenant. Ouch. If you own the property without an LLC, the tenant could have your wages garnished, force you to sell all your properties, and drive you to bankruptcy. You could end up eating cold beans out of a can under a bridge while pigeons sit on your shoulder—not a fun place to be. On the other hand, if the owner of that property was Main Street Investments LLC, rather than you personally, then the LLC would be the entity getting sued. The courts could make you sell that property, or other properties owned by that LLC, but they likely wouldn't be able to make you sell other properties owned by other LLCs, if you have them. They won't take your primary residence. You won't be eating cold beans. Sorry, pigeons.

Of course, this example is a bit overdramatized and unlikely to happen. And I don't actually mind eating cold beans. But it illustrates the fear that drives most investors to pursue an LLC. Even though it may sound like I'm encouraging you to establish an LLC, hold your horses. There are some other important factors to consider first.

The Problems with an LLC

LLCs are great; I won't deny it. However, they might not be great *for you*. There are some fairly important considerations to weigh before you jump on the LLC bandwagon.

Lending on an LLC Is Almost Impossible

That's right, if you plan on using a loan to acquire an investment property, it's unlikely you'll be able to have an LLC own the property. Most residential lenders (lenders who provide loans for one-to-four-unit properties) simply will not lend on a property that is part of an LLC, which forces you to turn to a commercial lender with higher fees, higher rates, and shorter terms—something you probably don't want to do.

Many investors simply transfer the ownership of a property to an LLC after purchasing the property in their primary name, but that presents some big risks as well. If the bank finds out (and they probably will, because of insurance paperwork), they might call your note due because of the due on sale clause. Of course, you didn't actually sell the property, but you did transfer the title from one entity (your name) to another (your LLC). In the past, this has never really been a problem, because banks have generally turned a blind eye to such transactions. However, this seems to be changing and is expected to only get worse as interest rates rise. If you plan to go this route, consider speaking with your bank and getting permission, in writing, to transfer your properties to an LLC after buying them. This is the only way you'll be truly protected from that dreaded due on sale clause.

What Are You Protecting?

New investors automatically think they need an LLC to protect themselves, but when you are first starting out, how much wealth do you really need to protect? Think about it. You have a property or two with very little equity. You have car payments. You don't have six figures in the bank. Yet you want to go through all this trouble to protect your "wealth"?

Additional Paperwork and Hassle

Although LLCs are definitely easier than corporations with regard to paperwork and taxes, they still add a lot of complications to the mix. This is especially true if the LLC involves multiple members who are not married, because an individual business tax return will be required for each member. Setting up the LLC takes money, maintaining it takes money, and filing taxes takes money—all this on a property you probably are not making much on in the first place. Imagine spending $2,000 per year on asset protection on a house that only cash flows $1,200 per year. Yes, an LLC can turn a good investment into a bad one.

The Truth About New Investors and LLCs

Here's the thing I've noticed: People like to set up LLCs because it makes them feel like they are taking action. But they aren't. In fact, the hurdle of setting up an LLC is probably the number one excuse people have for not taking action. "I want to invest in real estate, but I don't know what to do about an LLC." How absurd! The truth is this: People use the concept of an LLC as an excuse to avoid getting out there and taking action. It's easier to say, "I don't have an LLC yet, so I can't buy a property" than it is to say, "I'm scared." But this is often the truth.

Yes, LLCs are valuable. Yes, I have them. Yes, I recommend talking with someone about setting one up—at some point. However, LLCs are no substitute for taking action. If you don't have any wealth to protect, perhaps you don't need an LLC. When you find yourself building wealth and creating a sizable business, that's when an LLC will come in most handy. By that time, you'll be able to afford the proper attorneys and CPAs who can handle establishing the LLC correctly. And maybe at that time, they'll still tell you that you really don't need an LLC. Maybe they'll set you up with something different.

What Should You Use Instead of an LLC?

Let's recap the three benefits of an LLC:

1. Limited liability
2. Tax efficiency
3. Operational flexibility

What other legal structure can help you protect yourself from losing personal money if you get sued, and is also easy to manage and has a relatively simple tax structure?

I suggest two options: insurance and leverage. I'll talk about both, briefly.

Insurance

That's right, good insurance can help you avoid eating beans under a bridge with the pigeons. Get the right insurance, and get enough of it. Talk to a good insurance agent about your options, and let them know your fears. They'll be more than happy to sell you the best policy possible.

Leverage

When someone is going to sue you, what is their goal?

It's to get as much money from you as possible, of course. This is why leverage can actually be a big help in protecting your assets. By "leverage," I mean the down payment you use for your purchase. For example, if you owe $100,000 on a property, and the property is worth $110,000, you are highly leveraged. People often look at this like it's a bad thing, but in asset protection, it's a huge benefit. What kind of lawyer will go after someone, spend hundreds of hours litigating, and force them to sell their rental, only to find there is no blood to be squeezed from that turnip? On the other hand, if you own a rental property free and clear, and it's worth $110,000, suddenly the idea of suing you becomes much more exciting for an attorney, because they know there is a ton of money for them to take.

I'm not saying you should go increase the leverage on every property you own, but I am saying that when you are first starting out, you'll likely be very highly leveraged—and therefore not a large target for lawyers to come after.

So, Should You Get an LLC?

Unfortunately, I must conclude this section with the dreaded answer everyone hates: I don't know. To get a better answer, you should talk to an attorney and a CPA. Only they will be able to truly help you know if you are ready for an LLC. An LLC is a powerful legal entity, but only if it's set up correctly and actually beneficial to you. And there is no easy way for me to tell you if that's the case for you.

However, I encourage you not to let the LLC question stop you from moving forward with your real estate ambitions. Don't let it be an excuse, and don't let the fear of a lawsuit stop you from achieving your dreams.

Final Walk-Through of the Property

Finally, on the day of closing, I recommend setting up an appointment to walk through the property one last time. This will help you verify that everything is still the same and that nothing has changed since you made the original agreement. I would hate to see you buy a property only to show up and find that all the windows and doors have been removed. (It's happened, I'm sure!) If you are confident that the property is in the condition you expect, then it's time to move forward. But there is one more thing you may want to do before signing the documents, during this due diligence phase...

Plan the Rehab

If you wait until after you close on the property to plan the rehab, you'll already be behind schedule. During the due diligence process, start getting contractors into the property, and schedule them to begin working the day after closing. Make a plan for what should get fixed first, second, third, and so on. Get the materials list together and ready to order the day the property closes. (I don't recommend buying the materials before closing, though. If something goes wrong, you could have a lot of materials on your hands and no property.)

Sign the Docs

Your closing agent will likely call you a few days before closing to schedule the date and location where you'll sign all the paperwork. They'll also tell you the final amount of money you'll need to bring with you to close the deal. The process for signing all the paperwork depends greatly on the state in which you are buying, but most likely, it will take place at the attorney's or title company's office. You'll need to bring three important things to the meeting:

- Yourself and anyone else on the loan or title
- Your government-issued ID
- A certified check

Be sure to read over exactly what you are signing, because title companies and attorneys do make mistakes. Have the person organizing the documents go through all the math behind the numbers you are supposed to bring to closing. Also verify that the names and address are correct, as are the terms of who pays what. If it all looks good, sign your name on the dotted lines and hand over the check.

Once you have done this, the actual transfer of title could take anywhere from a few hours to a few days. The attorney or title company will let you know when they estimate it will close, and they will likely call you after it is finished. Your real estate agent will probably give you the keys, though your area might have a different custom for handing these over. Don't worry about it too much, just go with the flow. It'll all work out fine!

WRAPPING IT UP

Congratulations! You are now a rental property owner. How does it feel? Do yourself a favor and take your spouse out to dinner. Celebrate! This is an amazing thing, and I'm proud that you've made it this far. However, understand that the journey is not over but is just beginning. You are now a landlord—so it's time to get busy.

Chapter Seventeen

MANAGING YOUR RENTALS (PART I)

"Success is where preparation and opportunity meet."

—BOBBY UNSER

The year was 1978. In South London, an elderly woman's only precious cat ran up a tree and could not get down. She begged and pleaded with the cat for hours but soon discovered it was hopeless. Finally, she called the local fire station to request help. The firemen came to help the poor woman, and had cleverly and creatively devised a plan to get the cat out of the tree. Finally, the ladder went up and the cat came down in the arms of a heroic fireman. The neighbors cheered, the elderly woman was full of joy, and the firemen rejoiced in their accomplishment. The elderly woman treated the heroes to some afternoon tea, which they graciously accepted. Finally, as the afternoon waned, the firemen took their leave as the woman said a final goodbye. Still celebrating their victorious cat rescue and discussing the delicious snacks they had just enjoyed, the firemen backed out of the driveway—only to run over and kill the cat.

No matter how smart and clever you have been up to this point in your real estate investing, and no matter how much work you've invested, now is not the time to get sloppy. You must, at all costs, avoid killing the cat. As Babe Ruth famously said, "Yesterday's home runs don't win today's games." You've navigated the confusing world of real estate to buy a rental property, and now you are the proud owner of an income-producing asset. However, all of that time, money, and work could be jeopardized if you don't manage the property correctly. Now is when you must ratchet up your business, rather than wind down.

I have designed this chapter and the next to help you avoid killing everything you've spent so much time building, and you will do this through the systematic and professional management of your tenants. In this chapter, I will look specifically at the business side of property management and the things you must do before a tenant moves in. The foundation you build in your management business will ensure a long-lasting and profitable rental property experience. Let's get started with perhaps the most fundamental question: Should you manage your properties yourself or let someone else do it?

Self-Management versus Property Management

When you own a rental property, should you manage the property yourself or hire a professional to manage it for you? The response to this question, I'm afraid, is "there is no right answer, but there may be a right answer for you." Every person has different skills, personalities, and time availability. The purpose of this section is to help you make the best choice for you and your family.

Role of a Property Manager

First, let's address what a property manager actually does, though even that is tough to give a straight answer about. You see, property managers do a wide range of tasks depending on the manager and the owner with whom they are working. However, most of the time a property manager will be responsible for the following:

- Advertising vacant units
- Screening applicants
- Approving tenants and signing leases
- Handling phone calls from tenants
- Scheduling maintenance-related appointments

- Issuing late notices
- Filing evictions, if needed
- Keeping a record of income and expenses

They may also pay your property's bills, depending on the manger.

In addition, property managers offer numerous benefits, such as the following:

- They can clear up your day, allowing you to spend more time with family and friends, or at your day job.
- A property management company has the infrastructure in place to handle your rental, including office staff, paperwork, and signage.
- A property manager will have a reliable set of contractors with whom to work and can benefit from volume pricing.
- A property manager can give you more time to look for other deals, helping you focus exclusively on the task that brings in the most money for you.
- A property manager will have a lead system in place for attracting potential tenants. People will know their name, recognize their signs, and call them without even needing to advertise your property.

Sounds like a dream, right? Property management can be a powerful thing, allowing you to work on your business rather than in it. However, management does have some disadvantages.

Disadvantages of Property Management

- **Price.** Although the price for management depends greatly on where you live, management is usually in the 8 percent to 10 percent range, plus a fee when a new tenant moves in, usually between 50 percent and 100 percent of a month's rent. In other words, if the rent on your property is $1,200 per month, you might pay $120 per month plus $1,200 every time a unit turns over. Furthermore, some management companies charge a renewal fee each year, even if the tenant doesn't move. Clearly, the expense of a property manager can be a huge drain on your cash flow, and something you must budget for.

  For example, let's look at the numbers on a sample property: 123 Main Street. This property is a three-bedroom home that you purchased for $100,000 (with a $20,000 down payment), so you now have a mortgage payment of $500 per month. When you ran the numbers, you found that all the expenses (taxes, insurance, maintenance, CapEx, vacancy, etc.) came to $400 per month on average, over time. This means your total expenses on the property are $900 per month. If the home rents for $1,100 per month, you are looking at about $200 per month in cash flow, or $2,400 per year. On your $20,000 investment, this is a 12 percent cash-on-cash ROI. Not too bad, right?

Now let's factor in property management. If your local management company charges 10 percent of the rent, that's $110 per month. Your $200 per month in cash flow has now dropped to $90 per month, or $1,080 per year. On your $20,000 investment, you are looking at a cash-on-cash return of just 5.4 percent, a huge difference from what you thought you would be getting. However, is that difference in cash flow worth it for you? Could you invest your time elsewhere to make a better return? Or are you better off self-managing and keeping that extra income? These are questions you'll need to ask yourself.

- **No One Cares Like You Care.** The fact is this: No one will care as much about your property as you do. Your property manager will likely have hundreds, if not thousands, of properties to manage. Yours will not be special. When a potential tenant walks through the door, your property manager has no incentive to show your property over any other. They won't be as available to drive to your property to check it out as much as you might. It's not that they don't care; it's just that you are one in a bunch.

  Case in point, I use property management on just a few properties I own, as an experiment. Recently, a tenant of mine called the company and said that their gutters were detaching from the roof on one part of the house. The property manager got a bid from their main contractor to fix the problem, and the bid came in at $1,200. Now, I'm no contractor, but even I know that fixing this kind of gutter problem would require just a few screws and maybe one hour of work. $1,200? Someone was getting ripped off. I told the manager to get a second bid from someone else. The second bid? Just $115, and the person also took care of a few other issues while at the house. Now, had I not encouraged the second bid, the property manager would have blindly accepted the $1,200 price tag because they don't care as much as I care. The money is not coming out of their pocket, so they don't have the incentive to examine the bid to determine whether they are getting ripped off or not.

  Therefore, if you end up hiring a property manager, understand that your job is not 100 percent passive. You will still need to manage the manager and stay on top of them to make sure they are doing what they are supposed to do. Don't assume that property management means you can forget about the property and just collect checks.

- **Property Managers Are Terrible.** Okay, not all of them, but I would venture to say that most property managers are pretty bad at their job. Of course, if you begin managing your properties, you'll likely be terrible, too. But because it's your property, you'll learn and grow quickly from the on-the-job training. Therefore, if you are going to use a property manager, just remember this: most of them suck. You need to find the one that doesn't. A property manger will be one of the most important members of your team, so it's imperative you invest the time up front to find the right one. Treat it like a job interview. Get referrals and actually talk with those referrals. Ask the property manager hard questions in an interview. Don't settle for mediocre. If you are going to trust the most significant investment in your portfolio—and the key to your family's future wealth—to someone, shouldn't you do your homework first?

Property Manager Interview Questions

When you sit down with your potential property manager, I recommend starting with the following questions:

- What are your management fees?
- How do you communicate with owners? How frequently? What about?
- How many properties do you manage?
- How long have you been a property manager?
- Am I locked into a management contract with you? If so, how does that work?
- How many evictions do you have each month?
- What kind of reserves do you/does your company require?
- How long does a typical tenant stay in a property?
- How long do properties usually stay vacant before being rented?
- How do you screen tenants?
- Do you accept people who have had an eviction on their record?
- How do you handle maintenance requests?
- Is there a minimum charge for a maintenance visit?
- What do you do if a tenant doesn't pay rent?
- How do you market vacant properties?

These questions should serve as a starting point for your conversation, but don't let it end there. Dig in on each point until you truly understand the kind of manager they are. Write down the person's answers so you can review them later and compare your notes with the responses of other property managers (because, of course, you should interview more than one).

What Should You Do?

I wish I could give you a simple answer as to whether or not you should hire a property manager or do it yourself. But I don't know you. You might be a terrible manager. You might be really busy. Or you might be great.

However, I can say this: Managing tenants is not as difficult as it might sound if you treat it like a business. This means continually learning, growing, and networking. It means having systems in place to handle problems. It means always trying to improve.

In the rest of this chapter, I will focus on those who plan to self-manage. Even if you expect to hire a property manager, I recommend that you read through the rest of this chapter anyway so you can understand how I suggest doing things, and can better manage your manager and know whether they are doing a good job.

Business or Hobby: Getting in the Right Mindset

Now that we've got the "property management versus self-management" question out of the way, let's zoom in on the world of self-management. Let me ask you a question: Are you excited for middle-of-the-night phone calls, sleepless nights, and profitless rentals? If so, manage your properties the way most people do—as a hobby.

If, however, you want your rental property experience to be different, *you* will need to be different.

The difference between success and failure as a landlord often comes down to the method used to manage those rentals. Is this a hobby for you? Are you just doing this "on the fly," with no plan, direction, or purpose? Or is this a business for you, one you'll run with efficiency, systems, and processes? If you chose the former, like most landlords, prepare for some difficult years ahead. But if you chose the latter, welcome to the world of property management.

Managing tenants is a business. This means you need a process for doing things. Yes, I know you didn't get into real estate investing just to get back into the corporate world of systems and processes, but trust me, this is designed to help you work less and experience less stress in your management. Let me tell you about one kind of landlord, and you can decide whether you'd enjoy this life.

The buzzing cell phone wakes him up at 2:27 a.m. He picks up the phone, and the tenant on the other end of the line begins screaming about how someone is parked in their parking spot. He tells the tenant he is sorry and says, "There is nothing I can do." The tenant insists. He calls the other tenant upstairs, at 2:28 a.m., and asks them to move their car. They insist that they only parked there because the downstairs tenant was in *their* parking spot. But while they have the landlord on the phone, the upstairs tenant lets him know that, although rent is due tomorrow, they won't get paid until next week, so they'll need another extension. The landlord tells them to make sure they drop the rent off at his house next Friday, and it'll be fine.

But next Friday comes, and the rent doesn't show up. The landlord drives to the tenant's place, only to discover that the lawn—which is the landlord's responsibility—hasn't been mowed in almost a month. The landlord kicks himself for forgetting again and makes a mental note to try to come mow the lawn on Sunday. When he knocks, the chained door opens three inches, and a pair of unfamiliar eyes stares out blankly. The landlord assumes this must be the upstairs tenant's new girlfriend, whom the landlord didn't know was staying there. Smoke billows out of the partially opened door, and it doesn't smell like cigarette smoke. Her boyfriend isn't home, she says, and she isn't sure when he'll be back: "Might be a few days." The landlord asks her to ask the tenant to call and walks away shaking his head. He's used to this.

On his way down the steps, he's stopped by the other tenant, who again complains about the upstairs tenant parking in his spot too often. The landlord reassures him that he'll talk to the upstairs tenant about this and try to fix the problem. The tenant also reminds him that the bathtub faucet has been continually running for months, and the landlord promises once again that he'll come fix it soon. He just needs to wait for both tenants to pay rent so he can afford the new faucet.

As the landlord walks back to his car, defeated, he asks himself, "Is this really financial freedom? Is this really what I fought so hard for? Is this what I saved all my extra income to invest in?"

You are probably a bit depressed after reading this. Good! But you need to understand that this is reality for millions of landlords across the world. Defeated. Burned out. Broke.

Is this the life you want?

Of course not! The landlord in that story approached his business like a hobby, a side project, something he does when he finds time. He's deep inside his business and can't seem to get out. He's fighting a losing battle with his tenants and losing ground every day. But if there is one silver lining to this story, it's this: When this landlord goes bankrupt, and he most likely will, you and I will be there to get a great deal on his property, turn it around, and start managing it like a business.

We'll create office hours, have a system in place for parking, collect rent automatically, issue legal notices the day after a tenant is late, kick out bad tenants, move in great ones, raise the rent, hire the right people to do maintenance jobs, and work far less but make far more money.

I'll dedicate the rest of this chapter to the business of property management and how to deal with tenants. However, I cannot cover each and every scenario and situation you may come across. This is why I am spending so much time harping on this one fact: Treat your business like a business. If you can nail down that one basic principle and fully internalize it, you'll be able to handle all these situations on your own because you will be in the right mindset.

- Owning a business means creating a policy of how things are done—and sticking to that policy.
- Owning a business means having rules—and enforcing those rules.
- Owning a business means setting boundaries—and making sure others abide by those boundaries.
- Owning a business means continually finding ways to become more efficient and profitable.
- Owning a business means outsourcing the things you aren't good at or don't enjoy.
- Owning a business means being productive and maximizing every second.
- Owning a business means working *on* your rental business, not *in* your rental business.

Let's get into the specifics of managing your property. Although I am about to share a lot of specifics about how *I* manage my properties, you may find your own way to manage yours. The tools and techniques may differ, but as long as you remember that you are a business owner and not a hobbyist, you'll do great.

Getting a Property Ready to Rent

Before you can start giving tours of the property, it needs to be rent-ready. Trust me, if you start showing properties before they're fixed up and ready to go, you'll likely only attract tenants who are highly motivated to move in because of an eviction or some other less-than-positive reason. I once bought a vacant, incredibly ugly, purple triplex in the month of December, but because of the rainy winter weather, I couldn't paint it until spring. I decided to rent the property out, as it was, and paint it later. *Huge* mistake! I ended up evicting two of the first three tenants despite their solid applications and great tenant screenings. The simple fact is this: Bad tenants are the only ones attracted to bad properties.

Therefore, rather than placing tenants and then fixing the property up, fix it up and get it ready to rent immediately after purchasing it. This means having a thorough cleaning done, installing new blinds on the windows (if needed), getting the carpets professionally cleaned, ensuring that all appliances work, painting the interior and exterior (if needed), and performing whatever other task is necessary to make sure the property is in tip-top shape.

I recommend snapping as many photos as possible after the property has been rehabbed. This way, you'll have a reference point to look back on after the next tenant moves out, so you can see what has already been fixed and what has not. This will also help you market the unit, because you can use the photographs almost everywhere you advertise the property. If you own a high-quality camera (a DSLR), or have a friend or family member who does, I recommend using it to take the photos. There is a huge difference between a photo shot with a cell phone and one taken with a more professional-level camera.

I also recommend setting up a Google Voice phone number at this time. Google Voice is a completely free service that gives you a second phone number that can be forwarded to your cell phone, landline, or both. You can even set it up to ring one phone during part of the day and a different phone at another time. Or when you go on vacation, you can easily switch the phone to call your maintenance guy or someone else you designate.

Once the property is ready to show, you need to start getting tenants through the doors. But first you must attract those tenants through advertising.

Five Ways to Find Great Tenants

You may have found the real estate deal of the century. You may have achieved the best financing available. You may have the best plan, the best forms, the best mentor. But if you get the wrong tenant, you can lose it all. A common mistake with new landlords is to place just anyone in a unit. After all, they've worked so hard to get the rental property purchased, and now they have a looming mortgage payment and a vacant unit. Fill 'er up, right? Not so fast! You actually need to find the right tenant, not just any tenant. This begins with marketing.

Here I will outline my five favorite ways of attracting tenants to my properties. If I have a lot of vacancies, and I'm having trouble finding a tenant, I might do all five at once. If vacancies are fairly easy to fill, I might only do one or two. However, it's important for you to understand all five so you can adjust your marketing campaign to fit your local rental market.

1. Sign in the Yard

Perhaps the oldest method on this list for finding tenants—a sign in the yard—is also one of the most effective. You can pick up a "for rent" sign at almost any hardware store for around $5 and immediately start advertising your vacancy. I recommend including all the pertinent information about the unit on the sign directly, or as much as you can fit, to weed out those who won't qualify. For example, if you just place a phone number, every person who drives by will ask the same question: "How much?"

At a minimum, I like to include the rental price, the security deposit amount, the number of bedrooms, and my phone number. If I have space, I'll write out a couple of the qualification standards as well (which I'll talk about in a moment), such as "no smokers" or "650 credit score minimum." This will further limit the number of "tire kickers" who call and will help you get phone calls only from good prospects.

If you want to take your signage to a higher level, you can design and print a custom sign for around $20 with an online print shop such as www.vistaprint.com. This can help you stand out as a more "professional" landlord. I have about a dozen signs printed that have only our phone number, business name, business website, and "for rent" on them. When I use one of these signs, I try to attach a flyer box (a special box, usually with a see-through/clear front, meant to hold informational papers) to it (or near it) so people can get more information about the property.

One word of caution, by placing a "for rent" sign in the yard, you are letting everyone know that the property is vacant (or will soon be vacant). This, of course, increases the risk for vandalism, so many landlords choose not to advertise with a sign.

2. Craigslist

Lately, our number one driver of tenants happens to also be the least expensive: Craigslist. Craigslist is the world's largest classifieds website, and in most areas, it's completely free to post a "for rent" listing, which will be seen by hundreds or even thousands of potential tenants.

When you're creating your Craigslist ad, I recommend including as much information about the property as possible and uploading as many photos as you can. Spend some time making your ad stand out.

As with a sign, I recommend including as much information as possible about the property and the minimum standards you set regarding who can rent the property. This way, the tenant can learn all about the property and decide whether it's worth pursuing before calling you. However, I do not recommend including the address of the property in the listing, because this will only encourage vandalism. Craigslist allows you to instead include the street names of nearby cross streets so that prospective tenants can know the general area but still need to call you for the specific address.

3. Newspapers

Although newspapers may be dying a slow death, they may still be an incredibly effective strategy for driving tenants to your property. This, of course, depends on the cost of taking out a classified ad in one. In my local newspaper, I pay approximately $20 a week for a basic ad that looks like something like this:

2 Bedrm 1 Bth Apt in Aberdeen.
New paint, flooring, & lots of storage.
W/D Hkps. No pets, no smoke.
555-555-5555

The goal of a newspaper ad is to deliver the pertinent information in as short of a space as possible, so you'll want to abbreviate as many words as you can, as I've done in my example.

One tip that has worked well for me: Find out all the different advertising pricing options and devise a strategy based on that. For example, I discovered that taking out a "monthly ad" was only $80, but I could cancel it whenever the unit got rented. In other words, if I order it for a month but only use it for a week, I only pay $20, rather than the weekly rate of $50. Your local newspaper may have similar pricing strategies. I've even heard of landlords with multiple properties negotiating an "annual ad rate" and simply changing the ad to fit whichever property they currently have empty.

4. MLS

If you live in a large city, it's very possible that the MLS will be the main driver of tenants for your property. Although the MLS is best known for listing homes for sale through real estate agents, homes can also be listed for rent on the MLS, and real estate agents can help bring you tenants—for a price. You will typically need to pay the agent a fee when the property is rented, but this might be a small cost to get a great tenant. If you plan to use the MLS to list your property, talk with your real estate agent about how it's normally done in your area, as well as the typical prices you may end up paying.

5. Existing Tenants

If you already own a number of rental properties, your current tenants can be a great source of finding new tenants. When I am having a slow time getting a property rented out, I like to send a postcard to our existing tenants offering them the ability to "choose your neighbor." I also offer a cash reward if they refer someone who ends up renting from me, usually about $100. This money is only given after their friend has moved in and paid the rent plus deposit.

Accepting Phone Calls

When you receive a phone call from a prospective tenant, always pre-screen them. This means trying to qualify the tenant over the phone before spending time going to the house to show them. The easiest way to do this is by setting rental criteria and explaining that criteria over the phone. My criteria look like this:

- Their gross monthly income must be approximately three times or more the monthly rent.
- Applicants must have a favorable credit history (a score of 600 or higher).
- Applicants must have a source of income and be able to furnish acceptable proof of the required income.
- Applicants must have good references concerning rental payment, housekeeping, and property maintenance from all previous land-lords.
- The number of occupants per bedroom is limited to two (per Washington State law).
- Only non-smokers are considered.

You can read this list over the phone to the prospective tenant and ask them if they meet these qualifications. If they don't, don't rent to them. These qualifications are designed to take the emotion out of renting to someone, so stick with them. By allowing tenants who don't meet your minimum qualifications to move in, you are only setting yourself up for failure later on.

A note on discrimination: Be sure to not discriminate when you are advertising and screening for tenants. Federal law defines seven protected traits of people against whom you cannot discriminate, which include race, skin color, sex, national origin, religion, disability, and familial status. You cannot even ask questions about these terms without appearing discriminatory, so don't do it. Additional protected statuses (such as being on Section 8, marital status, and political affiliation) may also be protected, depending on the state you live in. Be sure to check with your state's fair housing laws.

Showing the Property to Tenants

Showing units can be difficult because, much of the time, potential tenants with whom you have arranged a meeting will simply not show up. To combat this, I use one of two techniques:

1. I give them the address to drive by first and tell them to call me

back if they are interested in seeing the inside. This eliminates the people who lose interest because of the location.

2. I try to "batch" all the showings within one time frame. I will tell all callers that I will be at the house from 5:00 to 5:30 on Friday afternoon, for example, and if they want to see it, they should show up then. Having multiple tenants look at a property at the same time can be a little bit awkward, but it creates a sense of competition and scarcity, which allows for more applications.

It's also a good idea to include the criteria and application process with the application. This allows the prospective tenant to easily understand how the process works and gives you yet another way to pre-screen for duds.

The Application Process

Give an application to every single person who is interested, even if you are not interested in them (this is another measure to ensure you will not be charged with discrimination). Encourage them to fill it out there, though the applicant will usually want to fill it out later, and drop it off or mail it to you. I try to discourage this, because it adds a lot of time, but sometimes the tenant will want to think about it, so have a plan in place to deal with this.

The Rental Application

An ideal rental application should have space for the tenant to fill in the following items for all adult applicants, at minimum:

- Name(s)
- Date of birth
- Social Security number
- Phone number
- Alternate phone number
- Previous addresses (past five years)
- Current employer (name, hire date, income, contact info)
- Past employer (name, hire date, income, contact info)
- Emergency contact information
- Release of information statement
- Signature
- Application fee

Always, I repeat, *always* take an application fee with the application. Don't even bother processing any part of the application unless the tenant has paid the application fee. The amount you charge must be reasonable and reflect the actual cost of you running the application, plus compensation for your time doing so. I recommend finding out what the local property management companies charge and asking for a similar amount. I charge at least $35 per adult. Be sure to check with your state laws and make sure there are no laws dictating how much you can charge.

Immediate Disqualifiers

When you receive an application from a tenant with the application fee, look the document over and check the important things before ordering the official background check. The obvious things are those you read to the tenant over the phone, which I covered earlier.

If you can quickly see that the rent for the house is $1,000 per month and the applicant makes only $1,800 per month in gross income, they clearly did not pass the income qualification. Sometimes this is because of a writing error or income they forgot to include, so be sure to clarify with them before rejecting the application. Chances are, however, that the tenant simply doesn't qualify and was hoping you wouldn't notice. If you did a thorough job of explaining the criteria over the phone with the applicant, and they still applied and didn't qualify, it's up to you if you want to return the application fee. However, don't bother running the background/credit check if they are disqualified because of one of the obvious criteria. I'll cover more on how to disqualify someone in just a moment.

Screening Tenants

Have you heard the story about the tenant who deliberately threw maggots down the stairs to the tenant below? Or the tenant who moved fifteen children into an 800-square-foot house? I did not make these stories up for your entertainment; they are true stories from actual BiggerPockets members, and are just a tiny sample of what a real estate investor must go through sometimes as a landlord. However, your experience doesn't have to be like these if you have a great tenant. Screening is how you separate the good from the bad, or at least try to.

Screening is about digging into an applicant's background and discovering who they really are outside of the application. After all, an application can only tell you so much, and data can be easily manipulated or falsified. Screening your tenant means looking into the information they provided, as well as analyzing outside information you can discover, and coming to a reasonable assumption regarding the kind of tenant they will be. I say "reasonable assumption" because there are no surefire ways of knowing the future quality of a tenant. As landlords, our job is to simply screen effectively and choose the best possible applicant for the property.

Deciding what kind of background or credit history you'll allow depends largely on your location and the strength of your market. If you have a lot of applicants to choose from, you can be pickier and only accept the most qualified tenant. However, if you are struggling to get applicants, you may need to lower your standards slightly (and I mean *slightly*) to move someone in. For me, I hold the person's rental history and income in a lot higher regard than I do their credit, because I live in a lower-income area where the vast majority of prospective tenants have terrible credit. Your area might be different, so if possible, talk with other local landlords or ask for advice on the BiggerPockets Forums.

The things I look closely at on the background and credit checks are these:

- Prior felonies
- Prior evictions filed
- Prior evictions carried out
- Bankruptcies
- Judgments
- Other criminal issues or a bad financial history

I make it a policy to never rent to a person with an eviction on their record or a recent felony (within seven years). Yes, people do change, but personally, I don't find the risk worth taking. I'll leave that risk to other landlords (and then buy their properties after they are foreclosed on and lose it all).

Verifying Income and Rental History

People often lie, especially when they want to get into a new rental and cannot qualify. As a result, verifying everything that the tenant writes on their application is vitally important. As I explained earlier, your application should include a "release of information" signature from your prospective tenant to allow you to properly check their claims.

Begin with their job. The application should include the name and phone number of their current employer, so call and speak with the company's manager, owner, or human resources manager. Many times, you will be required to fax over the release of information signature. The important questions to ask are these:

- How much do they currently make?
- How long have they worked there?
- Is this job considered temporary?

Next, call their previous landlords. Don't simply call their current landlord, because many landlords will lie or embellish the truth in an effort to get rid of bad tenants. Instead, call all their previous landlords for at least the past five years. Be sure to conduct a background check and credit check to see if any other addresses appear that might indicate they conveniently "forgot" to list a landlord they rented from. When talking with previous landlords, you might want to consider asking the following questions:

- How long did the tenant rent from you?
- What was their monthly rent?
- Did the tenant give proper notice when vacating?
- Did the tenant receive their security deposit back?
- Would you rent to this tenant again?

Accepting or Denying an Applicant

After doing a background check and verifying that the information listed on a potential tenant's application is correct, you will have a good idea of whether or not the tenant is worthy of your rental property. Sometimes, you will receive applications from multiple parties who all qualify. To avoid discrimination complaints, I recommend processing applications on a first-come, first-served basis, processing applications until you discover the tenant does not qualify and moving on to the next. Of course, you can choose to rent to the most qualified individual, but be sure that you can clearly demonstrate what (nondiscriminatory thing) made one better than the other.

When you deny an applicant, clearly documenting your reasons for doing so is important to avoid discrimination complaints. Always inform the tenant with a written notice. I always send a letter to the tenant stating that they did not meet the minimum requirements for tenancy for "such and such" reason. Be sure to keep a copy of all records pertaining to the prospective tenant so you can back up your reasons for denying them in the future, should you need to.

When you find an applicant who meets all your requirements, you can verbally let them know that they are approved. However, your job is not yet finished. Many times a good applicant will be approved but will find another place to rent, leaving you wondering what happened to them. Therefore, it is important to require a deposit to hold the vacant property. This deposit is nonrefundable and should be due within twenty-four hours of the tenant being accepted. Simply let the approved applicant know that you cannot hold the property indefinitely, so if they want to guarantee their position, they must pay the deposit within that time frame.

Some landlords actually require that this deposit be paid when the application is filled out, and the landlord simply returns the deposit if the tenant doesn't qualify. I don't personally use this technique, but it may work for your location if there are a lot of qualified applicants trying to rent your property.

This deposit will become the tenant's security deposit (which I will get to later), so it's not an unexpected or extra cost for the applicant. When you collect this deposit, be sure to sign two copies of a "deposit to hold agreement" that states what the deposit is for and what the terms are. Essentially, this document will declare that the applicant has until a clearly specified date to sign a lease agreement. If an agreement is not signed by that date, the deposit is forfeited to the landlord.

Both you and the prospective tenant will receive a copy of this agreement, which will serve as a receipt for the applicant. I try to schedule the lease signing for as soon as possible, to minimize the amount of time the property is left vacant and costing me money. Typically, I will not hold it longer than two weeks unless I absolutely love the tenant and don't want to lose them. This is up to you and your discretion.

To sign a rental lease with your tenants, you will need to have, of course, a lease. You can get a state-specific lease agreement from a number of sources. BiggerPockets has them available for your state at www.biggerpockets.com/landlord-forms or you can find them on other sites, such as www.ezlandlordforms.com, www.uslegalforms.com, a local paper supply company such as Staples or Office Depot, or your attorney.

Don't simply download a free lease off the internet. Each state has different rules and laws that govern the landlord-tenant policies in that state, so chances are that a lease found for free online may not be legally binding for you. Don't skimp on the quality of your lease.

Before purchasing your lease agreement, however, you need to decide whether you want a month-to-month rental agreement, a one-year lease, or something in between. Most landlords choose a one-year lease in an effort to keep their tenants in the home as long as possible and to minimize turnover. Others choose to offer only month-to-month leases, to maintain the ability to quickly and easily remove a tenant if things don't work out. Still others choose a six- or nine-month lease, which is often helpful in ensuring that a lease doesn't end during the holiday months of November through January, when vacancies are the most difficult to fill. This comes down to a personal choice, but no matter which lease term you choose, be sure to obtain the correct lease agreement form.

Although lease agreements generally vary in length and content, most contain the following information:

- Names of tenants
- Address of the rental property
- Lease term length
- Rent amount
- Security deposit amount
- Late fee description
- The move-in condition report
- Provisions for or against pets, utilities, smoking, and the like

You may also need to provide certain state and federal documents with your lease, depending on when your home was built and your state's laws. The U.S. Environmental Protection Agency requires that you give your tenant a pamphlet called "Protecting Your Family from Lead in the Home" if your property was built before 1978. Check with your local attorney for other state-specific forms you may be required to provide.

Signing a Lease Agreement

Schedule a time for the tenant to meet with you at the property or sign all papers at your attorney's office (showing professionalism and the seriousness of what they are signing). Don't sign at a coffee shop or via mail or email; actually meet at the property on the day they will be moving in or drive over from the attorney's office after signing. I find it helpful to go through the lease ahead of time, and mark all the signature or initial areas with Post-it notes or a highlighter so nothing is forgotten or missed.

When you meet with the tenant, walk them through each provision in the lease, step by step, and sign (with a blue pen) as you go. This may be time-consuming, but is will help protect you when the tenant says, "Well, I didn't know that" months down the road. You may consider having the tenant initial next to important items as well, such as a "no pet" policy. It's easy for a tenant to later forget details, so having them initial such things is helpful in jogging their memory later on.

Accepting the Rent

During the lease signing, when you get to the part that says how much the monthly rent is, this is a good time to collect the money for the first month's rent. You should have already received the tenant's security deposit (in the form of the "deposit to hold" when they were approved), so typically, this is when you would collect the first month's rent.

If a tenant moves into the property in the middle of the month, I don't prorate the amount they pay for that first month. Instead, I prorate the second month to match the first. In other words, every tenant pays a full month's rent when they move in, but when the time comes to pay the rent on the first of the following month, they will pay only for the amount of days they lived in the home the previous month. For example, if the rent is $1,200 per month, and they move in on January 10, they will pay a full $1,200 for rent when they move in but only $800 on February 1.

One final note on the rent—only accept rent in certified funds, such as a money order or a cashier's check. Don't take cash and don't accept personal checks, especially for the first month's rent. You do not want to move a tenant in and find out weeks later that the check was bad, forcing you to evict. This is a wise policy to have all around in your relationship with your tenants: certified funds only.

As for rent payments in the future, I recommend not picking up the rent in person, because this will only train the tenant to expect you each month. For my rentals, I used to mail monthly statements to the tenant, and they mailed their certified funds to my post office box. However, over time, I grew tired of the "my check is lost in the mail" story, so I switched to giving tenants another option: Property Management Software. Many property management software companies exist to help you keep track of your tasks, your tenants, and your expenses. Currently, we use a program called Buildium to manage our rental properties, but other services are excellent including Cozy.co, Appfolio, and RentManager. All of these programs can allow your tenant to pay rent online, including the option for a direct withdrawal each month from their checking account.

Many landlords have different techniques for collecting rent, so ultimately, you may change or adapt your style as you learn more and grow, or as technology advances.

The Move-In Condition Report

By this time, the rent and security deposit have been paid, and the lease has been signed. It's now important to do one final thing before handing over the keys: the move-in condition report. The move-in condition report is simply a paper that the tenant will sign that documents, in detail, the condition of the property. Allow the tenant to take some time walking through the property and inspecting it, perhaps even taking notes on the condition of each room. If there is a hole in a door, document it. If there is a light switch that doesn't work, document it. If there is a stain on the carpet, document it. The move-in condition report is designed to protect both your interests and the interests of the tenant when the time comes for the tenant to move out. As much as you might think you'll remember every detail of the home, trust me, you won't. By documenting everything and having the tenant sign off on that documentation, the tenant cannot come back to you later and say, "Oh, the giant hole in that wall was already there when I moved in."

For the same reason, I also recommend taking photos (or a video) of the property before handing over the keys. This will be further evidence in the future when the tenant moves out. In many states, a landlord cannot deduct any charges from the security deposit if a move-in condition report was not filled out when the tenant moved in. Do not make this mistake. Document, document, document.

Handing Over the Keys

When the tenant has filled out the entire lease agreement, both parties have signed it, the move-in condition report has been signed, and the rent has been paid, you can now hand over the keys to the tenant to allow them possession. Although the tenant may ask to do so, never let a tenant move things into the property before signing the lease and paying the rent. The consequences for failing to do this could be disastrous.

The process for moving a tenant into a property may seem overwhelming at first, but soon, the process will be second nature to you. I encourage you to take this application time seriously, because it will set a standard for how your tenant relationship will go for the next several years. By showing you are a professional at every step, your tenant will respect you and follow your rules, because you are the authority. This is the first step in "training your tenants," whereby you set the ground rules at the beginning of your relationship and ensure that they are aware you're not the kind of landlord they can walk all over.

Bookkeeping and Taxes

Perhaps the least sexy part of being a real estate entrepreneur is keeping track of the bookkeeping. Yes, I know you got into real estate to free yourself from bureaucracy, paperwork, TPS reports, and having a "job." I know you want to just sit back and wait for the checks to come in. However, if you don't do accurate accounting within your business, you could lose everything and, maybe worse, end up in jail. Besides, for a landlord, bookkeeping is designed to help you pay less taxes. That's right, less taxes. The better job you do at bookkeeping, the lower taxes you'll likely pay.

Bookkeeping is the practice of knowing where every dollar comes from and where it goes. Really, it's as simple as that. The way you track that, however, is where things can get a little complicated. Numerous tools are available out there to help you track your income and expenses.

- **Spreadsheet.** A good spreadsheet can help you keep an accurate record of the money that goes in and out of your business, though it generally must be designed from the ground up, so you need at least a basic understanding of how accounting for landlords works. The downsides of the spreadsheet model are that there is no automatic bank reconciliation, and you can't take the data and create numerous different reports like you might be able to do with some other methods I'll outline in a minute. However, when you are just getting started, using a basic spreadsheet might be enough for you. If so, I find it best to divide your spreadsheet into sections that correspond with the IRS's categories for income and expenses.

- **QuickBooks.** Many landlords choose to use professional accounting software such as QuickBooks to record everything. QuickBooks can be a bit overwhelming to learn and may feel like you are swatting a fly with a cannon, but once you learn the system, keeping track of income and expenses becomes increasingly easy, as does tax time (CPAs love landlords who use QuickBooks correctly). QuickBooks, however, is not designed specifically for landlords and rental properties, so it takes some heavy configuration to get it set up properly for you and your rental business.

If you are unfamiliar with how to use QuickBooks, I recommend taking an online course to learn the software. There are also several good training programs specifically designed to teach landlords how to use QuickBooks for their business, such as www.landlordaccounting.com.

- **Rental Property Software.** A third option used by landlords to track their income and expenses is online rental property software such as VerticalRent, Buildium, or Appfolio. These products are designed to help you manage your property (keeping track of tenants, leases, reminders, repairs, etc.), but each also contains basic accounting features. These programs let you prepare and print numerous reports, such as a rent roll and end-of-year tax statements. Most of these programs charge a monthly fee to manage your properties, so be sure to shop around to determine which would work best for you and your portfolio. For example, Buildium and VerticalRent are designed a little more for the smaller investor, while Appfolio is designed for the investor with dozens (or hundreds) of units.
- **Bookkeeper.** Finally, you might want to consider outsourcing your entire bookkeeping operation to someone professionally trained to do it. Although you will still need to accurately track receipts and income, you can hire a professional bookkeeper to keep it all in order, enter it into QuickBooks or another program, and get the paperwork ready for tax season. There are bookkeepers in nearly every town, but it would be best to find one with experience dealing with rental properties for other landlords or themselves.

Bookkeeping can be stressful and annoying for any landlord, but the more professional your bookkeeping is throughout the year, the easier tax season will be. In addition, the more expenses you accurately record, the less money you'll pay come tax season. Focus on doing your bookkeeping correctly from the start, and hire a professional if you don't want to do it yourself.

Paying Taxes

The IRS considers the cash flow you receive on your real estate income. Therefore, you must pay taxes on this money. The good news, however, is that the current IRS code is very generous to real estate investors, allowing you to deduct nearly all your expenses and even some unrealized expenses—namely, depreciation. This can help offset your cash flow and make your actual tax bill zero, if not less. The method for doing your taxes is beyond the scope of this book, but I will leave you with this: The more properties you have, the more difficult and complicated your taxes will be. I could no longer do my taxes even if I wanted to. The upside, however, is that when you are at the higher levels of this game, a good CPA should be able to help save you more money than they cost you.

WRAPPING IT UP

Preparation is key to the success of any venture, and landlording is no different. The topics I covered in this chapter may feel overwhelming, but trust me: The way you set up your landlording business from the beginning will define how your landlording business operates in the end. From finding the perfect tenant to setting up the books, the importance of preparation cannot be overstated. You've done so much great work so far, now is not the time to back over and kill the cat. Take special care during this part of your business development to ensure that the empire you've built stays strong.

No matter how well you set up and prepare your rental property, you will have problems. Things break, people lie, and conflicts will arise. In the next chapter, I will deal exclusively with those issues: how to handle problems with your rental property investing, because, trust me, you are going to have them.

Chapter Eighteen

MANAGING YOUR RENTALS (PART II)

"The tree that never had to fight
For sun and sky and air and light,
But stood out in the open plain
And always got its share of rain,
Never became a forest king
But lived and died a scrubby thing."

—DOUGLAS MALLOCH, "GOOD TIMBER"

Many years ago, researchers in Illinois planted a number of small trees inside a greenhouse, dividing the trees into three groups. Trees in the first group were supported firmly by a wooden stake to help them grow tall and straight. Those in the second group were not staked at all, but left to grow free. Trees in the third group, as in the second, were not staked but manually shaken back and forth for several minutes each day. After several months, the researchers looked at the three groups of trees and saw the inevitable: The staked trees in the first group were tall but weak. The trees in the second group were of medium height but also fairly weak. The trees in the third group, which had been shaken daily, had developed strong roots and a thick trunk that would help them grow tall and strong, though perhaps a bit more slowly than the other two groups.

The analogy should not be lost on you. Strength comes from adversity, as you have no doubt found in other areas of your life. Problems will arise, and how you deal with them is what defines your future. In this chapter, I will explore the many different problems you will encounter in your rental property business, specifically regarding the management of tenants. Problems will occur in your business, but how you overcome those difficulties will ultimately lead to your long-term success. Let's begin by talking about the most common problem you'll encounter: maintenance and repairs.

Maintenance and Repairs

As much as I wish rental properties stayed in tip-top shape forever, this just is not the case. One of your most important jobs as a landlord is to maintain the property and fix things when they break. Although this can be expensive and stressful, if you followed the analysis part of this book, you will have money set aside to handle these issues. If not, you'll need to come up with the cost from your own pocket. Either way, the repair must be fixed.

The Ten Most Common Repairs You'll Encounter

The most common repair requests we get from tenants are the following:

1. **Fridge/Stove/Dishwasher Not Working.** Appliances have a lot of moving parts, and therefore tend to break down fairly often. Although some issues can be fixed by the landlord themselves (replacing a burned-out light bulb, installing a new heating element), many issues will require a qualified appliance repair person. Unless a new appliance is needed, the typical cost to fix this sort of issue is between $50 and $100 per hour, and most repairs can be handled in one hour. If you do need a new appliance, consider buying a used one. Used appliance stores exist in almost every town and, especially in the case of stoves, can provide units that are just as good as new (though I never buy used dishwashers).

2. **Water Leak in Ceiling or Under Windows.** Water may be required for the human body to survive, but it's deadly to a rental property. If left unchecked, water can destroy wood, drywall, flooring, and virtually every other surface of your property. Even in small amounts,

moisture can cause mold to grow, which can be expensive to remediate if it gets out of control. When your tenant reports a water problem, make this your number one concern. Hire a qualified contractor to check the problem out and fix it immediately. When you're dealing with a water leak, don't hire the cheapest guy—hire the best. It's also a good idea to know whether your property has water supply lines in the ceiling, so if there is a leak, you can call a plumber instead of a roofing contractor.

3. **Water Leak Under Sink.** A water leak under a kitchen or bathroom sink can have one of two causes: the supply line (the pipe that brings water to the sink, both hot and cold) or the drain (the drain that takes the water from the sink and sends it out to the sewer). I estimate that 90 percent of water leaks are caused by the drain pipe not fitting together correctly. This is a fairly easy thing for you to learn how to fix (watch some YouTube videos to find out how) or hire a plumber, which should cost approximately $100.

4. **Water Drip from Faucets.** A slow drip from a sink or bathroom can end up costing you hundreds of dollars per year, so if you have a slow drip, get it fixed right away. In most cases, the problem can be solved with a $0.50 rubber washer and about an hour of work by a plumber (or you). However, occasionally, the entire faucet will need to be replaced. If this is the case, don't buy the $18 faucet that is mostly plastic. You'll just be tearing it out next summer and replacing it again. And again. And again.

5. **No Hot Water.** If the tenant loses their hot water, it's likely a problem with the hot water heater. If they need a new hot water heater, you'll spend approximately $600 for a plumber to replace it. However, it might just be the heating element inside the heater, in which case you can either replace it yourself for $20 and a couple hours of work, or hire a plumber for a couple hundred bucks to do it for you.

6. **Bugs/Rodents.** Dealing with pests can be one of the most annoying jobs for a landlord, because much of the time, it's the tenant's fault because they are dirty. Bugs and rodents like crumbs, so tenants with clean houses rarely have a problem. That said, it's still your responsibility to make sure that any infestation is taken care of. We tackle this issue on two fronts: educating the tenant *and* hiring a pest specialist to deal with the issue, which typically costs a few hundred dollars. Also be sure to seal up any holes, no matter how small, that bugs or rodents could use to get into the property. Many landlords include

in their lease that pest control is the tenant's responsibility after a certain number of weeks. This way, the landlord can say that it was definitively not the property's problem but must be the tenant's. I find this works okay in single-family houses, but in multifamily units, it can be impossible to find out where the bugs originated from, because they travel through walls easily.

7. **Garbage Disposals.** These technological wonders may be great for grinding up food in your house, but they are a constant thorn in the side of landlords. They break all the time. I believe this is mostly because tenants put things into them that never belong in a garbage disposal. ("I didn't know I wasn't supposed to put whole chicken bones down there!") For this reason, I try to remove garbage disposals from my properties whenever possible. However, if your garbage disposal breaks while a tenant is in the property and you need to fix it, there are generally two things that could be wrong. First, it might just be "stuck" and need an Allen wrench to unstick it. Or the motor might be burned out, in which case you'll need a new disposal, which might run a couple hundred bucks, including installation by a handyman.

8. **Toilet Water Leaks.** Toilets may be made of long-lasting porcelain, but the tank parts are generally cheap pieces of plastic that break all the time. If a toilet is running (water can be heard going through it 24/7, or the tank refills with water on its own every so often), it's most likely a problem with the flapper. Typically, these kinds of problems can be fixed with less than $20 in parts and an hour of labor by a plumber, handyman, or you.

9. **Clogged Toilet.** If your tenant clogs their toilet, this is *not* your responsibility. Problems that are caused by the tenant are the tenant's responsibility, so inform them that they need to call a plumber to deal with the issue. Or call a plumber yourself and bill the tenant for the cost. However, if the drains seem to be clogged in the bathtub or bathroom sink as well, this is a good indication that the problem may lie with your drain pipe, such as a collapsed pipe or a tree root that has grown through it. (I once had a tenant who flushed huge rocks down the toilet. This caused a major problem for me—and resulted in a hefty plumber's bill.)

10. **Furnace Repairs.** Heat is vital, so a furnace repair (especially during the winter) is one of the most important repairs on this list. If a furnace stops working, it could be something as simple as the pilot light

going out or as complicated as a gas leak. When your tenant calls, get a furnace repair specialist out to the property immediately. Also, many furnace problems would have never happened had the furnace filter been replaced often, so be sure your tenant knows how and when to do this.

You'll likely encounter more problems than I've listed here while owning rental properties, but these ten likely represent 99 percent of the issues you'll face. None of them, by themselves, are that expensive to fix. However, if left untreated, each of these can end up costing you thousands or even tens of thousands of dollars in damage. Treat each of these items with care and address them immediately. Your tenant, and your wallet, will thank you.

Landlord versus Tenant Responsibilities

Not all repairs are the responsibility of the landlord. Your job is to provide a safe, habitable property that is up to code. For example, unless your local jurisdiction specifically requires it, you do not have to provide new paint if a tenant's child draws all over the wall. You don't need to fix a piece of torn carpet if the tenant tears it. You don't need to provide new blinds because the tenant doesn't like the color. Unless your lease or local laws require you to fix these items, doing so is up to you.

However, items such as smoke detectors, heat, appliances, plumbing—these are your responsibilities to maintain. I recommend that you get a copy of your state's landlord-tenant laws and read them thoroughly to understand what is, and is not, required in your area. Furthermore, repairs that are needed because the tenant broke something can be made the responsibility of the tenant. For example, if a tenant breaks a window while moving some furniture, you are not responsible for the cost. However, unless you want your window covered with cardboard and duct tape for the next six months, you may want to hire the contractor to fix the issue and bill the tenant (I highly recommend that).

While the landlord definitely has certain responsibilities with regard to the condition of the property, so does the tenant. It is the tenant's responsibility to report problems when they occur, and if they don't, the cost of fixing those issues could be placed on the tenant (depending on your state's laws). Your tenant also must keep the property reasonably clean and safe, and make sure they don't misuse the systems in the property, such as by overloading electrical outlets or flushing large objects down a toilet.

Annual Preventative Maintenance

In addition to fixing problems when they happen, there is another category of repair that, as a landlord, you'll need to make sure gets done: preventative maintenance. In other words, these are tasks that need to be accomplished on a regular basis, usually annually, whether or not anything is broken. They are preventative measures, not necessarily repairs.

Accomplishing these projects annually will keep your property's future repair needs to a minimum and allow your property to run like a well-oiled machine. It will help you save money over time, because you'll spot problems before they become an issue. I recommend giving the following list to your handyman once a year for each unit you own. Keep in mind, this list is just a sample of some of the ongoing property maintenance you *may* need to do. Not all will apply to your property, and your property may have additional concerns. But this is a good place to start.

Interior

- Change furnace filters (probably more than once per year)
- Vacuum dust from fridge coils
- Replace smoke detector batteries
- Check to make sure carbon monoxide detector is installed and working
- Sweep the fireplace
- Ensure that lint from the dryer vent has a clear path to outside
- Flush water heater
- Check expiration date on fire extinguisher
- Repair any broken grout or caulk in bathroom
- Tighten any handles, knobs, racks, etc.
- Remove showerheads and clean sediment
- Check weather stripping on all doors and windows, and repair as needed

Exterior

- Clean gutters and remove all leaves and junk from inside
- Check siding and roofing for visible signs of problems
- Check sump pump and make sure it is still operational
- Test garage door opener, including auto-reverse function
- Check window screens and repair as necessary
- Look for signs of termites or other bugs
- Check trees for power line interference
- Recaulk any doors or windows as needed
- Trim up the landscaping
- Inspect the crawl space; look for bugs and water leaks
- Touch up peeling or damaged paint
- Fertilize the lawn
- Close off any openings to the crawlspace
- Check water valves (in both the fall and spring)
- Wash exterior with garden hose and mildew cleaner

By executing this preventative maintenance checklist each year, you will be able to catch problems before they become expensive fixes, while at the same time keeping your property looking great. Plus, your tenants will appreciate your dedication in helping their home look and operate the best. It's a true win-win.

Dealing with Difficult Tenants

One of the toughest parts of being a landlord is dealing with difficult tenants. No one enjoys confrontation or drama. But unless you outsource your tenant interaction to a property manager, you will have to expect to handle such situations yourself.

Of course, the best way to minimize drama with tenants is through proper tenant screening and allowing only the best tenants to rent from you. However, even with the highest screening standards and practices, bad tenants will make their way into your property. Therefore, the next best way to minimize bad tenants is by effectively training them.

Training Your Tenants

My dog Charlie is an adorable Yorkie who weighs less than ten pounds.

Although he's kind of a stupid dog, every head in the room invariably turns whenever he jumps in the air, rolls over, "speaks," or does any of his other special tricks. That's the fun advantage dogs have over cats— their trainability.

Like dogs, tenants need to also be trained. It may sound demeaning, but we are all trained to do certain things. We obey the speed limit, don't talk on our cell phone in the movie theater, and cover our mouth when we sneeze. Properly training your tenants can make all the difference in the world between being successful in real estate and being absolutely miserable. But how do you train a tenant? Tenants are trained the same way Charlie was: Establish rules, reward good behavior, and apply punishment when rules are broken. Therefore, the first step is establishing your rules via the lease agreement. Make sure your tenant has a copy of their lease and that it contains all the rules and regulations you want followed. Then, make sure you enforce them. Just like when a bad parent refuses to punish their kid for misbehaving and ends up with an unruly kid on their hands, when you fail to enforce a rule for your tenant, you will find yourself dealing with selfish, spoiled, and entitled tenants.

The easiest way of punishing tenants is through fees—late fees, non-compliance fees, etc. Now, many landlords struggle with applying fees, especially when the tenant calls and says they can't pay rent for one reason or another. However, you will find that when your policy is to never budge on the rent, suddenly all those excuses just disappear.

When I first started in real estate, I tried to be "nice" all the time. But trying to be the nice guy screwed me over time and time again. As soon as I made the decision to enforce every fee, late payments dropped from almost a dozen a month down to none. Late fees are rare now, and when they occur, tenants don't call and complain. They know the rules.

But even well-trained kids, pets, and people cause problems. No matter how well you screen and how well you train, you will still need to deal with issues as they arise. In this section, I want to discuss five of the most common problems you'll likely encounter as a landlord, and share my best tips on training your tenants to abide by your rules.

1. Late Rent

Late rent is not okay. You cannot allow a tenant to pay rent late on a consistent basis. I don't say this just for your benefit, but also for your tenant's. If you let them pay late, you are training them that this is okay. They will pay later and later, until pretty soon, they are three months behind. When you allow late rent, you just make the problem worse for everyone. You might think you are being a jerk by enforcing on-time payments, but trust me, you are doing your tenant a favor. Of course, this is one of those areas of landlording that I, and millions of other landlords, will tell you is important, but you will still probably ignore it until you discover the truth for yourself. It's hard to be strict, but in the end, it truly is the best scenario for everyone.

When I first began landlording, a lot of tenants paid late. Tenants would call, and I'd give them a few more days. They would tell me a story about why the rent was late, and I'd sympathize and waive the late fee. I worked out payment plans. And then I stopped being Mr. Nice Guy and—here's a novel concept—started simply following the rental agreement. Once the tenants knew I was serious and that there was a penalty to paying late, the late payments stopped almost completely. Late rent is fairly rare now, because the tenants have been properly trained. And that's the key.

When the rent is due but doesn't come in, immediately serve a notice to pay or vacate. Each state is different, but most require a notice to be served on the front door of the property that tells the tenant they have three to five days to pay or vacate. This form will probably also list the late fee they now owe because of being late. The amount of the late fee should be defined in their lease. Don't just make one up. When the set number of days is up, and they still have not paid, it's time to get them out of there. You have a few choices:

1. Work out a payment plan
2. Ask them to leave
3. Pay them to leave (cash for keys)
4. Evict them

I don't recommend option one. Trying to work out a payment plan has never worked for me. It shows that you are soft on the rules and trains them that, the next time, they can just "work something out" again. I don't recommend this except in extreme cases.

Option two is to simply ask them to leave. Simply talk with the tenant and let them know, "Hey, this is not working out. Let's just go our separate ways, okay?" This rarely works, but it's worth a conversation. Maybe they feel they are stuck between a rock and a hard place, because they have a lease and they don't want to break it, but they also can't afford the rent. By letting them know that you are okay with them leaving, maybe they'll take you up on the offer. If not, I usually move quickly to option three.

Option three is commonly known in the landlord space as "cash for keys." It is the act of paying your tenant to vacate the property. Yes, seriously. I know this goes against everything you want to do to a tenant who is causing you so much financial pain and stress, but don't let your pride get in the way of the almighty dollar. It's just business, and paying the tenant to leave may be a cheaper option. An eviction can cost between $1,000 and $3,000 just for the attorney, and depending on your state, it could take several months of lost rent to get them out. When the eviction finally does go through, chances are the tenant will have trashed the unit and left a huge mess for you to have to pay to have cleaned. An eviction could easily end up costing you $5,000 or more at the end of the day. Instead, why not offer the tenant a few hundred bucks to walk away quickly, saving their record from having an eviction on it? Of course, if you offer them money, do so on the contingency that they leave quickly (within a day or two) and that the property be "move-in ready" for the next tenant. Then, don't hand over the cash until they have vacated, given you the keys, and signed a release letting you know they have moved out, and you have inspected the unit to make sure it wasn't trashed. Cash for keys may damage your ego a little, but it can save you thousands of dollars and keep your stress level at a minimum.

Sometimes, though, you will simply have to evict a tenant. No one likes to evict, and as I mentioned, the process can be very expensive and lengthy. You can do the eviction yourself, but I don't recommend it for new investors because there are so many legal steps you must take, and if you do any of them incorrectly or in the wrong order, you could be forced to start your eviction over from the beginning, costing you even more time and money. Instead, use an attorney who is well trained in evicting tenants. After the initial notice is taped to their door or you've given it to them in person, and after the number of days required by your state is over, call up your attorney and explain the situation. They will likely want a copy of the lease, as well as all the information about the tenant that you have. After you hand that over, you are done. You can sit back and wait for the attorney to handle the eviction.

2. Neighbor Conflicts

If you are buying a multifamily property, it's likely you'll get complaints from one tenant about the other, such as the following:

- The tenant upstairs walks too loud.
- The other tenant parks in my parking spot.
- The tenant downstairs is having sex too loudly at 2 a.m.
- They keep throwing trash in my yard.
- I don't like their kids playing near my garden gnome.

Sometimes, having tenants feels a bit like running a day care. (I should know: My mom did day care in our house for my entire childhood.) Although there is no cure-all solution for this kind of drama, here are a few tips for handling it.

- **Let Them Figure It Out.** When I'm not renting out a unit, I let most calls go to voicemail and then call the tenant back. If it's a tenant complaining about something another tenant is doing, I will often wait a couple days to call them back (unless it is an emergency). About 90 percent of the time, the tenants handle the situation themselves.
- **Be Direct.** If one tenant is doing something that violates their rental contract, be direct and firm with them. In most states, there is a "notice to comply" form you can deliver to the tenant that basically says, "You have X days to stop this, or you'll be evicted." This usually gets their attention.
- **You Can't Solve Everything.** With many issues, I just tell the tenant, "Sorry, there is nothing I can do." For example, if a tenant complains about another tenant walking too loudly across their floor, I can't tell the upstairs tenant to tiptoe around their unit.
- **Fire a Tenant.** If one tenant is constantly causing problems, fire them! Ask them to move, pay them to move, or when their rental lease comes up, simply let them know you will not be renewing their lease, so they'll need to move. About 10 percent of your tenants will cause 90 percent of the drama, so don't hang on to that 10 percent. Fire them and move on.

3. Moving in Unapproved Pets or People

This happens more often than you might think. Tenant Gary moves in his girlfriend, Rhonda. Rhonda moves in her cat, Baxter. But neither Rhonda nor Baxter were approved to live in the property. What do you do?

When a tenant moves a person into their unit, the new person must be approved by you, the landlord. In other words, they need to fill out an application, pay the screening fee, and go through the same process as any new tenant. Otherwise, you have no idea who is living in your property. How would you like to find out you are renting to a level-three sex offender? That's bad for business.

If you notice that a tenant has moved someone else into their unit without telling you first, you must address this promptly. Send a letter that states the problem and give them a short time frame in which to fix it. Include an application and insist that it is filled out. If the tenant ignores you, post a legal notice to comply, in accordance with your state's laws, and then evict them if they don't. Again, this is all about training the tenant.

As for pets, this can be hard if you are an animal lover (like I am), but you must make the tenant abide by the contract they signed with you. If pets *are* allowed in the property, make sure the tenant pays the required fee, if you have one, and that the pet is licensed. If pets are not allowed, send a "notice to comply" form and give them a short deadline by which to remove the animal. You are not being cold and heartless, you are simply protecting your investment.

Since we're on the topic of pets, let's talk about that.

I absolutely love my pets. I'm a total "animal person" and couldn't imagine life without them. However, although pets can be man's best friend, they definitely are not always a landlord's best friend. Pets cause additional wear and tear on a building, make noises that irritate the neighbors, and can bite people, which can trigger a lawsuit. If not taken care of properly, pets can also cause a property to smell pretty bad—not to mention they can chew up pieces of building material not meant for consumption.

Should you accept pets?

For me, the answer is generally no. However, there are times when I will accept them, and the logic may seem a bit backward: The nicer the property, the greater chance I'll allow a pet. In my experience, dirty people have dirty pets, but clean people have clean pets. In general, nicer properties attract nicer tenants, who take better care of their pets.

Ironically, as I was typing the previous paragraph this morning, my dog jumped off the couch and proceeded to throw up on the floor. Seriously. I set down my laptop, carefully cleaned up the mess, and came back to my writing—no smell, no stain, no problem. However, had that happened with a dirty tenant, I would expect to find the remains of that puke when the tenant moved out. I don't know how people can live that way, but trust me, they do.

I never allow pets in a multifamily property—period. Although I might like tenant A and could allow them to get a cat, which likely wouldn't be a problem, tenant B will see that I allow pets and move in a big, angry German Shepherd. Then I'd have to be the jerk who makes them get rid of their dog and must try to explain why I allowed the other tenant to have a pet but not them.

If the property is a nice single-family home, I may allow a pet under a few conditions:

1. The tenants are high-quality tenants: I've seen their previous house and they have great references.

2. I usually set a twenty-pound limit for dogs, to keep out the big, more dangerous breeds.

3. If finding a non-pet tenant seems hard. If I have a number of vacancies, I may allow a pet to help me fill the vacancy faster. Typically, stable people tend to have pets, and I want stable people, so I might trade the risk of a pet to get a house filled faster. As an added bonus, good, stable tenants who have pets tend to have a hard time finding rentals that will take them. Therefore, those tenants tend to stay a lot longer.

4. I always charge a nonrefundable pet fee when the tenant moves in. Right now, that fee is $300 per pet. This may seem steep, but trust me, "animal people" will pay it. I might give a slight discount if it's two cats or a small dog and a small cat (like $300 total), but I always charge a fee. Be sure to check with your state's laws as to whether you can charge a nonrefundable fee for this. If not, just add it to the security deposit.

The pet must be licensed with the city and current on all its shots, and the tenant must sign my "pet addendum."

I wish pets could live in all my properties. They are so cute and innocent. But the problem is not with the pets; the problem is with the pet owners. Left unchecked and uncared for, pets can cause immense damage to your property and rob cash flow from your pocket every year. Think long and hard before allowing a pet in your rental, and if you allow it, take the precautions necessary to ensure you don't get screwed at the end of the tenancy.

Of course, when I'm talking about pets, I'm not talking about renting to people with service animals. Service animals are protected by Federal Law and a tenant with a service animal cannot be denied the ability to have that animal, or you could face some serious discrimination charges.

4. Breaking a Lease

Let's say that a tenant has signed a one-year lease with you, but in the seventh month, they find a new place and ask to leave. What should you do? Stick to the lease. The lease is a legal contract between you and your tenant, which is something you must remind your tenant. Tell them that it's fine if they move, but they must continue paying rent until their lease is done or until you get the unit re-rented to another person. Let them know that you'll do your best to get the property rented to another family, but you can't guarantee how long that will take.

Of course, you probably will not end up taking a tenant to small claims court if they do break their lease; you'll probably just keep their security deposit and take the loss. But you don't need to let them know that.

5. Drugs

Drugs are never fun to deal with, but this is a situation you likely will encounter as a landlord, no matter what class of tenant you rent to. The fact is this: Some of your tenants will likely do drugs. Most of the time, you'll never know until it's too late and they begin using their rent money for drugs, coming up with all sorts of excuses as to why the rent is late. Stick to your policy.

If you suspect drug dealing in your property (this is usually obvious because of the heavy traffic your tenant receives, usually from people who stay for just a minute or two), you have a few choices. You could try to evict them and get them out of the property, but you then run into the challenge of having to convince a judge that they are dealing. If the judge decides to be lenient and give the tenant "one more chance," you might waste a lot of time and money for nothing.

Instead, I follow the same steps I outlined earlier when a tenant doesn't pay rent. First, I ask them to leave or simply don't renew their lease if they are at the end of their term or are paying month-to-month. If I can't simply ask them to leave, I'll pay them to leave. I'm not going to confront them on my suspicions of drug dealing. I'll simply let them know I'm doing some restructuring and need them to move out promptly. If they still won't move, I could wait until their lease is up or go the eviction route. If you find yourself in this situation, no matter what you do, don't let them stay long. A drug dealer can cause you to lose good tenants and put a serious delay on your ability to build wealth. And of course, there is always "cash for keys," where you would pay the tenant to move out. For a drug-dealing ruffian, this might just do the trick.

If You Are Unhappy, Your System Is Broken

Hopefully, by now, you've picked up on the fact that systems are incredibly important to me. I'm a huge believer in running your rental business *as* a business, which means having processes, checklists, and ways of doing things that are repeatable and explainable. When a tenant pays rent late, I have a defined process for dealing with the problem, because I have a system in place for it. When a tenant wants to move in a dog, I likewise have a process for handling that request. When I want to buy a new rental property, I have a process. Systems and processes make business easy and fun. A good system allows you to work less and enjoy life more.

Of course, not everything you encounter can be planned for ahead of time. For example, I recently had a tenant call and tell me, "Hey, Brandon, I just saw another tenant in the apartment complex sitting in his bedroom, pointing a shotgun out the window." I don't have a specific process or checklist for that, so it was a problem I had to deal with on the fly. Problems cause stress, stress causes chaos, and chaos causes unhappiness. I don't want to be unhappy, and I'm sure you don't, either. I want to explain something that will revolutionize your life:

If you are unhappy, your system is broken.

In other words, if something in your business is causing you stress, you either, most likely, don't have a system for that issue, or you are not following your system. Either way, it's broken. I don't get stressed out anymore when tenants pay rent late, because I have a system. However, I did recently discover a system I have not yet perfected: finding contractors.

I was recently rehabbing a home that I plan to rent out. Although I've been using several different contractors on the project, as the property neared completion, my contractors stopped showing up. The tenant had already paid the first month's rent and was ready to move in, but the house was not done. I called every contractor I could, but no one would show up. I ended up picking up my tools, heading to the house, and finishing the job with my wife. The whole time, I was stressed and irritated, thinking, "I should be working on my book right now" and "I should be finding other great rental property deals right now." Instead, I was doing hard physical labor that I didn't really want to do. That's when it occurred to me: My system was broken. Rather than being mad, I changed my attitude to that of "Okay, how do I fix this system so this doesn't happen again? How do I make this process easier and more reliable next time?" I brainstormed about a half-dozen solutions and began writing down my new system for making sure contractors finish the job, including making sure paydays were given only *after* certain benchmarks were achieved, thereby incentivizing the contractors to finish if they wanted to get paid. Next time, I'll also likely hire a project manager to handle the contractor relations, something I recognize is a weakness of mine.

Will this work for me? I don't know, but next time I have a large rehab of a rental property, I'm going to try it out and test the new system. And I'll continue to tweak it and test it until the rehab process on a large property is as smooth and easy as dealing with a tenant paying their rent late.

WRAPPING IT UP

As you build your investment business, problems are going to occur. Going back to the trees I described at the beginning of this chapter, the strongest trees grew from being shaken. Don't think of problems as irritations, but as opportunities to strengthen your system. And the stronger your system, the greater your ability will be to scale and the less work you'll need to do to build wealth.

Stop being unhappy, stressed, and surrounded by chaos. Systematize everything, and find peace in your business.

I could have concluded this book here, but managing your properties is not the end of the game. Someday, you'll need to do something with your rental property. In the next chapter, I will focus on the end goal and everyone's favorite part: building serious wealth.

Chapter Nineteen
EXIT STRATEGIES AND 1031 EXCHANGES

> *"I was at this casino minding my own business, and this guy came up to me and said, 'You're gonna have to move, you're blocking a fire exit.' As though if there was a fire, I wasn't gonna run. If you're flammable and have legs, you are never blocking a fire exit."*
>
> —MITCH HEDBERG

Widely considered one of the most influential military leaders in human history, Alexander the Great began his conquest of the Middle East at the age of 20, and a decade later, he controlled one of the largest empires the world had ever seen. But then it all fell apart because of poor long-term planning. At the age of 33, the great king was struck by a severe fever and died. Because he had not appointed an heir to take over the vast empire he had forged, the Macedonian kingdom fell into a forty-year civil war.

Although I don't expect civil war to erupt in your life because of bad planning, the truth is the same: Poor long-term planning results in chaos. In this chapter, I will help you peer into the future and look at the possible choices you have for relinquishing your throne, so to best prepare for the day that you do. After all, chances are that you don't want to hang on to your property forever. This book has focused primarily on buying the asset that will take you into retirement (hopefully at an early age), but the fact is that you didn't get into real estate to own a bunch of rentals. You got into real estate for the benefits that those rentals can provide, namely financial freedom, wealth, and security for you and your family. As a result, sometimes you will need to get rid of properties to either trade up to larger deals, trade down to fewer properties, or simply to ride the wave of "buy low, sell high." Let's talk about some of the best exit strategies for your rental portfolio.

Hold Forever

Speaking about stocks, billionaire Warren Buffett once said, "Our favorite holding period is forever." Personally, I don't think this is a terrible strategy for real estate investors, either. It's entirely possible to hold on to your property forever. Perhaps your kids will inherit the property after you go, or perhaps the property will be sold upon your death and the money distributed amongst your family. Although there is nothing wrong with this plan, I encourage you to keep a few things in mind:

1. Understand that, as you age, it will become more and more difficult for you to be involved with the property. Your hands (and mind) will not work the same way, and it would be a pity to lose everything you've worked so hard for at the end of your life. Be sure to structure your investments in such a way that they become 99.9 percent passive for you later in your life. This means either owning properties that require very little involvement (such as some commercial real estate) or using property managers to take care of your properties for you. You may also decide to "trade up" into easier-to-manage properties, which I'll talk about in a moment when I discuss the 1031 exchange.

2. If you plan to hold on to your properties forever, be sure to consult with some expert asset-protection lawyers who can structure your rental business in such a way that taxes will be minimal, or non-existent, for your descendants.

What if you don't want to simply keep your properties forever? One common tactic many investors use to keep the cash flow flowing without the day-to-day management of tenants is selling with seller financing.

Seller Financing

Once you pay your property off and no longer have a bank loan, you can easily transition to the role of "the bank" and sell your property using seller financing. In other words, the same strategy I explained in Chapter 13 in my discussion of creative ways to finance your rental you can use to sell your rental.

Seller financing has a few key benefits over a regular sale:

1. **Possibly higher sales price.** When selling a property with seller financing, you may be able to get a higher sales price, because the buyer is more concerned about the terms.
2. **Lower tax bill.** If you were to sell the property outright, you might be hit with a huge tax bill. Instead, with seller financing, you pay only on the income received in a given year.
3. **Ongoing passive income.** Although selling all your properties and suddenly having a million dollars in the bank might feel nice, that money will only last so long. By selling using seller financing, you turn that equity into passive monthly income that will last you long into retirement.

If you plan to use seller financing, just be sure to hire a lawyer and do your homework, because there are numerous laws that must be followed, as well as some general best practices that are beyond the scope of this book. Also, the person you sell to matters, so screen them carefully and require a sizable down payment.

Cash Out

At some point, you could simply cash in your chips and exit the real estate game. Sell the properties you have, pay the hefty tax bill, and move your money into a savings account, stock market, or another passive investment. Or, you could use that money to become a private money lender or hard money lender, assisting other real estate investors in building their dreams while you collect interest on a secured asset that you understand, having been in the game for many years.

Finally, let's talk about one of the most common strategies real estate investors use to build wealth: the 1031 exchange. Although this isn't necessarily an exit strategy only, I felt it best fit this chapter, because, ultimately, the 1031 exchange can save you millions of dollars in taxes and ensure your wealth is transferred to your heirs with the least possible taxation.

The 1031 Exchange

If you decide to sell a rental property at some point, you will need to pay taxes on that gain.

Bummer.

This might not be a big deal if you are a terrible investor or have had some bad luck that kept you from achieving any financial gain. But I hope that, instead, you are a smart real estate investor. You aren't going to make some measly profit or sell at a loss. You will rock this game and make some serious moola when you sell! In short, you will have so much cash that you'll need to get yourself some bigger pockets. (See what I did there?)

But then, Uncle Sam is going to come knocking for his piece of the pie. And trust me, he's got quite an appetite.

But don't fret. I've got some good news: The IRS wants to partner with you on that money by allowing you to do a 1031 exchange.

Seriously? Partner? With the IRS?

Yep—through a 1031 exchange.

A 1031 exchange (pronounced "ten-thirty-one exchange"), is a tax strategy so named because of its inclusion in Section 1031 of the IRS tax code. It is also commonly known as a "Starker exchange" or a "like-kind exchange." In essence, a 1031 exchange allows an investor to "defer" paying any taxes on the profit of a property when it is sold, as long as another "like-kind" asset is purchased using the profit received. I'll explain exactly what that means in just a moment, but let's cover the big picture first.

First, understand that the 1031 exchange is not just for real estate, though that is how it is most commonly used. In reality, a person could use a 1031 exchange to defer taxes on numerous asset types, from paintings to businesses to cattle to automobiles, but given that this book is specifically about real estate, we'll keep our focus on that.

I mentioned that the IRS wants to "partner" with you. Now, the IRS doesn't come right out and say that anywhere, but in a way, that's exactly what they are doing. When you make money, you must pay taxes on that income. But if you follow the strict rules of a 1031 exchange, the IRS is basically telling you (in a whiny, nasally voice, of course): "Hey, you have obviously been doing pretty well with this real estate thing. Why don't you hang on to our money for a while and reinvest it in your next deal? This will help you make more money next time, and we'll get an even bigger share down the road. Unless you want to partner again on another deal after that."

This is what is meant by "deferred" taxes. The taxes will still be due someday (unless you die before you pay, but I'll discuss that scenario later), but until that point, it can be extremely advantageous to keep using what would otherwise be the government's money to invest in properties. In addition to the government "partnering" with you, the entire U.S. tax system is designed to encourage particular behaviors in society by rewarding or penalizing people for certain actions. In this case, the U.S. government rewards real estate investors, because we are providing housing for the masses.

The logical reason for the 1031 exchange makes sense. After all, if you make $100,000 on a property and then use that $100,000 to buy another property, you are clearly not out spending your $100,000 on shiny new toys. In fact, as I'll discuss in a minute, the money never even touches your bank account after the sale of the property, but is instead held by an "intermediary." The IRS, in all its benevolence, has decided to be fair and not require us to pay those taxes *yet*.

Nice guys, the IRS, right? Well, maybe. I'll get to that.

In addition to tax savings, the 1031 exchange offers several other benefits. It can allow a real estate investor to shift the focus of their investing without incurring the tax liability. For example, perhaps you are investing in properties that are low income and thus high maintenance. You could exchange the high-maintenance investment for a low-maintenance investment without needing to pay a significant amount of taxes. Or perhaps you want to move your investments from one location to another without the IRS knocking. The 1031 makes this possible.

1031 Exchange Examples

Because 1031 exchanges can be slightly complicated, I want to share stories from a couple of BiggerPockets members who used the 1031 exchange to defer a lot of money on the sales of their real estate investments.

1031 Exchange Example 1

In July of 2013, Jason Mak purchased an eighty-one-unit apartment building in Riverside, California. Paying $3.1 million for the property, he immediately set out to make improvements. He evicted bad tenants and improved management efficiencies, while also enhancing the physical condition of the property, adding a new roof, painting, landscaping, installing an elevator, and performing other valuable refinements. After increasing occupancy from 60 percent to 95 percent and stabilizing the entire operation, Jason sold the property for $5.5 million in the spring of 2015. Overall, he netted a final profit of $2 million on the two-year apartment turnaround.

Had Jason simply sold this deal, he would have needed to pay close to $600,000 in capital gains tax—but he knew better. Jason used a 1031 exchange to parlay his cash into two new properties: a twenty-four-unit apartment building and an upscale office building. Although he reduced the number of units he managed by doing so, Jason was able to buy nicer properties in significantly better locations that will be easier to manage and increase his ability to grow wealth.

1031 Exchange Example 2

In 2012, Serge Shukat purchased a newer single-family home in Casa Grande, Arizona, for $70,000. The home was a foreclosed property that quickly climbed in value. When Serge sold the home two years later for $135,000, he cleared almost $60,000 in profit. According to Serge, he would have had to pay close to $15,000 in capital gains tax, plus an additional $3,000 or so for the recapture of depreciation (which we'll talk about in a moment). Instead, Serge spent $600 on the 1031 exchange process and was able to roll his entire profit into the purchase of a newer, larger single-family home *and* a 2006 mobile home on one acre of land. Essentially, he turned one $1,000-per-month rental into two that gross $1,950 per month.

1031 Exchange Rules

If you plan to use a 1031, understand that you *must* follow some pretty strict rules. If you don't, you won't get the tax-deferred exchange. It's as simple as that. Let's talk about those 1031 exchange rules now.

1. "Like-Kind" Stipulation

The IRS requires that the property being sold (the "relinquished" property) and the property being acquired (the "replacement" property) be "like-kind" assets. In other words, you can't trade a car dealership for a rental house, because they are different kinds of assets. However, you can exchange almost any type of investment real estate for any other type of investment real estate. For example,

- exchanging a duplex for an apartment complex
- exchanging a piece of raw land for a rental house
- exchanging a vacation rental property for a strip mall

Also, keep in mind that the property must be an investment, not your primary or secondary home. In addition, both properties must be located within the United States to qualify.

Sorry, house flippers—properties that are designed for quick purchase and resale do not count.

2. Required Value of the Replacement Property

For you to be able to completely avoid paying any taxes on the sale of your property, the IRS requires that the replacement property acquired be of equal or greater value than the property being relinquished, though that value could be spread out over multiple properties.

For example, let's say you have a property that you are going to sell for $1,000,000. To get the full benefit of the 1031 exchange, you must buy at least $1,000,000 worth of like-kind real estate. That could be an apartment complex costing more than $1,000,000 or four different properties of $250,000 or more each—it doesn't matter. (Also note that acquisition costs, such as inspections, escrow fees, and commissions, do count toward the total cost of the replacement property.)

Technically, you could carry out a partial 1031 exchange and actually purchase something of lower value, but you would need to pay taxes on the difference. For example, if the relinquished property is sold for $1,000,000 and you purchase a new property through the 1031 exchange for $900,000, you will need to pay the normal capital gains tax(es) on the $100,000 difference. This extra $100,000 is known as "boot."

Finally, understand that when I talk about the sales price of a relinquished property, I am talking about the *entire* sales price, not just the profit you made. In other words, let's say you purchased a piece of property for $100,000 and sold it later for $200,000. The replacement property (or combined properties) would need to be greater than $200,000, not just the $100,000 in profit you made.

Now that you understand the price range, it's time to start looking for a replacement property—and you better hurry up.

3. The Forty-Five-Day Identification Window

The IRS imposes a very strict timeline on identifying the property you plan to buy: forty-five days.

That's right, you must identify the property you plan to close on within forty-five days or lose the entire benefit of the 1031 exchange.

If you are an experienced investor, you probably recognize that this is not a lot of time to find a property, especially in today's hot market. Sometimes I will go six months without buying a property, simply because I can't find a deal worthy of buying. I think this is a great indication that the creators of this rule didn't invest in real estate, but this forty-five-day rule is unlikely to change anytime soon, so just understand that the day you sell your relinquished property, the clock starts ticking.

Of course, you will likely have more time than just forty-five days to begin looking, because the timer doesn't start until the day you sell your property. You will probably list your property for sale several months before closing, so if you are confident that you want to do a 1031 exchange, start looking for deals long before your property is officially sold. Ideally, the day you list the property for sale would be the day you begin your search, or as my friend Serge Shukat told me, consider selling an asset using the 1031 exchange after you find a new deal to purchase. Keep in mind that you can also negotiate a long escrow period on the property you are selling, giving you more time before the countdown begins.

In addition to adhering to the countdown the IRS places on real estate investors, you must follow some strict procedures in this process. For example, you are allowed to officially identify three potential deals, which is helpful in case the first one doesn't work out. If you only identify one deal, and something happens later in the due diligence period, you might miss out on the entire 1031 exchange.

A few exceptions to this rule exist, known as the 95 percent rule and the 200 percent rule. These exceptions state that you can identify more than three properties, but you are required to actually purchase 95 percent of those you identify, or the total combined cost of all those identified properties must be less than 200 percent of the sales price of your relinquished property. For example, if you formally identify twenty different potential properties, you would either have to purchase nineteen of those (95 percent of the twenty) or the combined value of all twenty would need to be less than 200 percent of your sales price. I'm sure you can imagine the difficulty in both these scenarios, but because they are exceptions to the rule, they are seldom used.

What exactly does "identifying" a property mean? This is what the IRS says on this point:

> *"The identification must be in writing, signed by you and delivered to a person involved in the exchange like the seller of the replacement property or the qualified intermediary. However, notice to your attorney, real estate agent, accountant or similar persons acting as your agent is not sufficient."*[7]

Once you have identified the properties, you'll need to move forward with closing, because another timer will have already begun ticking: the 180-day closing window.

4. *The 180-Day Closing Window*

We discussed earlier that the clock for the forty-five-day window starts ticking the moment a relinquished property is sold. At this same moment, another clock, known as the 180-day closing window, also begins counting down. The IRS requires that the new replacement property be fully purchased (the title officially transferred) within 180 days of the sale of the relinquished property. This rule, along with the forty-five-day rule, is strictly enforced, and your entire 1031 exchange will fail if you do not adhere to both rules.

5. *Necessity of an Intermediary*

Finally, one of the most important rules governing the entire 1031 exchange process is this: You may not touch the profit from the relinquished property's sale if you hope to avoid the taxes.

Although you may have up to 180 days between the sale of the relinquished property and the purchase of the replacement property, **the**

---

[7] http://www.irs.gov/uac/Like-Kind-Exchanges-Under-IRC-Code-Section-1031

proceeds may never enter your bank account or an account controlled by you. Instead, you must use a *qualified intermediary*. An intermediary is someone who holds on to your money while you wait to buy the new property.

Of course, a lot of people out there would love to hold on to your money for you, but I recommend using a qualified intermediary, also known as an accommodator. Hundreds of companies can serve this role for you, as a quick Google search will reveal. I recommend going with an established company that has a long history and a solid reputation to avoid fraud or other unfortunate situations.

Also keep in mind that although the IRS doesn't specifically state what a qualified intermediary is, they do define what a qualified intermediary is not. A qualified intermediary cannot be you, your agent, your broker, your spouse, your family member, your investment banker, your employee, your business associate, or anyone who has had one of these roles in the previous two years.[8]

How to Do a 1031 Exchange, Step by Step

At this point, we've covered all the dirty details about 1031 exchanges, so let's put it all together and walk through, step by step, the process for carrying one out. Be aware that the following is just a general outline, so specific deals will likely vary slightly from this process.

1. **Decide to Sell and Do a 1031 Exchange.** Not every purchase is worth doing a 1031 exchange. After all, with all the requirements, costs, and countdown timers, simply paying the tax and moving on may be advantageous. That is definitely a discussion for you to have with your accountant.

2. **List Your Property for Sale.** You then list your property for sale, as you ordinarily would. Your agent will likely include language in the listing paperwork regarding your desire to do a 1031 exchange and the buyer's needed willingness to play along.

3. **Begin Looking for Replacement Properties.** Remember, the moment the relinquished property is sold, the forty-five-day countdown begins. Therefore, you should begin looking for deals immediately.

4. **Find a Qualified Intermediary.** Look for someone professional with a good reputation.

---

8 http://www.irs.gov/uac/Like-Kind-Exchanges-Under-IRC-Code-Section-1031

5. **Negotiate and Accept an Offer.** When someone agrees to buy your property, you will need to make sure the paperwork clearly states that a 1031 exchange is taking place on your end, and the buyer will need to comply. Although the buyer does not need to do a lot of work, they may need to sign off on certain paperwork, such as assignments or disclosures.

6. **Close on the Sale of Your Relinquished Property.** The title company or attorney will handle the closing, as with any other real estate transaction, except that your qualified intermediary will be actively involved in the process, and the funds will transfer to their bank account, not yours.

7. **Identify up to Three Properties within Forty-Five Days.** Now is the time to officially designate the properties you might pursue. Keep in mind, you can identify up to three properties, or more if you close on 95 percent of them or the total combined value of the identified properties is less than 200 percent of the sales price of your relinquished property.

8. **Sign a Contract on the First-Choice Property.** Most likely, of the three properties you identify, one will stand out as your first choice. You will need to get that property under contract and open escrow, making sure the seller knows you are purchasing through a 1031 exchange. You could also go under contract on all three of your identified properties, using contingency clauses to back out on the ones you later decide not to pursue.

9. **Let Your Qualified Intermediary Work with the Title Company.** You, your agent, and your qualified intermediary will work with the title company or closing attorney to make sure to dot all the "Is" and cross all the "Ts." This is actually a fairly simple process, one that your qualified intermediary should be familiar with.

10. **Close on the Replacement Property.** Finally, the qualified intermediary will wire your money over to the title company or attorney, and the property will close as in a normal transaction, deferring your need to pay the taxes until some point in the future, if ever. (I'll talk about the "end game" in a moment.)

The beauty of the 1031 exchange is that you can repeat this process over and over again on properties and continue deferring taxes indefinitely. This can help you build some serious wealth over time, greater than if you simply paid the taxes each time.

How a 1031 Exchange Can Make You Millions

In this section, I'll present a timeline for two different investors who bought and sold properties over a twenty-five-year span. The investors in both scenarios start with the same amount of money ($50,000), buy the same property (a $250,000 deal, second column below), have the same growth (5 percent equity growth each year, reflected in the third column below), and reinvest their profit (fourth column below) plus their previous down payments as a 30 percent down payment on their next deal (fifth column). But each ends up with a very different amount because of the taxes. (For simplicity, I do not include closing costs, depreciation, loan paydown, cash flow, or other obvious sources of income and expenses in this diagram. This is simply to illustrate a point.)

INVESTOR #1

Years	Purchase Price	Sold For	Profit	Equity to Reinvest (1031 Used)
1 to 5	$250,000.00	$319,070.39	$69,070.39	$119,070.39
6 to 10	$595, 351.95	$759,836.72	$164,484.77	$283,555.16
11 to 15	$1,417,775.79	$1,809,481.10	$391,705.31	$675,260.47
16 to 20	$3,376,302.35	$4,309,112.44	$932,810.09	$1,608,070.56
21 to 25	$8,040,352.79	$10,261,754.02	$2,221,401.23	$3,829,471.79

Investor #1 purchased a $250,000 property with his $50,000 down payment. After five years, he sold it for $319,070.39. He was able to use the entire profit and his equity he'd built thus far to put a 30 percent down payment on his next deal. This continued for twenty-five years with no tax due, because he continually used the 1031 exchange. Now let's take a look at the numbers for Investor #2, who chose not to use the 1031 exchange.

Years	Purchase Price	Sold For	Profit	Profit to Reinvest (15% Tax Paid)
1 to 5	$250,000.00	$319,070.39	$69,070.39	$119,070.39
6 to 10	$553,549.16	$693,721.77	$150,172.61	$236,356.55
11 to 15	$1,181,782.76	$1,508,287.54	$326,504.79	$513,885.62
16 to 20	$2,569,428.10	$3,279,313.71	$709,885.61	$1,117,288.39
21 to 25	$5,586,441.95	$7,129,872.66	$1,543,430.91	$2,429,204.66

After twenty-five years, Investor #2 ended up with just less than $2.5 million. Although this is still a respectable sum of money, notice that this investor trails Investor #1 by more than $1,000,000. This is because Investor #1 was able to put the government's money to work by using a 1031 exchange, helping him build greater wealth.

Now, what happens to Investor #1 at the end of year twenty-five? After all, the 1031 exchange is simply a method of tax deferral, not tax avoidance. Or is it? Let's talk about that next.

The 1031 Exchange End Game

In our examples, Investor #1 ended year twenty-five with $3.8 million, while Investor #2 ended with $2.4 million. But what happens after that? Typically, there are two common scenarios for any real estate investor when they are done with their investment career.

1. Cash Out

Some investors decide to exit the real estate game entirely, cashing in their chips and walking out the door. In other words, they decide that they will pay the IRS what they owe after selling all their properties. However, at this point, they are not simply paying the taxes on that final property's profit but (put very simplistically) on *all* the properties for which they have ever used the 1031 exchange. Because the "cost basis" of a property is carried forward on every deal, that final tax bill will likely be exceptionally large.

Keep in mind that if you opt for this end game strategy—cashing in your investments and paying the tax—you will still likely have significantly more income than if you had paid taxes each time you sold a property.

2. Die and Pass It All On

That's right, many investors simply choose to hold their properties until the day they die, and to pass the properties on to their heirs. The benefit of this approach is that current inheritance laws allow the heirs to receive the property on a "stepped-up basis," which means the tax consequences virtually disappear.

For example, let's say the adjusted basis on a property, after numerous 1031 exchanges and lots of time, is $200,000, and the property is worth $3,000,000. If the owner sold the property five minutes before dying, they would owe taxes on the $2.8 million in gain. But if the estate passes to the investor's heirs, the basis is automatically bumped up to the fair market value, or $3,000,000. The heirs could then sell the property and pay little, if any, tax. Of course, there are special rules and fine print that accompany this (especially for the exceptionally wealthy), so be sure to talk with a qualified professional about your estate planning.

Understandably, not every investor wants to hold on to properties until they die. I know I don't want to be dealing with tenants when I'm 40 years old, so being a 100-year-old landlord is absurd. How does one get around this?

You do it by trading up into properties that are significantly easier to manage. For example, perhaps you could 1031 exchange your equity into a multimillion-dollar shopping mall, as part of a syndication with hundreds of other investors. Or trade it into an NNN lease commercial investment where the tenant pays everything, and you sit back and collect a check.

There are hundreds of ways to make money with real estate, so simply trading up to a more passive method sounds pretty good to me.

Final Thoughts on the 1031 Exchange

I've just spent multiple pages giving you more information about 1031 exchanges than you probably ever wanted to know. You should feel proud: You now know more about this option than 99.99 percent of the U.S. population. Hopefully, by now, you have all the knowledge you need to decide whether a 1031 is right for you and, if so, how to accomplish such a task.

A 1031 exchange may be slightly complicated, but the long-term benefits of using this tax loophole can pack a tremendous punch in helping create your future wealth, and should be considered by all serious real estate investors who are in this game for the long haul. But remember, if you are considering a 1031 exchange in your future, please speak with a qualified tax professional about your options.

WRAPPING IT UP

Real estate investing is an exciting game, but it's a means to an end. Whatever your goals are in life, I sincerely hope real estate investing can help you achieve them. And once you have reached your goals, you will need to decide where to go next. Onward and upward? Or retirement on the beach with your loved ones? The choice of how you liquidate your assets will be one you'll need to make with careful consideration and planning, which can begin right now. Like Alexander the Great and the fall of the Macedonian Empire, you don't want your real estate empire to fall apart someday because of poor planning. Begin looking at your future today and decide how you will best exit the game safely, securely, and financially whole.

Chapter Twenty
FINAL THOUGHTS

"Life's like a movie, write your own ending. Keep believing, keep pretending."

—JIM HENSON

Over the past 100,000 words or so, we've gone on a journey that began with just changing the way you thought about real estate, then progressed through the process of building a plan, networking, and eventually buying your deal and managing it effectively. I hope you now have all the tools you need to begin building your rental property portfolio so you can achieve everything you could ever want in life.

But this isn't over just yet.

In this final chapter, I want to talk about the rest of your life as a rental property owner. After all, simply finding and acquiring great properties is not enough to give you long-lasting success. You must live successfully to maintain that level and grow over time. Let's talk about what comes next in your life, after the acquisition, in a section I'll call "the five success principles of rental property ownership." I believe these five principles will help you continue to achieve your goals with rental properties until the day you exit the game forever.

The Five Success Principles of Rental Ownership

The character of Uncle Ben from the *Spider-Man* comics and movies once said, "With great power comes great responsibility."

Although he may have been giving Spider-Man advice on kicking bad guys' backsides, the same principle applies to real estate investors. You stumbled upon something incredibly powerful when you decided to get into real estate investing. Most of your family and friends will never flip the switch in their head to take control of their financial destiny. In much of the world, even those who know about the power of real estate couldn't do anything about it.

But you—you are incredibly blessed with great power, which means you've got some responsibilities now. Maybe you don't yet feel that you are "successful," but that's okay. If you cultivate these habits now, they can help you develop into the kind of investor who is successful. Fake it till you make it, right? Therefore, the following are the five responsibilities every rental property owner must maintain throughout their investing life.

1. Manage Effectively

The first responsibility you'll have as you become an experienced real estate investor is to manage your portfolio effectively. Whether you have a property manager in place or you manage your own tenants, you are *still* a manager.

Owning a rental property is a lot like walking a tightrope. You need to keep walking on that thin line, and when a gust of wind comes from the left and pushes you to the right, you must lean to the left so you balance yourself and don't fall off.

In your rental property business, "gusts of wind" can take many forms. Thieving employees, bad property managers, natural disasters, fires, economic depressions, and other such factors can throw your investing off kilter, forcing you to step in and maintain stability. Don't assume that just because you own some rentals that you can sit back and relax on a beach 365 days a year.

Yes, the goal may be financial freedom, but that freedom requires some ongoing work.

2. Increase Income

As you move through your investment life, one of your tasks will be to increase the income your rental properties generate. And I'm not talking about just raising the rent, though that is obviously the largest aspect of increased income.

First, you need to ensure that your property is always being rented at the market rate, not below. Maybe you think that by offering below-market rent, you'll deal with less drama, which may be true. But how much are you sacrificing? This becomes increasingly problematic the more units you have. If you own fifty units, and each is under market by just $25, that's $1,250 you are missing out on each month, or $15,000 per year. At a 10 percent cap rate, that's $150,000 in value you are not receiving because of just $25 a month.

Of course, you must also be cognizant of being priced *too* high. Just as I advocate raising the rent to stay current, you must be quick to decrease the rent if needed to fill units. As I've mentioned at other times in this book, vacancy will be one of your biggest cash-flow killers, and keeping your rent competitive is the easiest way to keep vacancy rates down. It may be a bit of a balancing act, but learning to maximize your income is incredibly important for your entire investment life.

3. Decrease Expenses

Another task you'll need to continually stay on top of is decreasing expenses. I'm not saying you should spend all your time pinching pennies, and some landlords take this way too far. You shouldn't sacrifice your tenant's right to enjoy their property just because you want to save money. However, you can cut costs in numerous other ways as a landlord, such as the following:

- Transferring the responsibility of certain utility payments (water, garbage, electricity, etc.) to the tenant.
- Switching your garbage pickup to a larger can with fewer collections
- Negotiating lower rates with vendors in exchange for longer contracts or exclusivity
- Switching to energy-efficient appliances when you are responsible for paying for the electricity
- Switching to low-flow toilets and implementing other water-saving techniques to keep the water bill down
- Shopping around for better insurance rates
- Challenging your property tax bill if you feel it is too high

These are just some ways you can decrease expenses as a real estate investor. No one else will likely do these tasks for you, but small changes can sometimes result in a massive boost to your bottom line.

4. Execute Your Plan

In Chapters 2 and 3, I talked about building a plan and compared investing in real estate without a plan to the act of driving across the country without a road map. Hopefully, you've created a plan for yourself and have a goal for where you want to go. However, just having the plan is not enough. Now you need to carry it out.

I recommend reviewing your goals on a daily basis and monitoring your progress on a monthly basis. In other words, if your goal is to achieve $1,000,000 in net worth, where are you right now? On episode 113 of the *BiggerPockets Podcast*, real estate investor and author Jay Papasan described how keeping track of his net worth daily has made the greatest impact on his life and his investing. Smart dude!

Your plan will likely change over the course of your career, as it should. Life happens, and it can throw curveballs into your plan. Kids are born, natural disasters happen, your physical abilities slow down, and you become increasingly aware of your own mortality—these things can all play a role in your plan. However, a goal without a plan is just a wish, so even if your plan changes, keep working it and don't give up.

5. Give Back

Finally, I believe that every investor has a duty and obligation to give back to others, regardless of the level of success they have achieved. You can give back in multiple ways, but I encourage you to look at giving back both educationally and financially.

- **Educationally.** You might have just purchased your first deal, but that puts you miles ahead of 90 percent of the rest of the population who have never owned a real estate investment. Give back and share what you've learned! This is the spirit of the BiggerPockets community, where people from all different experience levels can share, learn, and grow together. Tell your story, help others, and encourage them to achieve the success you've seen.
- **Financially.** I believe strongly in giving back financially. If life has rewarded you, I feel you should give back financially to help those with fewer opportunities than you. Do some research and find an

organization you can trust to use your money to make a difference in the world. Not only is this good for the world, it's also good for your heart, helping keep you grounded and focused on the things in life that really matter. It's easy for real estate investors to get so focused on money and success that they lose sight of the bigger picture. And you don't need to be a millionaire to start giving back. Do it today! I recommend starting with giving 10 percent of your income to a good cause, and see where that takes you.

You'll never get to the end of your life and say, "Man, I wish I hadn't given back so much." Cultivate an attitude of generosity in yourself and become the kind of person who contributes to society. After all, much of the success you'll achieve in life was facilitated by someone else giving back and helping pave the way for you. It's now your turn to pay it forward.

Will You Take Action?

Let me end this book by asking you a very simple question: What do you wish you had in life?

A new car? A nicer house? More time to spend with the family? An early retirement? More time and money to travel? Less time spent at work?

These may be great things to desire for your life, but just wishing for them is not enough. As I originally noted in the prologue of this book, Michael Jordan once said, "Some people want it to happen. Some wish it would happen. Others make it happen."

Which kind of person are you?

You've just read an entire book on the step-by-step method for building wealth through real estate. You've learned how to get your mind in the right place. You've learned how to make a plan that will help you reach your financial goals. You've learned how to find properties that best meet your criteria, and how to analyze those deals to make sure they make sense. Finally, you've learned how to finance those properties and, once purchased, how to manage them to make sure they continue to operate at peak performance for you.

I've poured my heart and soul into this book and given you every single piece of information I know about real estate investing. I've told you stories about other investors who have found success through real estate. And you have access to the BiggerPockets community, including the incredible BiggerPockets Forums, where you can reach out to others any time you have questions or concerns about your next step. In other words, you've been given every single piece of the puzzle, handed to you on a silver plate.

But there is one thing you are still missing—action.

Without action, you are just another book reader. Without action, you are just another wantrapreneur. Without action, you are just a wisher, a dreamer. Without action, you are destined to continue down the same path as everyone else. Without action, you are stuck.

Books are great, and you've taken an important and valuable step in reading this one. Hopefully, you'll pass it on to a friend, or go back and reread it, this time with a highlighter and pen in hand. Still, a book is just a stack of papers, wrapped in cardboard and covered in ink. It's what you do with the information in it that matters.

Take action!

Don't sit on the bench while others take the field. Get out there and make it happen. Don't wish it, don't want it—*do* it.

ACKNOWLEDGMENTS

"Feeling gratitude and not expressing it is like wrapping a present and not giving it."

—WILLIAM ARTHUR WARD

Writing a book is hard, but certain key people have made it much easier.

I want to thank Josh Dorkin, the founder of BiggerPockets, for his encouragement and guidance in putting this book together, as well as the rest of the BiggerPockets Publishing Team, who have been amazing to work with on this project: Katie Miller, Kaylee Pratt, Scott Trench, Taylor Hugo, and Wendy Dunning.

And, of course, to my amazing, thoughtful, intelligent, spunky wife Heather, without whom this book never would have been completed.

Thanks to the hundreds of real estate investors whose words, actions, and encouragement made their way into my head over the past decade and, thus, into the pages of this book.

Finally, everything I have, everything I am, everything I will ever be I owe entirely to the grace of God.

Read the Rest of
The Rental Kit Series

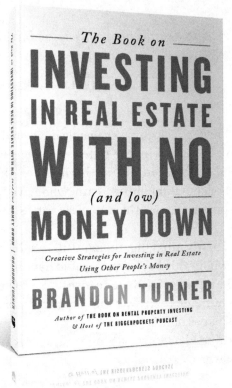

The Book on Investing in Real Estate with No (and Low) Money Down

Is your lack of cash holding you back from your real estate dreams? Discover the creative real estate financing techniques that savvy investors are using to do more deals, more often. Active real estate investor and co-host of The BiggerPockets Podcast, Brandon Turner, dives into multiple financing methods that professional investors use to tap into current real estate markets. Not only will you be able to navigate the world of creative real estate finance, but you'll get more mileage out of any real estate investment strategy!